Pro XAML with C#

Application Development Strategies

Buddy James

Lori Lalonde

Apress®

Pro XAML with C#: Application Development Strategies

ISBN-13 (pbk): 978-1-4302-6776-8

ISBN-13 (electronic): 978-1-4302-6775-1

Managing Director: Welmoed Spahr
Lead Editor: Gwenan Spearing
Development Editor: Gary Schwartz
Technical Reviewer: Fabio Claudio Ferracchiati
Editorial Board: Steve Anglin, Mark Beckner, Gary Cornell, Louise Corrigan, Jim DeWolf, Jonathan Gennick, Robert Hutchinson, Michelle Lowman, James Markham, Susan McDermott, Matthew Moodie, Jeffrey Pepper, Douglas Pundick, Ben Renow-Clarke, Gwenan Spearing, Matt Wade, Steve Weiss
Coordinating Editor: Melissa Maldonado
Copy Editor: Kim Wimpsett
Compositor: SPi Global
Indexer: SPi Global
Artist: SPi Global

Distributed to the book trade worldwide by Springer Science+Business Media New York, 233 Spring Street, 6th Floor, New York, NY 10013. Phone 1-800-SPRINGER, fax (201) 348-4505, e-mail orders-ny@springer-sbm.com, or visit www.springeronline.com. Apress Media, LLC is a California LLC and the sole member (owner) is Springer Science + Business Media Finance Inc (SSBM Finance Inc). SSBM Finance Inc is a Delaware corporation.

For information on translations, please e-mail rights@apress.com, or visit www.apress.com.

Apress and friends of ED books may be purchased in bulk for academic, corporate, or promotional use. eBook versions and licenses are also available for most titles. For more information, reference our Special Bulk Sales–eBook Licensing web page at www.apress.com/bulk-sales.

Any source code or other supplementary material referenced by the author in this text is available to readers at www.apress.com. For detailed information about how to locate your book's source code, go to www.apress.com/source-code/.

Contents at a Glance

About the Authors.. xiii

About the Technical Reviewer xv

Acknowledgments xvii

Introduction xix

■Part I: Getting Started 1

■Chapter 1: What Is XAML?... 3

■Chapter 2: Software Craftsmanship 15

■Part II: Laying the Groundwork.. 25

■Chapter 3: Domain-Driven Design 27

■Chapter 4: Design Patterns.. 37

■Chapter 5: Unit Testing 57

■Chapter 6: Advanced Unit Testing and Test-Driven Development....... 77

■Chapter 7: Exception Handling and Logging....................................... 97

■Part III: Completing the User Interface Layer 123

■Chapter 8: The WPF User Interface 125

■Chapter 9: The Windows Phone User Interface 159

■Chapter 10: The Windows User Interface 195

■Chapter 11: Deploying and Maintaining Your Application 219

Index...265

Contents

About the Authors.. xiii

About the Technical Reviewer xv

Acknowledgments xvii

Introduction xix

■Part I: Getting Started 1

■Chapter 1: What Is XAML? 3

A Brief History of Windows User Interface Design 3

Extensible Application Markup Language 3

    Separation of User Interface Concerns.. 4

    Declarative vs. Imperative Programming 4

    To Code-Behind or Not to Code-Behind? 7

    The MVVM Design Pattern 7

Summary.. 13

■Chapter 2: Software Craftsmanship 15

Software as an Art and a Science 15

SOLID Object-Oriented Design 15

To Unit Test or Not to Unit Test?.. 16

    Test-Driven Development 16

Meet the Team... 21

    The Development Manager... 21

    The Business Analyst 21

    The Junior Developer.. 21

The Guru 21

The DBA... 22

The First Team Design Meeting.. 22

Scrum Agile Methodologies.. 23

How to "Talk the Talk" When It Comes to Gathering Requirements 23

User Stories and How to Create Them... 24

Summary.. 24

■Part II: Laying the Groundwork.. 25

■Chapter 3: Domain-Driven Design 27

Introducing Domain-Driven Design 27

What Is Domain-Driven Design?.. 28

Before Domain-Driven Design 28

Business User? Who's That?.. 29

The Domain Model in Domain-Driven Design... 30

The Source Code Is the Design Documentation.. 30

Domain Entities 30

Domain Aggregate Roots 32

Domain Value Objects 34

Domain Services... 34

Domain Events.. 36

CQRS: Command Query Responsibility Segregation... 36

Summary.. 36

■Chapter 4: Design Patterns.. 37

Architecture Types.. 37

Layered Architecture 38

User Interface Layer 39

Presentation Layer.. 39

Service Layer... 39

Domain Layer...39

Infrastructure Layer..40

Design Patterns Used Throughout the Book...40

The Repository Pattern...40

The Adapter Pattern...43

The MVVM Design Pattern..44

ICommand: The Cure for the Common Event Handler..49

Summary...55

Chapter 5: Unit Testing...57

Debugging Strategies...57

Defensive Programming...58

System Testing...58

Regression Testing..59

User Acceptance Testing..59

Unit Tests to the Rescue..59

Unit Testing Basics..60

Characteristics of a Great Unit Test..61

Automated Unit Test Execution..61

Unit Test Execution Speed...61

K.I.S.S. Your Unit Tests..64

All Team Members Should Be Able to Execute Unit Tests...65

Great Unit Tests Survive the Test of Time...65

Unit Test Fixtures..65

Unit Testing Frameworks...65

NUnit..65

Microsoft Unit Testing Project Template...73

Summary...76

■**Chapter 6: Advanced Unit Testing and Test-Driven Development** **77**

Test Fixtures Are Classes Too 77

Use Inheritance to Avoid Duplicate Code.. 77

Unit Testing Classes That Have Dependencies 80

    Dealing with Dependencies 80

    Repository Pattern 85

    Stubs 86

    Mock Objects 87

Using the Moq Framework 87

    Using the Mock Class to Set Up Your Dependencies 88

Design by Testing: Test-Driven Development 93

Summary 95

■**Chapter 7: Exception Handling and Logging** **97**

Enterprise Library Exception Handling Application Block 97

    Installing the Exception Handling Application Block 98

    Installing the Enterprise Configuration Console 99

    Configuring Policies, Exception Types, and Handlers 100

    Modifying the Code 109

    Configuring the Logging Exception Handler 112

Logging Options for Windows Device Apps 117

    Visual Studio Application Insights 118

Summary 122

■**Part III: Completing the User Interface Layer** **123**

■**Chapter 8: The WPF User Interface** **125**

The Basics 125

    Application Class 125

    Windows, Pages, and User Controls 127

    The Code-Behind File 128

    First Look 129

XAML Designer 131

Container Controls 131

Layouts 134

Resources and Styles 146

Resources 146

Styles 148

Data Binding 151

XAML Markup 152

ViewModel and INotifyPropertyChanged 153

DataContext 154

Dependency Properties 156

Summary 158

Chapter 9: The Windows Phone User Interface 159

The Basics 160

Windows Phone 8.1 SDK 160

Multiresolution Support 161

Scaling 164

Themes, Resources, and Styles 166

Background and Accent Colors 167

Theme Resources 168

Predefined Styles 170

Application Architecture 170

Page Orientation 171

Navigation 172

Caching Pages 176

Templates 176

DataTemplate 176

ItemTemplate 177

Displaying Collections 178

    ListView 178

    GridView 183

Presentation Controls 185

    Hub 186

    Pivot 188

Application Bar 191

Summary 193

■Chapter 10: The Windows User Interface 195

The Basics 195

    Windows Software Development Kit 195

    Developer License 196

    Basic Design Principles 197

    Gestures 201

Managing Layouts 201

    Visual States 202

    Storyboards and Animations 203

    OnSizeChanged 205

Searching Data 206

Flyouts 210

    The Basics 211

    Usage and Syntax 211

    Programmatic Display 213

    Flyout Styles 214

Contracts 215

    Share Contract 215

    Settings Contract 217

Summary 217

■**Chapter 11: Deploying and Maintaining Your Application** **219**

Version Control 219

The Basics 219

Choosing a Version Control System 221

Continuous Integration 225

"Johnny Broke the Build!" 226

Configure a CI Build 226

Queue a Build 234

Deploying WPF Applications Using ClickOnce 235

Publishing Apps to the Windows Store 238

Windows Dev Center 238

Summary 264

Index **265**

About the Authors

Buddy James is a software engineer, author, blogger, mentor, thought leader, and technologist. He is a Microsoft Certified Solutions Developer, Microsoft Certified Applications Developer, and Microsoft Certified Professional. Buddy began programming at the age of 13 with QBasic. He became a professional developer in 2002 and has since gained experience with many technologies. He has worked with the .NET Framework since version 1.1. Buddy is passionate about software development. When he's not working, he writes articles for his blog at http://refactorthis.net. Follow Buddy on Twitter @budbjames.

Lori Lalonde is an Apress author, independent consultant, blogger, international conference speaker, Xamarin Certified Developer, and Microsoft MVP. She is also the founder and president of Solola Solutions Inc. She began her career in software in 1997 and hasn't looked back since. Her experience spans numerous industries and a variety of technologies, with a primary focus on the Microsoft .NET platform since 2002. Lori is actively involved in the local community, serves as the User Group Leader of Canada's Technology Triangle .NET User Group, and participates in local Women in Technology groups. Whether mentoring junior colleagues or writing about her experiences in the industry on her blog, she is always happy to share her knowledge with the greater community. You can follow Lori on Twitter @loriblalonde and check out her blog at http://geekswithblogs.net/lorilalonde.

About the Technical Reviewer

Fabio Claudio Ferracchiati is a senior consultant and a senior analyst/developer using Microsoft technologies. He works at BluArancio SpA (www.bluarancio.com) as a senior analyst/developer and Microsoft Dynamics CRM specialist. He is a Microsoft Certified Solution Developer for .NET, a Microsoft Certified Application Developer for .NET, a Microsoft Certified Professional, and a prolific author and technical reviewer. Over the past ten years, he's written articles for Italian and international magazines and coauthored more than ten books on a variety of computer topics.

Acknowledgments

I would like to thank Gwenan Spearing for the opportunity to be part of this book. Thank you to Melissa Maldonado for keeping the project on task. Thanks to Gary Schwartz and Fabio Ferracchiati. Your feedback was essential to the success of this project. Thank you to everyone at Apress for an awesome opportunity.

I'd like to thank Lori Lalonde for her hard work in coauthoring this book. She brought a great deal of experience to the table and did a wonderful job.

I'd like to thank my parents for supporting me and my passion for programming. Finally, I'd like to dedicate this book to the memory of my grandmother, Daisy Burns.

—*Buddy James*

First and foremost, I would like to thank Gwenan Spearing, who brought me onto this book project.
It is because of your support and encouragement that I have coauthored two Apress books, simply because you reached out and asked me to write for Apress.

Thanks to Buddy James for entrusting me to help him complete this book, which was his project and vision all along.

Thanks to the entire team at Apress that had a hand in the making of this book: Melissa Maldonado, Gary Schwartz, Fabio Ferracchiati, and the countless others behind the scenes.

Last but not least, thanks to my family for putting up with me during the writing of this book.
Your support means the world to me.

—*Lori Lalonde*

Introduction

I started developing applications in .NET, using WinForms and ASP.NET. WinForms was a great improvement over Visual Basic 6. ASP.NET WebForms introduced a form-focused, event-driven user interface model similar to WinForms. A major difference was the way in which the user interface was defined.

Visual Studio offered WYSIWYG design support for both technologies. The key difference was that WinForms user interfaces were represented in procedural C# and ASP.NET WebForms that were built in declarative HTML. I've always loved the expressive nature of HTML. Even though I preferred developing user interfaces for the Web, desktop applications seemed to offer more power. I like to have complete access to the computer's resources.

Microsoft released WPF with the .NET Framework version 3.0. I will admit that there was a bit of a transition for me. WPF was a little intimidating. I had to think about things in a completely different manner. The lessons that I learned went beyond the new controls and events. As I learned about data binding, I began to learn about the Model View View Model design pattern, also known as MVVM.

When Microsoft released Windows 8 and Windows Phone 8, I was thrilled to learn that XAML was one of the language choices. Microsoft also introduced the Windows Runtime libraries, also known as WinRT. WinRT offered APIs to support new devices such as tablets and phones. With the release of Windows 8.1 and Windows Phone 8.1, the ability to create Universal Applications projects enabled developers to create Windows Store and Windows Phone applications that share common code, assets, and XAML UIs between both platforms.

The Universal Application development experience has been improved in Windows 10 to allow you to create one project that can be deployed to both Windows Store and Windows Phone devices. If you are developing for your desktop, tablet, or phone, you can use XAML to design the user's experience.

—Buddy James

What This Book Covers

This book was written with two goals in mind. First, we wanted to cover the XAML-based user interface technologies. The second goal was to introduce some common software development practices and design patterns that are used in the enterprise today. We will also cover some development tools and libraries that you can use to aid you in your work.

Chapter 1: What Is XAML?

This chapter is an introduction to XAML. We explain the difference between declarative and procedural programming. We discuss how XAML development is different than other Microsoft development technologies. There is a brief introduction to the MVVM design pattern and how the data binding capabilities of XAML support the implementation of the pattern.

Chapter 2: Software Craftsmanship

Software development is constantly changing. This chapter discusses agile development methodologies and the problems that they solve. We cover object-oriented design goals and how leading your design by developing unit tests first can assist you in achieving these goals. We cover development teams and requirements gathering in this chapter as well.

Chapter 3: Domain-Driven Design

Programming professionally is more about solving business problems than writing source code. Domain-Driven Design is a set of software design principles that support agile development practices where customer participation is required to ensure that you deliver applications that meet the needs and expectations of your clients. We briefly cover some of the software design principles that are used in Domain-Driven Design.

Chapter 4: Design Patterns

Design patterns offer uniform solutions to common problems in software development. This chapter covers layered architecture and several design patterns to assist you in your development efforts. We present an MVVM example in WPF to illustrate the benefits of design patterns in XAML-based applications.

Chapter 5: Unit Testing

Unit testing can help you reduce the number of bugs that you introduce into your software during development. Writing unit tests can also improve your design by illustrating the ways in which your classes are meant to be used.

Chapter 6: Advanced Unit Testing and Test-Driven Development

This chapter builds on the last one by introducing some of the advanced topics in unit testing. This chapter provides an introduction to mocks and stubs, which allow you to write unit tests that execute in the same way each time, even if your code relies on third-party APIs and components. We cover unit testing in Visual Studio as well as NUnit. There is also an in-depth look at Test-Driven Development.

Chapter 7: Exception Handling and Logging

Exception handling is a fundamental task in .NET development, and it safeguards against unexpected application crashes. It is equally important to record data associated with any exceptions, which will assist with troubleshooting issues that arise in production. This chapter covers the Microsoft patterns and practices Exception Handling Application Block, as well as the Logging application block and its usage within WPF applications. We wrap up the chapter with alternative approaches to handling exceptions and logging within your Windows Store applications.

Chapter 8: The WPF User Interface

This chapter provides an introduction to WPF development using XAML to design your user interfaces. WPF-specific controls and design concerns are covered. We also demonstrate how XAML resources and styles allow you to create a common look and feel across your entire application. The chapter concludes with a detailed discussion on data binding techniques to manage data flow within the application.

Chapter 9: The Windows Phone User Interface

This chapter covers Windows Phone development concepts using XAML and C#. We discuss the basic structure of a Windows Phone Store application and how you can design your application for various screen sizes and page orientations. The various presentation controls are covered, and we show how you can use them to display application content while maximizing screen real estate. We also demonstrate how to display data collections and how to configure the Application Bar.

Chapter 10: The Windows User Interface

Windows Store applications are fundamentally different than desktop-based applications. The user interface design standards promote simple, clean user interfaces that are focused on content. In this chapter, we provide you with the basics you need to get your environment set up for Windows 8.1 development. We also cover topics that are specific to Windows Store applications, such as flyouts, Windows 8.1 contracts, and how to adapt to different layouts.

Chapter 11: Deploying and Maintaining Your Application

The last chapter of the book is dedicated to the deployment and maintenance of your application. Source control best practices are explained, as well as an overview of the popular version control systems, TFS and Git. You will learn how to deploy WPF applications using ClickOnce deployment, as well as how to submit your Windows 8.1 and Windows Phone 8.1 applications to the Windows Store.

Who This Book Is For

This book is for all .NET developers who are interested in developing software using Microsoft's XAML-based technologies. The book requires a working knowledge of C#. To get the most out of this book, we recommend some experience with at least one XAML-based technology.

The examples in this book were developed using Visual Studio 2012 and Visual Studio 2013. You will need experience designing and compiling applications in Visual Studio to build the example source code. The minimum framework version when developing WPF applications is .NET Framework 3.0. The minimum framework version when developing Windows 8.1 and Windows Phone 8.1 applications is .NET Framework 4.5.1.

PART I

■ ■ ■

Getting Started

CHAPTER 1

■ ■ ■

What Is XAML?

This chapter is a "crash course" in Extensible Application Markup Language (XAML). If you are experienced in writing applications using XAML-based technologies, feel free to skim the chapter and pick the parts that interest you. If you don't have experience writing XAML-based applications, then this chapter is a prerequisite for the rest of the book.

A Brief History of Windows User Interface Design

Before XAML was introduced to the development community, Windows desktop applications were mainly created using the WinForms technology. The WinForms design paradigm is similar to Visual Basic 6–style graphical user interfaces (GUIs) of old. You work within a what-you-see-is-what-you-get (WYSIWYG) interface that allows you to drag controls from a toolbox and drop them on the window.

Visual Studio serialized the user interface in the designer as C# code that contained object declarations for all user interface controls along with property values and other details required to represent the user interface. This meant that if you were working in an environment where the team was made up of designers and developers, collaboration between the two groups was difficult. If a designer wanted to apply a common theme to a user interface, they would often create bitmap mock-ups and divide the mock-ups into smaller bitmaps to be used for each control on the form. These bitmaps would then need to be applied to each control as some property, such as the background. This process was tedious and inefficient. Bitmap-based designs don't scale well, and resizing the controls on a form caused the associated bitmaps to resize, which would often result in degraded image quality. Enter XAML.

Extensible Application Markup Language

XAML (pronounced "zammle") is based on Extensible Markup Language (XML) and is for designing user interface layouts. XAML is known as a *declarative language*. It is almost always used in conjunction with another type of programming language known as an *imperative language*, such as C#, VB.NET, C++, and so forth.

XAML-based technologies covered in this book include the following:

- *Windows Presentation Foundation (WPF)*: XAML + C# + WPF assemblies
- *Windows 8.1/Windows Store development*: XAML + C# + Windows Store assemblies
- *Windows Phone 8.1*: XAML + C# + Windows Phone assemblies

Each of these technologies uses XAML in combination with another .NET programming language, such as C# or VB.NET, to create desktop, tablet, and mobile applications with stunning and unique user interfaces as well as elegant and intuitive user experience designs, which were nearly impossible to achieve prior to the introduction of XAML and WPF in .NET 3.0.

Since XAML is an XML-based declarative markup language, it adds a completely new paradigm to Windows-based user interface (UI) development. XAML is verbose and thus easily read by humans. This is helpful when you need to edit XAML by hand. Moreover, the XML basis of XAML makes it an easy language for which WYSIWYG editors can be created.

I know, I know—right now you are probably thinking, "XML may be easy to read, but what about the performance of my application? XML is too verbose!" This is true. XML can cause performance problems when parsing; however, the XAML parser will compile your XAML into a binary format called Binary Application Markup Language (BAML) that is used during the execution of your application. BAML drastically reduces the size of your XAML code, and this helps to eliminate the performance problems associated with traditional XML parsing. BAML is tokenized as well so that duplicate references throughout the BAML code can be replaced by much smaller tokens. This in turn makes BAML code even smaller and thus faster during application execution.

Separation of User Interface Concerns

One of the great things about this new user interface design paradigm is the synergy it provides between developers and designers. Unlike technologies of the past, XAML includes code-behind associations, although this is not a requirement. In contrast to WinForms, XAML does not require the designer to create a C# representation of the user interface. XAML is designed to be all that is needed to define the look and feel of your user interface. This aspect of XAML, along with important new features such as data binding, routed events, and attached properties, which we'll discuss throughout the book, allows XAML-based applications to take advantage of user interface design patterns that allow the complete separation of the user interface design (XAML) and presentation layer logic (C#).

This book will focus on the Model-View-ViewModel (MVVM) design pattern, which will be covered in depth in later chapters. There are other design patterns that you can use with XAML based user interfaces that allow you to separate your user interface design from the presentation layer logic, and you should definitely look into some of them. Table 1-1 provides references to two other great design patterns that you should explore.

Table 1-1. *User Interface Design Pattern References*

Design Pattern Name	Reference URL
Model-View-Controller (MVC)	https://msdn.microsoft.com/en-us/library/ff649643.aspx
Model-View-Presenter (MVP)	https://msdn.microsoft.com/en-us/magazine/cc188690.aspx

Declarative vs. Imperative Programming

In declarative programming, the source code is written in a way that expresses the desired outcome of the code with little or no emphasis on the actual implementation. This leaves the framework to deal with parsing the declarative source code and handling the "heavy lifting" required to instantiate objects and set properties on the these objects, which are defined in the XAML elements.

Imperative programming is the opposite of declarative programming. If declarative programming can be thought of as declaring *what* the desired outcome is, imperative programming can be viewed as writing lines of code that represent the instructions of *how* to achieve the desired outcome.

A great example of a declarative language and an imperative language working together is XAML and C#. Whether you are developing a smart client desktop application using WPF, a Windows Store app for use with tablets such as the Microsoft Surface Pro, or a mobile application using Windows Phone, any of these applications can be developed using a mixture of XAML and C#.

■ **Note** When it comes to the imperative .NET languages, you are not limited to C#. Depending on the target platform, you can use C#, VB.NET, and even F#. A search of the Internet reveals that C# is generally the language of choice when using WPF, Windows Store apps, and Windows Phone 8, so that's the language we'll use for the code examples throughout this book.

Let's begin by looking at the declarative XAML markup used to define a WPF Window. Listing 1-1 shows a basic WPF Window with a grid and a button control written declaratively in XAML.

Listing 1-1. Declarative Source Code Written in XAML

```
<Window x:Class="WpfApplication1.MainWindow"
        xmlns="http://schemas.microsoft.com/winfx/2006/xaml/presentation"
        xmlns:x="http://schemas.microsoft.com/winfx/2006/xaml"
        Title="MainWindow" Height="350" Width="525">
    <Grid>
        <Button Name="btnOK">
            <TextBlock Name="ButtonText" FontSize="100">
                Click Me!
            </TextBlock>
        </Button>
    </Grid>
</Window>
```

If you don't have experience with XAML, don't worry about the syntax. Instead, note the aspects of declarative programming. You see what looks to be an XML file that contains a root element called Window. The elements in XAML are associated with a class in which the parser will create an instance of the specified type during runtime. The attributes of these elements are directly linked to the properties of the object that the element represents.

The element has attributes as well as nested elements. The nested elements can also be used as property values of the parent element's instance. For example, notice that there is a Grid element, and within the start and end of the Grid element tags, there is a Button element. Much like the other elements, the Button element has a nested TextBlock element. In this case, the TextBlock element represents an instance of the TextBlock type that is assigned to the Content property of the Button element's object instance.

Perhaps an example will assist in explaining how elements defined in XAML and their attributes and nested elements are related to object instances and property values. Just as Listing 1-1 shows the XAML definition of a WPF window using declarative programming, Listing 1-2 contains C# code to build a WPF window imperatively, which is identical to the window created declaratively in Listing 1-1.

Listing 1-2. Creating a WPF Window Using Imperative Source Code Written in C#

```csharp
using System;
using System.Collections.Generic;
using System.Linq;
using System.Text;
using System.Threading.Tasks;
using System.Windows;
using System.Windows.Controls;
using System.Windows.Data;
using System.Windows.Documents;
using System.Windows.Input;
using System.Windows.Media;
using System.Windows.Media.Imaging;
using System.Windows.Navigation;
using System.Windows.Shapes;

namespace WpfApplication1
{
    //Equivalent to the MainWindow element
    public class CSMainWindow : Window
    {
        private Grid _ContentGrid;
        private Button _BtnClickOk;
        private TextBlock _ButtonText;

        public CSMainWindow()
        {
            //Set the window properties
            SetValue(TitleProperty, "CSMainWindow");
            this.Height = 350;
            this.Width = 525;

            //Instantiate each object (element) in the Window
            _ButtonText = new TextBlock();
            _ButtonText.Text = "Click Me!";
            _ButtonText.FontSize = 100.0;

            _BtnClickOk = new Button();
            _BtnClickOk.Content = _ButtonText;

            _ContentGrid = new Grid();
            _ContentGrid.Children.Add(_BtnClickOk);

            this.Content = _ContentGrid;

        }
    }
}
```

As you can see, the C# code is imperative, which means that the application is expressed in lines of code where each line illustrates *how* the control instances are created. It also shows the properties and the order in which the property values are set in order to accomplish the same WPF Window layout as in Listing 1-1.

Let's compare this to the XAML in Listing 1-1. The declarative style of the XAML Window definition doesn't require you to instantiate any control instances. Instead, you express the controls that you need as XML elements. Also, the Button element contains a nested element of type TextBlock, which in turn has a nested string value to be displayed as the text of the button. This is what is meant when we say that declarative code describes *what* should appear in the window, without the need for any implementation details like object creation. The XAML parser handles creating the required object instances (Window, Grid, Button, and TextBlock). The XAML parser also evaluates nested elements, and then it decides which property the nested object will populate.

As you can see, declarative XAML is very different from other .NET programming languages. However, it's pretty impressive to see the parser make complex condition-based decisions about the objects and property values that are created/transformed when building the WPF Window output upon program execution. "Intelligent" XAML parsing combined with the power of the C# presentation layer logic (code-behind event handlers and view models), along with the domain logic and infrastructure code, explain why XAML and C# are a commonly used design combination for the technologies you will be using to build a solid, robust, loosely coupled, and highly testable line-of-business application throughout this book.

To Code-Behind or Not to Code-Behind?

The separation of concerns that XAML creates between the user interface design and presentation layer logic allows you to design loosely coupled, unit-test-friendly applications, which are much easier to create since XAML came along. This allows designers to develop the user interface with design tools such as Visual Studio or Expression Blend to create the XAML, leaving programmers to work simultaneously in C# to build the presentation layer logic to respond to user interactions as well as the code to update the user interface upon requests from the domain logic or from external systems.

XAML files have code-behind files that work almost exactly like WinForms and WebForms code-behind files. The difference is that a user interface can be created without adding any code to the code-behind file. In fact, there are many MVVM purists who will suggest you never write code in the code-behind files of your XAML-based projects. The main reason for this is to create a complete separation of concerns between your user interface design and the presentation layer logic. For example, in a WinForms application, you can specify a Button's click event handler in the code-behind of the form. This tightly couples the presentation layer logic to the user interface. These types of dependencies create presentation layer logic that is hard to unit test. It also makes it harder to switch between different user interface platforms without reproducing the event handlers. Although you can do the same thing in XAML, there are better options to keep your user interface concerns separate from your presentation layer logic.

One option is to bypass the code-behind completely and use data binding to bind the Command property of a Button to an ICommand implementation in a separate class. These data-binding techniques can be expressed 100 percent declaratively in XAML, meaning that you are not tied to a specific code-behind file. This lets you write reusable view models that handle all presentation layer user interaction logic, and they are also easily unit tested. This now brings us to our discussion of the MVVM design pattern.

The MVVM Design Pattern

The MVVM design pattern is based on the Presentation Model design pattern. John Gossman created it specifically for XAML and WPF. The MVVM pattern allows you to separate your domain model's business logic (the *model*) from the user interface (the *view*) by adding a layer of abstraction that encapsulates all of the logic required by the user interface, and it processes requests from the user to perform actions on, or retrieve data from, the model. When using MVVM, the view is represented by XAML. The view is directly dependent on the *view model*; however, the view model is view agnostic. You should not have any user interface elements or other dependencies related to the view in the view model. The view model's public interface should be well defined. Any change to the view model's public interface could result in a change of the view. The view model will work with the application service layer to modify or retrieve data from the model. The model or domain model should only contain code that is relative to the business domain at hand. It's important not to allow any of the user interface–related code from the view or view model to sneak its way into the domain model. The domain model should be isolated from any code that does not relate to the business domain. See Figure 1-1, which represents the communication between the different parts of the MVVM design pattern.

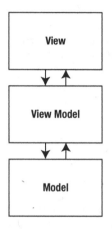

Figure 1-1. *The flow of communication when using the MVVM design pattern*

As you can see, the view will declaratively create an instance of the view model. The view model's properties will be data-bound to controls declared in the view. The data binding will allow for automatic updating of view control display values as well as binding user interface control events and commands related to user interaction to the methods and properties of the view model. The view model will respond to user interaction events to interact with the model. The view model will communicate with the model to make changes and report updates to the model. This allows for a complete separation of the user interface, presentation layer logic, and domain model of your application.

Basic MVVM Implementation in WPF

In this section, you will see how to create a bare-bones MVVM implementation using WPF and C#. This example will illustrate the key concepts of the MVVM design pattern. The view will be represented as a WPF Window. The view model will contain properties that provide data to display in the view using data binding. Notice that there is no code-behind needed; only XAML, the view model, and the model, which represents a class called PersonModel, are required. Remember that this is a basic example of MVVM, so don't be concerned if you don't understand everything in the example. There will be many more examples and explanations throughout this book. Listing 1-3 displays the WPF application markup.

Listing 1-3. The XAML for App.xaml

```
<Application x:Class="BasicMVVMWPF.App"
             xmlns="http://schemas.microsoft.com/winfx/2006/xaml/presentation"
             xmlns:x="http://schemas.microsoft.com/winfx/2006/xaml"
             StartupUri="MainWindow.xaml">
    <Application.Resources>

    </Application.Resources>
</Application>
```

As you can see, the `Application` class can hold application-level resources such as styles and templates. The main purpose for the `Application` class in this example is to provide the main startup object of the application, which is specified in the `StartupUri` attribute. Next up is Listing 1-4, where you see the definition of the `MainWindow.xaml` file, which represents the view.

Listing 1-4. The XAML for MainWindow.xaml (the View)

```
<Window
    xmlns="http://schemas.microsoft.com/winfx/2006/xaml/presentation"
    xmlns:x="http://schemas.microsoft.com/winfx/2006/xaml"
    xmlns:d="http://schemas.microsoft.com/expression/blend/2008" xmlns:mc="http://schemas.
openxmlformats.org/markup-compatibility/2006" mc:Ignorable="d" x:Class="BasicMVVMWPF.
MainWindow"
    xmlns:vm="clr-namespace:BasicMVVMWPF"
    Title="MainWindow" Height="350" Width="525">
    <Window.Resources>
        <vm:MainWindowViewModel x:Key="viewModel" />
    </Window.Resources>
    <Grid>
        <Grid.RowDefinitions>
            <!--Header row-->
            <RowDefinition />
            <!--Content row-->
            <RowDefinition />
            <!--Footer row-->
            <RowDefinition />
        </Grid.RowDefinitions>

        <TextBox x:Name="txtInstructions"
                 Text="This is the View of the application." FontSize="20" Grid.Row="0" />
        <Grid DataContext="{StaticResource ResourceKey=viewModel}" Height="236"
VerticalAlignment="Top" Grid.RowSpan="3" Margin="0,54,0,0">
            <Grid.RowDefinitions>
                <RowDefinition Height="44*" />
                <RowDefinition Height="34*" />
                <RowDefinition Height="40*" />
                <RowDefinition Height="39*" />
                <RowDefinition Height="40*" />
                <RowDefinition Height="39*" />
            </Grid.RowDefinitions>
```

```
            <TextBlock x:Name="txtFullNameDescription" Text="The field below represents the
person's full name"
                    FontSize="20" Grid.Row="0" />
            <TextBlock x:Name="txtPersonFullName" Text="{Binding FullName}"
                    FontSize="20" Grid.Row="1" />
            <TextBlock x:Name="txtFirstNameDescription" Text="The field below represents the
person's first name"
                    FontSize="20" Grid.Row="2" />
            <TextBox x:Name="txtFirstName"
                    Text="{Binding FirstName}" FontSize="20" Grid.Row="3"  />
            <TextBlock x:Name="txtLastNameDescription" Text="The field below represents the
person's last name"
                    FontSize="20" Grid.Row="4" />
            <TextBox x:Name="txtLastName"
                    Text="{Binding LastName}" FontSize="20" Grid.Row="5" />
        </Grid>
    </Grid>
</Window>
```

Here you have a WPF window with two Grid objects for controlling the layout of the TextBox and
TextBlock elements. You add a new XML namespace (xmlns:vm) and, instead of referencing a uniform
resource identifier (URI), you reference the namespace of the view model. Now you can access any class
defined under that namespace in XAML. In the Window.Resources element, you add a resource to the view
model and give the resource a key value of viewModel so that you can access the resource in XAML. You
set the DataContext property equal to the viewModel resource. Now, when you use data binding on other
controls in the Grid, the binding will reference a property on the view model by the same property name.
Now take a look at Listing 1-5, which is the source code for the model class.

Listing 1-5. The C# Source Code for PersonModel.cs (the Model)

```csharp
using System;
using System.Collections.Generic;
using System.ComponentModel;
using System.Linq;
using System.Text;
using System.Threading.Tasks;

namespace BasicMVVMWPF
{
    public class PersonModel : INotifyPropertyChanged
    {
        private string _FirstName;
        private string _LastName;

        public string FirstName
        {
            get { return _FirstName; }
            set
            {
                _FirstName = value;
                OnPropertyChanged("FirstName");
            }
        }
```

```
    public string LastName
    {
        get { return _LastName; }
        set
        {
            _LastName = value;
            OnPropertyChanged("LastName");
        }
    }


    public event PropertyChangedEventHandler PropertyChanged;

    public void OnPropertyChanged(string propertyName)
    {
        if (PropertyChanged != null)
            PropertyChanged(this, new PropertyChangedEventArgs(propertyName));

    }
  }
}
```

As you can see, the model is simple. It represents a Person entity. There are two properties exposed, FirstName and LastName. The class implements the interface InotifyPropertyChanged, which allows the model to alert the view model of any property changes. Finally, Listing 1-6 shows the source code for the view model class.

Listing 1-6. The C# Code for MainWindowViewModel.cs (the View Model)

```
using System;
using System.Collections.Generic;
using System.ComponentModel;
using System.Linq;
using System.Text;
using System.Threading.Tasks;

namespace BasicMVVMWPF
{
    public class MainWindowViewModel : INotifyPropertyChanged
    {
        private PersonModel _Model;
        private string _FullName;

        public MainWindowViewModel()
        {
            _Model = new PersonModel
            {
                FirstName = "Buddy",
                LastName = "James"
            };

            this.FullName = string.Format("{0} {1}", _Model.FirstName, _Model.LastName);
        }
```

```csharp
        public string FirstName
        {
            get { return _Model.FirstName; }
            set
            {
                _Model.FirstName = value;
                this.FullName = string.Format("{0} {1}", _Model.FirstName, _Model.LastName);

                OnPropertyChanged("FirstName");
            }
        }

        public string LastName
        {
            get { return _Model.LastName; }
            set
            {
                _Model.LastName = value;
                this.FullName = string.Format("{0} {1}", _Model.FirstName, _Model.LastName);

                OnPropertyChanged("LastName");
            }
        }

        public string FullName
        {
            get { return _FullName; }
            set
            {
                _FullName = value;
                OnPropertyChanged("FullName");
            }
        }

        public event PropertyChangedEventHandler PropertyChanged;

        public void OnPropertyChanged(string propertyName)
        {
            if (PropertyChanged != null)
                PropertyChanged(this, new PropertyChangedEventArgs(propertyName));

        }
    }
}
```

The view model's source applies the same techniques as the model. You implement the INotifyPropertyChanged interface to alert the view of changes to the properties (via data binding). You also include a new property named FullName, which will return the first and last names when one of those values changes. The first and last names are represented as TextBox controls in the view, so their values can be changed. The FullName property is represented by a TextBlock, which means that the user can't modify the value. Nevertheless, because of the data binding to the view model, you can instantly see the FullName TextBlock's Text property change when you modify either the TextBox for the first or last name.

Summary

In this chapter, you looked at the XAML language. We talked about the differences between declarative programming and imperative programming and how both can work together using XAML and C#. We touched upon data binding and the MVVM design pattern, which allows you to separate the user interface definition (view), the user interaction logic (view model), and the domain business logic (model) using the view model abstraction.

In the next chapter, you will look at some of the design patterns and other design techniques that you'll use to create a line-of-business application that can share code between WPF, Windows Store, and Windows Phone.

CHAPTER 2

■ ■ ■

Software Craftsmanship

"The proof is in the pudding!"

Software as an Art and a Science

Now that we've covered the Extensible Application Markup Language (XAML) and its different "dialects," or anomalies that exist between WPF, Windows 8.1/Windows Store, and Windows Phone 8.1 XAML, we can concentrate on the design patterns and industry best practices that you'll use throughout the rest of this book to design and develop a "smart client" line-of-business (LOB) application. The primary idea of this book is to take you through the experience of working with a virtual (fictional) team. Doing so will aid you in learning the key concepts involved by presenting some of the common issues that you will face and providing you with tips that will resonate with you no matter what area of IT you work in.

The patterns and paradigms presented in this book will provide you with the information you'll need to design and develop robust, reusable, business domain–related software solutions that solve problems found in the enterprise while using effective design methodologies, design patterns, and other tools that are used throughout the software development community.

The book will offer tips and tricks on how to achieve the highest level of user interface layer component reuse between the three XAML-based target platforms. The applications in this book are designed with flexibility in mind. The book will concentrate on the SOLID object-oriented design principles to aid you when designing the classes that make up your applications. The ultimate goal is to illustrate how to design applications that are divided into logical layers that promote a clear separation of concerns. Physically, the layers will represents class libraries that are concise, flexible, extensible, and loosely coupled from other components throughout the system. This will maximize code reuse throughout your organization, as well as make your code easier to write unit tests for.

SOLID Object-Oriented Design

The *S* in SOLID stands for the Single Responsibility principle. This principle means that a class should have one and only one responsibility. As an example, your `Order` class shouldn't be concerned with how yearly reports are printed. This would be the responsibility of a class called `ReportPrintService`. The `Order` class should be responsible only for describing an order in the system.

The *O* in SOLID stands for the Open/Close principle. This means you should design your code to be open to extensibility and closed to modification. You may ask yourself, "How can I make a class open to being extended without modifying the code?" There are several ways to assist you with this principle. For instance, you could create a base class and inherit from the base class to implement methods on your own. Our favorite approach is a design pattern called the Decorator pattern. You can find the official definition at `http://sourcemaking.com/design_patterns/decorator`.

"The Decorator Pattern attaches additional responsibilities to an object dynamically. Decorators provide a flexible alternative to subclass for extending functionality."

We will provide a full example of this pattern, as well as other useful design patterns, later in this chapter. The *L* in SOLID stands for the Liskov substitution principle. This means you should be able to reference an instance of your class as any base class or any interface in which the class implements. The *I* in SOLID stands for the Interface Segregation principle, which states that when possible, you should code to an interface rather than a concrete implementation. Finally, the *D* in SOLID stands for the Dependency Inversion principle, which promotes two patterns: Dependency Injection (DI) and Inversion of Control.

■ **Note** The SOLID object design principles represent an acronym in which each letter represents a principle to consider when designing a class, property, or method in object-oriented design.

To Unit Test or Not to Unit Test?

The topic of unit testing spurs debates where each participant feels strongly about their stance. One party might say, "Unit tests sound great in theory, but I don't have time to meet deadlines *and* write unit tests from which I gain nothing!" Another individual may insist, "Unit tests are the best thing since sliced bread and the butter that you put on it!" A third party may make the claim, "I've written code for more than 20 years just fine without unit tests." Finally, there may be an individual who believes, "With unit tests, I know the moment that a bug is introduced into the system, as well as where to find it." These are just a few of the arguments that come to mind.

There is no absolute "correct" answer. Honestly, does unit testing add extra development time? Generally, the answer is "yes." Does unit testing help reduce the bugs in an application? There have been many studies that suggest that unit testing does in fact help make your code less error prone. Just like anything else, unit testing takes practice to gain proficiency, which means that your unit tests will provide quality protection only when they are quality tests. You have to know what to test and what unit tests are redundant or misleading. Practice makes perfect!

Test-Driven Development

While we are on the topic of unit tests, we're obligated to talk a bit about Test-Driven Development (TDD). TDD is a software development paradigm in which you write unit tests *before* you even implement the class under testing. If you write each test before the method you are testing, you guarantee that all methods will be covered with a unit test.

There is another benefit to using TDD that many people overlook. If you write a unit test for the method `PrintService.PrintReport()` before a `PrintService.PrintReport()` exists, then you are designing the method and the public contract of the `PrintService` class. This design is based on how you would naturally imagine the class should be used. Thus, not only do you guarantee that each method has at least one unit test associated with it, you also get to design your classes based on how you would use the class. When the unit test is finished, it can serve as a succinct example of how the class should be used.

There is more to TDD than writing unit tests first, so here are the rules for TDD:

- The first rule to consider is "Make sure that the unit test fails." Obviously, if you write the test before the class under testing even exists, your solution will not compile. This isn't the same as the first failure you are after, so you'll want to create an empty class declaration for the classes used in the test so that it will build properly. Once the test builds, then run it to experience the first failure. Once your test fails, the next step is to make the smallest change possible to the class under test and then run it again. Do this until the test passes. The key to this process is the importance of making small incremental changes until the test passes. If you were to get your unit test to build and fail the first time, then you would move forward to make the test pass. We recommend that you then write the entire method quickly, trying to anticipate issues and other ideas for the class that you would then implement. Instead of making small incremental changes to achieve a passing unit test, make one big change and even add some fields or methods that you know will be coming up. So, what's the big deal? Well, when you make the smallest changes possible in an incremental fashion, you will add only what is absolutely necessary, which will greatly reduce the size and complexity of your code.

- Now it's time to refactor the method. Since you used small, incremental changes, you should refactor the method that you've created to make sure that it is clean and concise. Thus, the cycle goes like this: Red ➤ Green ➤ Refactor ➤ Retest.

  - *Red*: The unit test failed because of no implementation.

  - *Green*: The unit test passes after small, incremental changes. The small incremental changes guarantee that you don't jump ahead of yourself and that you add only the code that is needed to make the test pass, and this can reduce complexity.

  - *Refactor*: Go back and refactor your new code to clean up the implementation, and test again to make sure your refactoring didn't break anything.

  - *Retest*: Move on to your next test.

Imagine that you wanted to write an application that would accept a user's name during login and return a welcome message to the user. A TDD style would go something like this:

1. Create a new blank solution in Visual Studio.

2. Create a class library for the functionality of the program, create a new unit test project for the solution, and add a reference to the class library so that the test can actually use the library to test it.

3. Rename the default unit test class that is created with the unit test project.

4. Create your first test, which would looking something like the one shown in Listing 2-1.

Listing 2-1. GreetingTests.cs

```csharp
using System;
using Microsoft.VisualStudio.TestPlatform.UnitTestFramework;
using ApressXaml.Usb;

namespace ApressXaml.Usb.UnitTests
{
    [TestClass]
    public class GreetingTests
    {
        private IUserLoginService _UserLoginService;

        [TestInitialize]
        public void Test_Init()
        {
            _UserLoginService = new UserLoginService();
        }

        [TestMethod]
        public void If_A_Name_Length_GreaterThan_0_Then_Service:Returns_Message()
        {
            if (_UserLoginService == null)
                throw new NullReferenceException();

            var validName = "Buddy";

            var actualGreeting = _UserLoginService.GreetUser(validName);
            var expectedGreeting = "Hello Buddy!";

            Assert.AreEqual(expectedGreeting, actualGreeting, "The user greeting is incorrect");
        }
    }
}
```

As you can see, there is a simple test class here. You create an IUserLoginServer interface and a UserLoginService class in the class library so that the solution will compile. Nevertheless, there is no implementation, so the test will fail at first (which is what you want to happen).

Now that the test has successfully failed, it's time to make small incremental changes until the test passes, as shown in Listing 2-2.

Listing 2-2. Empty IUserLoginService.cs Interface Definition

```
using System;
using System.Collections.Generic;
using System.Linq;
using System.Text;

namespace ApressXaml.Usb
{
    public interface IUserLoginService
    {
        string GreetUser(string userName);
    }
}
```

As you can see in Listing 2-3, the only thing that exists in the class is the GreetUser method declaration. This is required for the solution to build so that the test can fail. Now, you need to make the smallest change possible to make the test pass. This should be pretty easy.

Listing 2-3. Empty UserLoginService.cs Class Definition

```
using System;
using System.Collections.Generic;
using System.Linq;
using System.Text;

namespace ApressXaml.Usb
{
    public class UserLoginService : IUserLoginService
    {
        public string GreetUser(string validName)
        {
            throw new NotImplementedException();
        }
    }
}
```

Replace the line in which the NonImplementedException is thrown with the functionality that is expected in the unit test. Listing 2-4 shows the class with this small change added.

Listing 2-4. UserLoginService.cs with Small, Incremental Change to Make the Test Pass

```
using System;
using System.Collections.Generic;
using System.Linq;
using System.Text;

namespace ApressXaml.Usb
{
    public class UserLoginService : IUserLoginService
    {
        public string GreetUser(string validName)
        {
            return string.Format("Hello {0}!", validName);
        }
    }
}
```

As you can see, only one line of code is different, and when the test is run again, it passes. However, look at the code for a moment. There are no null reference checks on the validName parameter. This validName parameter should have a name that fits better with its purpose, and you should always check for null values.

This is the part of TDD that was hard for us to get used to. Starting out, we would have identified these issues and resolved them on the first edit of the class. Through much practice, however, we have learned to wait until the refactor stage of the process so that we can reap the benefits of changing only the minimum amount of code on each iteration until the test passes.

Now that it's time to refactor the method, make the modifications shown in Listing 2-5, and retest until all tests pass. Then move on to the next test and, in return, the next feature.

Listing 2-5. The Final Version of the UserLoginService.cs After Refactoring and Retesting

```
using System;
using System.Collections.Generic;
using System.Linq;
using System.Text;

namespace ApressXaml.Usb
{
    public class UserLoginService : IUserLoginService
    {
        public string GreetUser(string userName)
        {
            if (string.IsNullOrEmpty(userName))
                throw new ArgumentNullException("userName");

            if (userName.Length == 0)
                throw new ArgumentException("userName cannot be empty.");

            return string.Format("Hello {0}!", userName);
        }
    }
}
```

As you can see, you've added some defensive programming (null reference checks), renamed the parameter, and changed the method's return type. Once you've finished these refactorings, the test is rerun, and this time it passes. That's how we prefer to use TDD. You will write many more unit tests in this book before the solution is complete.

Meet the Team

Design methodologies and design patterns are the major components of any software project, but before we get into the design patterns that we will use in this book, let's meet our virtual team! The scenario is that you've recently accepted an offer from Acme Systems to assist in the development of several line-of-business applications. The company has recently changed owners, and they've decided to bring all enterprise systems development in-house. The team is filled with individuals who have their own roles to play, have their own opinions, and bring different levels of experience to their jobs.

The Development Manager

The *development manager* is the person to whom you report. The development manager's job is to manage all of the resources allocated for this new company initiative. The development manager must stay on top of people, project budgets, and timelines.

The Business Analyst

The *business analyst* knows the business. Even more important, the business analyst knows what questions to ask the business users in order to get useful information regarding the software project. The business analyst will take requirements-gathering questions from the developers, provide explanations on why they are problematic, and offer solutions. The business analyst's role is to emphasize the importance of gaining knowledge of the business domain to ensure that the users' needs are met.

The Junior Developer

The *junior developer* is an entry-level .NET programmer with the least amount of experience on the team. The junior developer is fresh out of college. This is the developer's first job in software development. Everyone says that the junior developer is a quick learner who loves doing software development. The junior developer is enthusiastic, which can sometimes be misinterpreted as being overzealous—but this individual means well. The junior developer stays on top of all of the newest technologies and is quick to suggest their use on projects. The junior developer will look to you for guidance, and in pointing out mistakes, you can learn something new too. Most people can relate to the junior developer; after all, everyone was that person once in their careers.

The Guru

The *guru* works magic with the keyboard. The guru's experience includes all of the design patterns and technologies used throughout the book. The guru is the "go-to" guy (yes, pun intended) for anything related to software (and then some). The guru can be stubborn when it comes to software development, though this individual has been known to adopt a new technology after personally considering all of the important factors. The guru is a bit of an introvert; however, when asked, this individual is happy to provide guidance to the team.

The DBA

The *DBA* works in the realm of data access and storage. The DBA holds the keys to the database (yes, pun intended again). The DBA is in control of data access–related decisions from database server types used to the schemas, roles, users, and permissions. The DBA is in charge of schema change requests during development. The DBA is also responsible for database backup and restoration (disaster recovery). You must always remember that the DBA is not only in charge of new systems but also of old legacy systems.

The First Team Design Meeting

The first design meeting consists of you, the junior developer, the guru, the business analyst, the DBA, the product champion, and the development manager.

During this meeting, the team's agenda is as follows:

- Have the team meet and get acquainted with one another

- Discuss the business problem that will be solved by the team

- Identify each person's role on the team

- Discuss any project deadlines that exist

- Decide on a team development paradigm

- Create meeting schedules

- Decide on the methods of communication that the team will use

- Decide on technologies that will be used (based on the information that's been given)

In the first meeting, you will learn about the business problem that needs to be solved. Aside from the product champion, the business analyst has the greatest knowledge of the business's processes on the team. The product champion is an employee of the client and is considered a "power user." These individuals have been chosen to allocate time every week to assist with the development of the solution.

As the meeting starts, the business analyst explains the details of the business problem to be solved. "As many of you know, Acme has decided to bring all system development in-house. This decision came about when it was discovered that a mandatory accounting system update broke integration with the in-house purchasing requisition system used throughout Acme Systems."

The plan is to rewrite the entire accounting system over the course of one year. The decision to start with the purchasing requisition system was made because the old solution no longer works with the legacy system.

If there is anything that we've learned over the last ten years in software development, it is this: if you provide a software developer with 20 reams of printed UML diagrams and other legacy-style design artifacts and you request that they create a software solution, nine times out of ten you will end up with an application that makes perfect sense to the developer and yet still does not click with business users' ideas of what the system should be. This is because typical software developers are experts in software development, not in the business domain in which they are solving a business problem. Developers don't think like users.

The point is that you need feedback from a user of the system, and you need the feedback often during the development of the software solution. With constant feedback during development, you can rest assured that you are developing for the users' needs.

Scrum Agile Methodologies

All team members have experience with the Scrum agile team paradigm, so they decide to use Scrum and agile methodologies. As such, it's decided that the team will work in two-week sprints, or iterations, of development and that they will use Team Foundation Services (TFS) 2013 to record the product backlog, plan and schedule sprints, and create user stories and tasks, as well as for source control for the application.

TFS is a great choice because of its awesome integration with Visual Studio. It's a one-stop shop for tracking issues, tracking bugs, recording user stories, and providing estimates. You can create a user story through its life cycle, from creation through creating specific child tasks that contain all of the information you need to develop the story, all the way through acceptance testing.

The integration of TFS with SharePoint adds a nice web-friendly user interface. You can create Excel spreadsheets that display graphs relating to sprints completed and the remainder of your product backlog. The SharePoint TFS portal has a wiki that the team can use to capture important information regarding the project. You can plan sprints from the Web and much more.

One of the features of TFS is an absolute godsend—its integration with Microsoft Office. You can create queries to retrieve a subset of TFS work items and export the list to an Excel spreadsheet. The spreadsheet will allow you to work on batch item creation with little effort as compared to entering 50-plus user stories manually. Furthermore, some people will demand a spreadsheet over a URL to all of the information they could possibly need. Ah, the communal spreadsheet—one spreadsheet, one network share, and four different users. You may have been there are smiling and gritting your teeth. Those of you who haven't been there, be thankful.

The team decides that the software will be created with as much unit test coverage as possible, and they will use the mstest functionality built into Visual Studio to maintain the unit tests. The team requests another meeting in two weeks to work with the product champion to create user stories and identify other requirements.

■ **Note**   TFS is Microsoft's source control solution. It provides work item tracking, automated builds, and much more.

How to "Talk the Talk" When It Comes to Gathering Requirements

As a developer, I'm sure you've realized that users of your business applications line don't care that you implemented a linked list from scratch while writing the program. They care about how the system is used, the results it produces, and the speed at which the results are produced. Thus, it's important for developers to work closely with business users to learn as much as possible about the business side of a user's day-to-day workload and how to create software to improve their jobs.

One major component to doing this is simply vocabulary. During brainstorming sessions, be sure to identify nouns and verbs as the business analyst and end user explain the system. If you ask a question and the answer starts with something like "Do you mean a _____?" these are the terms that you need to identify and record so that they can later become part of your ubiquitous language (see Chapter 3).

The more you know about the business side of the problem for which you are creating a solution, the better your chances are of success. Try to study the business domain in nonprogramming terms. Perhaps offer to buy the business analyst or the business user lunch so that you can discuss any questions you may have. Try to speak their language.

User Stories and How to Create Them

In agile development, a *user story* is basically a simplified use case. It represents an interaction between the user and the system. Sometimes, a user story will even represent an interaction between two systems!

The Anatomy of a Good User Story

There are many well-known traits of a good user story. First, a user story must serve a value to the business. This means the user story should be written using the ubiquitous language of the business domain so that anyone involved can understand the request.

Another key to a great user story is brevity. The idea isn't to hash out every aspect of the design and development of a user story's features. Rather, you should capture just enough information to be able to refer to the user story later on during development, and if the feature makes the cut, then use the user story to start planning the design of the feature. Had you created the user story with the feature's design choice at the start and the user story didn't make the cut, you would have lost all of the time working on a feature's design that would not be implemented. Keep it short, sweet, and in the terms of the business domain.

When consulting, we use index cards when we're creating user stories. You can even ask the business user if they wouldn't mind trying to write the stories on these cards in their own words. If the user explains the user story, you definitely capture what the user wants and in the business domain's terms. If you're writing them yourself, you can write a story title, the date, and then a brief description. Remember, the idea is not to capture all of the important details; the point is to write enough to remember how to ask for the details when they are needed.

Summary

Indeed, software development is both an art and a science. Over the last ten years, there have been major advancements in programming styles, software design, and requirements gathering. Somewhere along the way, we learned to stop creating massive amounts of work at the beginning of a project. Instead, we began to understand that change is nearly guaranteed, and the current style of design was neither conducive nor friendly to change. These changes ruined estimates and then budgets and ultimately produced software that the user had to learn to "deal with" rather than enjoy.

Now we have agile methodologies that put the business first. Without a business problem, there is no software solution to build. We've learned that user involvement in design is vital to a business application line and that it's best to be involved with a selected user to show progress and to receive feedback immediately.

There's another software design style that lines right up with our newfound views of a business-centric software development solution. It's called Domain-Driven Design (DDD), and we will discuss this design methodology in the next chapter.

PART II

Laying the Groundwork

CHAPTER 3

■■■

Domain-Driven Design

We don't write code; we solve business problems.

Introducing Domain-Driven Design

How do you measure the success of a software project? Do you rely solely on deploying the solution on schedule? Does the quantity and quality of design documents, such as a vision and scope document, package diagrams, component diagrams, key feature class diagrams, and other various Unified Modeling Language (UML) diagrams provide an indicator of a project's success or failure? Have you seen the documentation created in a waterfall design–based software development project? I think trying to keep all of these documents in sync with the constantly changing requirements of a system is a nightmare. No thanks; I'd rather sleep at night.

I believe a software project is considered a success when the resulting application provides the value requested by the user to improve business processes. Oftentimes it makes life much easier for users by streamlining their workflow and allowing them to be more productive (being on schedule and on budget doesn't hurt either).

Over the past ten years, there has been an evolution in application development. Object-oriented design is mature and here to stay. The industry has welcomed the idea of design patterns with open arms. Of all of the new paradigms, however, none has put more into practice than has Domain-Driven Design (DDD).

■ **Caution** Domain-Driven Design is a vast collection of rules, terms, guidelines, and patterns. In fact, in order to cover the paradigm completely, I would need to write a book on the subject. This book contains only an overview of DDD. This book provides enough coverage to enable you to understand the architecture of the sample line-of-business applications that you are going to develop. Nonetheless, I strongly recommend that you pick up a copy of *Domain-Driven Design: Tackling Complexity in the Heart of Software* by Eric Evans (Prentice Hall, 2003). This was the first book on DDD and is commonly referred to as the "blue book." It is *the* book for learning every aspect of Domain-Driven Design, and it contains the first official introduction to the collective concepts that represent DDD.

What Is Domain-Driven Design?

Simply put, *Domain-Driven Design* is a framework for designing and developing software solutions in which the design is built around the entities that make up the business domain. DDD provides a set of guidelines that help align your software design and implementation with the expectations of the customer.

Once you've built a domain model based on the core entities that make up the business domain, you then work to add support for the relationships between the entities and how they are supposed to interact with each other and the rest of the system. You work closely with a business analyst and, if you are lucky, the people who will actually use the finished product in order to make sure that you deliver what the user expects. Feedback is an excellent way to determine what the client wants, so you should schedule receiving feedback from the client as often as possible.

If you follow agile methodologies like Scrum, as you will do throughout the book, then the purpose of each sprint is to deliver a scheduled set of features derived from user stories. At the end of each sprint, you should have a working piece of software that delivers at least one feature that the end user should be able to test and on which they should be able to provide feedback. If you deploy the features delivered in each sprint and receive direct feedback regarding development, you will know right away if you start to stray from alignment with the client's needs regarding the solution that you are developing.

For you to develop software for a specific business domain, you must take time to learn the current processes, rules, constraints, and terminology of the domain. This requires the team to have access to a business analyst or, even better, a user of the proposed system who can explain how things work, specifically in terms relating to the business and not to software development.

Before Domain-Driven Design

Before DDD, business analysts would gather requirements for the application to be developed. The business analyst would then work with an architect to create a verbose set of software design documents and UML diagrams. They would design every aspect of the application before writing a single line of code. The design documentation would serve as a way to create the project schedule, generate the plan for the required resources, and fashion the project budget.

As time went on, it became clear that this approach wasn't very effective. In light of all of the time spent on creating design documents, these projects would rarely even consider how to handle a change of requirements. Developers would rely on a "requirements freeze," which meant that, after a certain point, requirements would not change. The problem with this approach is that not only can requirements change, but they usually do!

The practice of designing a software solution from beginning to end before writing any code can be compared to the process of designing and constructing a house. When you build a house, you work with a contractor and make all of the decisions regarding the details of the design of the house. Once the computer-aided design (CAD) drawings are created and the client has signed off on the design plans, the contractor and construction team will then begin to build the house. Following along with this example, imagine that the contractor is 40 percent finished with the house and the client requests a modification that requires a change to the foundation's layout. Indeed, I would not want to be the contractor facing this dilemma!

This is where it becomes clear that older software design and development paradigms aren't really optimal design styles because requirements are likely to change throughout the development process. Application requirements don't experience change only during design and development. Technology is constantly changing. It's possible that you may need to change virtually any aspect of a software solution at any given moment in response to a change in technology, such as the release of a new NoSQL database storage engine, a cloud-based file system, or perhaps an update to the implementations of external system dependencies.

Oftentimes, a user will think they need a specific feature. However, when they receive the final application, only then are the design flaws brought to light. In these instances, the client will have to learn to work around the bad design decisions that were made when the requirements were gathered at the beginning of the project. For this reason, Domain-Driven Design advocates use agile development practices to interact with the user throughout the development life cycle in order to obtain feedback as the software is developed.

The point is that change is part of software development, and Domain-Driven Design (along with agile methodologies) introduces a set of guidelines that promotes developing software that is flexible and extensible in order to minimize the effects of changes to the requirements.

UML Hell and Stale "Requirements Documents"

Unified Modeling Language provides standards to communicate software development design artifacts in a predefined graphical format. I'll admit it, up until this point, I have not painted the best picture of UML. The truth is, I like UML. It's when UML is overused that I have a problem with it. When UML began to gain traction with object-oriented software design and analysis methodologies, many people considered UML to be the "magic bullet" to good design. As a result, there was a lot of time wasted making diagrams that were never looked at after their initial release.

Changes to requirements, along with large volumes of useless design diagrams, create several problems when developing software solutions, one of which is stale documentation.

You are more likely to update design documents if they are essential to the project. Domain-Driven Design promotes combining the model with the implementation. Your code should express the design details of your model clearly.

Business User? Who's That?

Who are the business users? They are some of the most important people involved in the process of creating a line-of-business application. They are a group of people who have to deal with the issues associated with the business problem that your software solution is designed to solve. I can safely say that for projects on which I've worked, the direct involvement of a potential user to whom I was able to direct questions freely and receive constant and consistent feedback were easily the best and most rewarding. The resulting solutions were tailor-made for the business user's needs. A happy client is the best indicator regarding the success of a software development project.

The fact of the matter is that you don't always have the advantage of working directly with a business user. Generally, you work with a business analyst instead. If the analyst has a clear picture of the business domain, then you can still achieve great success in your development projects. The key point is that with Domain-Driven Design, the entire team needs to be on the same page regarding the entities, the processes, the external systems, and, most importantly, the ubiquitous language regarding the business's terminology as it relates to the context of the business domain problem space.

Ubiquitous Language

When working on a business problem, you can ask five different users, with five different roles, to define a particular domain entity, and you may receive five completely different answers. That's because certain terms and definitions when used in the context of one user's role may vary completely when used in the context of a different user's role.

This concept applies to the development team as well. When working as a team to learn and understand the ins and outs of a business domain, it's important to understand that there will be gaps in the ways that each individual relates to a particular business concept and therefore how they understand it.

The solution involves working as a team to create a ubiquitous language that covers the gaps in various interpretations of business terms. A *ubiquitous language* is a dictionary full of business terms that are related to the domain in which you are working to create a domain model. This will form a standard, unified language to be used when referring to domain terminology, which will prevent confusion and promote consistency in the domain model.

The Domain Model in Domain-Driven Design

What is a domain model? A *domain model* is a loosely coupled component that embodies all entities, value objects, aggregate roots, and domain services, which are used to describe the business domain in which you are creating a software solution. The domain model is the core of the Domain-Driven Design paradigm. The domain model is source code that uses business terminology from your ubiquitous language to "model" the business domain in code.

The domain model should encapsulate only the constructs that are relevant to the business domain. This separation of concerns is extremely important. When the domain is modeled purely from business entities, it can easily be changed based upon user requests. When you ensure that your domain model is loosely coupled with other parts of the system, the model can easily be reused in future software solutions created to solve new business problems.

The Source Code Is the Design Documentation

In Domain-Driven Design, the source code represents the domain model, and therefore it serves as the documentation. There are various other documents that you can create as part of your process; however, the code should be clear and based on the business domain such that the design speaks for itself. This is another instance in which unit testing comes into play when writing an application. For instance, a new developer can look at unit tests to see how any class is meant to be used—any constraints, argument value ranges, expected exceptions, and so on.

Domain Entities

The *domain entity* sits at the core of Domain-Driven Design. During requirements-gathering sessions, you and your team should work with the business analyst or user to discuss the business processes related to the task at hand. As you do this, you will identify nouns that will later represent terms in your ubiquitous language and eventually a class in your system.

Domain entities have specific rules regarding their design. An entity should represent something in the business domain that has a unique identity. For instance, if you were working on an order placement system, you would have an entity called Order. The class should provide only the properties and methods for which it is responsible.

A domain entity should be ignorant regarding how and when it is persisted to the data store. This is a guideline that you often need to ignore when creating entities. For instance, if you plan to save and retrieve an entity from the data source, then you will generally encapsulate an ID property of some sort that relates to the database. This ID property has nothing to do with the business; however, it is a convenience when saving and retrieving an object. Remember, just like any other design methodologies, these are guidelines, not laws. You have to decide what works best for you.

Domain entities should be cohesive units of code that represent unique entities in the domain. An entity should know how to validate its state as well as be aware of the way that it interacts with any collaborating entities or value objects. The less your entities know about other parts of the system, the better. This cohesion assists in creating domain entities that can be used in other applications.

As you can see in Listing 3-1, the Employee entity is as simple as it needs to be. We've included a unique identifier and the relevant attributes that describe the employee. Always try to keep your entities as simple as possible, adding complexity only when necessary.

Listing 3-1. Example of a Person Entity in C#

```csharp
using System;
using System.Collections.Generic;
using System.Linq;
using System.Text;
using System.Threading.Tasks;

namespace Purchasing.Domain
{
    public class Employee
    {
        public enum EmployeeRoleType
        {
            GeneralEmployee = 0,
            TeamLeader = 1,
            Supervisor = 2
        }

        private int _Id;
        private string _FirstName;
        private string _LastName;
        private EmployeeRoleType _Role;

        public int Id
        {
            get { return _Id; }
        }

        public string FirstName
        {
            get { return _FirstName; }
            set { _FirstName = value; }
        }

        public string LastName
        {
            get { return _LastName; }
            set { _LastName = value; }
        }
```

```
    public EmployeeRoleType Role
    {
        get { return _Role; }
        set { _Role = value; }
    }

    public Employee(int id)
    {
        _Id = id;
    }
  }
}
```

Domain Aggregate Roots

One of the tougher aspects of modeling the domain in source code is modeling references effectively to other entities. In most domains, you will find an entity that contains a private field that represents a collection of child entities or value objects. How can you model such references so that a modification to the state of any referenced entity is correctly propagated throughout the entire chain of references? This is where aggregate roots come into play.

An *aggregate* in the context of Domain-Driven Design is a collection of associated objects that are bound together for the purposes of modeling data modifications. Every aggregate has a root and a boundary. The root entity is the only object in the aggregate that can be referenced by objects outside of the aggregate boundary. Of course, inside the aggregate boundary, entities can reference each other. Otherwise, there would be no way to model complex associations.

Take, for instance, the Order entity mentioned earlier. This entity may have a collection of OrderItem entity objects. Each OrderItem entity could have an associated Product entity, and so on. In this example, the Order entity serves as the aggregate root. The Order entity is the only entity in the aggregate boundary in which an object outside of the boundary may hold a reference, such as a property or field.

The aggregate root entity may transiently pass a reference to a child entity to be used in a single operation, in which the calling object may not hold on to the reference. The aggregate root's identity must be global while the entities throughout the boundary should have local identities. The root entity is responsible for checking all invariants or constraints throughout the aggregate's boundary.

The aggregate roots should be the only entities that can be retrieved by a database query. All other entities of the aggregate must be loaded by following the associations of the aggregate. Finally, if any modifications are made to an object within the aggregate and the modifications are committed, all of the invariants or constraints must be satisfied. As long as the aggregate root controls all access to objects in the aggregate boundary, then there is one point of change for the data, and you can be sure that all invariants are enforced.

Here in Listing 3-2, you have an Order aggregate root entity that holds a reference to a collection of LineItem entities. The only way to access any information regarding the collection of LineItem objects is through the aggregate root Order entity object.

Listing 3-2. *Aggregate Root That Represents an Order Placed by a Customer*

```csharp
using System;
using System.Collections.Generic;
using System.Linq;
using System.Text;
using System.Threading.Tasks;

namespace Purchasing.Domain
{
    /// <summary>
    /// Represents a customer's order
    /// </summary>
    public class Order
    {
        #region "private members"

        private int _Id;
        private IList<LineItem> _LineItems;
        private double _OrderTotal;

        #endregion

        #region "public properties"

        public int Id
        {
            get { return _Id; }
        }

        public int LineItemCount
        {
            get
            {
                return _LineItems.Count();
            }
        }

        #endregion

        #region "constructor"

        public Order()
        {
            _LineItems = new List<LineItem>();
        }

        public Order(int id)
        {
            _Id = id;
            _LineItems = new List<LineItem>();
        }
```

```
    #endregion

    #region "public methods"

    public void AddLineItem(LineItem lineItem)
    {
        _LineItems.Add(lineItem);
    }

    public double CalculateOrderTotal()
    {
        foreach (var lineItem in _LineItems)
        {
            _OrderTotal += lineItem.Price;
        }

        return _OrderTotal;
    }

    #endregion
    }
}
```

Domain Value Objects

A *value object* in the domain model is an object similar to an entity; the difference is that an entity has a unique identity and a value object does not. A well-known example of a value object would be a class that represents a customer's address. The Customer object is clearly an entity because it has an identity and life cycle, which is tracked in the domain. The Address object, however, may describe the address of any customer, person, or business. An Address value object would have properties for street, house number, postal or ZIP code, state, country, and so on. When it comes to modeling value objects, you care about the attributes. Value objects should be immutable in order to make sharing references and different instances of the value safe.

When you make a value object immutable, it means you don't change the reference to it. If modifications need to be made, you must replace the reference with a new instance of the value object. Some other great examples of value objects are lists that are used in your application, such as a drop-down list that is bound to a collection of State value objects, which allow the user to select a state. The collection of State value objects can be shared with any part of the system that needs to present a list of states. A drop-down box that allows the user to pick a color is another good example of where you would want to create a value object (in this case, the class would be Color).

Domain Services

Oftentimes, there are operations that belong in the domain; however, they don't match up with any specific entity. You create these operations as methods that belong to classes called *domain services*. Domain services are often used to orchestrate operations that involve one or more entities. These service objects contain methods that represent actions that work with multiple domain objects to accomplish an activity specified in the model.

When it comes to domain services, you must be careful that you don't get lazy. For example, instead of identifying an activity as a behavior or responsibility of an entity or value object, you simply create a service. At the same time, services assist you by providing a place to implement operations that belong in the domain but that don't belong to any specific entity or value object. If you were to add a method to an entity simply because you couldn't find anywhere else to put the functionality, you would complicate the entity and the responsibilities of the entity would become cloudy. It's much better to model this type of functionality as a domain service to protect the integrity of the domain model.

Domain services must be stateless. It shouldn't matter how an instance of a domain service has been used prior to using the instance of the service. The service will use data from the entities in which it operates; however, it does not hold any state-related properties itself. This reduces complexity by removing the need to worry about when an instance of the service was created or which operations have been executed and in what order.

The methods of domain services should be named using the ubiquitous language of the domain model. We usually name our domain services with the suffix of *Service*. A couple of examples of domain service names are PurchasingService and ReportService.

In Listing 3-3, you see OrderService, which is a domain service that works with an Order aggregate root Order entity and an IOrderRepository instance to save the Order and generate an Invoice entity. (We'll discuss the Repository pattern in the next chapter.)

Listing 3-3. OrderService.cs Domain Service

```csharp
using System;
using System.Collections.Generic;
using System.Linq;
using System.Text;
using System.Threading.Tasks;
using Purchasing.Domain.Service.Interfaces;

namespace Purchasing.Domain.Service
{
    public class OrderService : IOrderService
    {
        private IOrderRepository _OrderRepository;

        public OrderService(IOrderRepository orderRepository)
        {
            _OrderRepository = orderRepository;
        }

        public Invoice CreateInvoice(Order order)
        {
            _OrderRepository.AddOrder(order);
            _OrderRepository.Commit();

            var invoice =
                new Invoice { OrderTotal = order.CalculateOrderTotal() };

            return invoice;
        }
    }
}
```

Domain Events

Domain events are domain objects that represent the occurrence of an event that is important to the domain. Domain events are objects that contain all of the attributes required to express the event that has occurred.

Domain events are powerful because they provide a way of notifying any part of the system when an event occurs about which the system needs to be aware. Moreover, depending on your event dispatching and subscription systems, events can transcend logical layers, physical tiers, and so forth. Events also provide assistance when adhering to the rules of aggregate root persistence. We will discuss specific design patterns for event publication and subscription in the next chapter.

CQRS: Command Query Responsibility Segregation

Command Query Responsibility Segregation (CQRS) is a design philosophy in which operations are divided into two types: commands that change the domain entity data and query-related operations that read data from the domain. The idea is to model your classes based on these two fundamental types of operations. You end up with services that contain only commands and with services that contain only queries. Essentially, what you are left with is an abstraction of all commands and an abstraction of all queries. In some instances, a sharp definition can improve the clarity of the domain model. We will not use CQRS in this book; however, it is important to be aware of the concept for your reference.

Summary

Domain-Driven Design is not a "magic bullet." Still, once you invest the time required to use DDD effectively, you and your team will create software solutions that are well aligned with the requests of users. You will create loosely coupled components, which can be used throughout the enterprise when new applications are created.

For all of the advantages to using DDD, there are also some valid concerns, including the following:

- The need to climb a steep learning curve.

- An absolute commitment to DDD among the team members.

- A willingness of team members to invest the time necessary to learn the principles of DDD.

- To use DDD effectively, the entire team must share an understanding of the business domain. As design progresses, there will be questions raised and modifications required based on the answers to those questions. The team must have access to someone with deep knowledge of the business domain in order to validate the assumptions made throughout the entire project life cycle.

As you can see, there is a lot to learn with DDD. We're confident that this chapter has provided enough information to whet your appetite to continue to learn and practice this awesome design methodology. Nevertheless, like most other things in life, the only way for you to learn DDD is to practice it. We hope that we've provided enough background for you to follow along with the reasons behind the design decisions that you will make throughout the rest of this book.

Next up, we will cover the design patterns used in modern applications that work hand-in-hand with Domain-Driven Design.

CHAPTER 4

■ ■ ■

Design Patterns

A design pattern in programming is the equivalent of a recipe in cooking. Can you make chocolate chip cookies without following a recipe? Of course, you can. However, you will be investing a lot of time and effort into trying to solve an issue that's already been solved. You will basically reinvent the wheel, we mean, the cookie.

Not only do design patterns assist developers in solving common problems when developing software, they also establish a ubiquitous language to use when discussing a particular implementation. Design patterns are written in such a way that there are universal terms associated with the implementation details of the solution. This will promote efficiency among your development team. For instance, if your entire team is well versed in design patterns and the vocabulary that is used to describe the problems and solutions, it's much easier to communicate ideas or problems without resorting to using a whiteboard. This absence of ambiguity can benefit junior developers too. If the team speaks the same language, then experience levels are irrelevant.

If you know what a design pattern is, then chances are you've heard of the Gang of Four. Just in case you haven't, the Gang of Four is a group of authors who collaborated to write *Design Patterns: Elements of Reusable Object-Oriented Software* (Addison-Wesley Professional, 1995), the de facto book on design patterns. This is a must-have reference for any software developer. There are 23 design patterns in the book. However, the book you are currently reading is not about design patterns, so we will cover only the patterns that are relevant to the application that you'll be building throughout the rest of the book. Before we cover the design patterns that you will use, it's important for us to discuss the different types of architectures used in modern domain-driven applications.

Architecture Types

If you are a software developer writing a line-of-business (LOB) application, chances are that you are familiar with the concept of *n-tier application design*. This style of design describes software that separates common application components into libraries, which allows different parts of your application to reside on multiple computers or servers.

In the past, it was common for line-of-business systems to keep all application resources on the same machine as the application's executable. These resources include INI files, Access databases, trace logs, and other pieces of data required for the application to solve a business problem. As technology prices have dropped and computer literacy has increased, there is now more data than ever, and that data is growing exponentially. It's no longer practical to keep an application's data on a single user's workstation.

These days, most businesses have full departments dedicated to information technology. In a typical office environment, nearly all employees have their own PC, which they use to run the applications that allow them to do their day-to-day work. This creates the need for centralized databases and other shared resources that can handle access from multiple users.

Most applications communicate with some sort of server. These servers include relational database management systems (RDBMSs), web servers for web applications and services, Active Directory domain controllers for authorization and authentication, and many other types of servers.

Since most LOB applications use more than one machine to accomplish a task, the software development community has created several architectural designs to take advantage of these distributed resources. Two of the most common architectural designs include the *Layered architecture* and the *Hexagonal/Ports and Adapters architecture*. These architectures are similar in that they both work to separate the domain model, also known as *business objects*, from the standard boilerplate code used to handle common tasks, such as data access or file system access. We'll discuss these two architecture types now and illustrate the pros and cons associated with each type.

Layered Architecture

The older, and more common, architectural style is the Layered architecture. When using the Layered architecture design, you separate your application into distinct logical boundaries. Each layer is often created as a class library (DLL); however, this is not always the case. One of the benefits of this separation of similar components is the ability to execute application programming interface (API) calls on multiple computers. This distributed execution promotes scalability and, in some circumstances, provides performance gains for the end user. One thing to understand is that you aren't required to use multiple computers to implement the Layered architecture. There are many applications in which the code from all layers resides on the same machine as the application's executable. Still, the logical separation of each layer promotes loose coupling between application components and code reuse through the class libraries. An application that uses the Layered architecture typically consists of the layers shown in Figure 4-1.

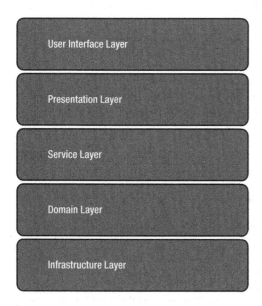

Figure 4-1. *Typical Layered architecture*

User Interface Layer

As you can see, there are five layers. In Extensible Application Markup Language (XAML) applications, the *user interface layer* consists of the XAML-based views of your applications. A view can represent a window, page, user control, or any other file that consists of XAML markup to define the visual aspects of your application. Generally, the user interface layer is light, with very little logic. So, where do you put the code that handles input from the user? This is the job of the presentation layer.

■ **Note** There are some implementations of the Layered architecture in which the user interface layer and the presentation layer are combined. This is often found in WinForms applications and some web applications. You could even take this approach with XAML-based applications; however, as you will see, the awesome features that were introduced with Windows Presentation Foundation (WPF) and XAML made way for a new paradigm for creating unit test–friendly applications with rich user interfaces and components that can be built with no event handlers in the code-behind. This separation of the user interface from the user interface logic makes XAML-based applications a prime candidate for the five-layer approach.

Presentation Layer

The *presentation layer* is used to handle any logic that occurs as a result of an action in the user interface layer. This includes the user clicking a button, a window resizing, a finger tap, reorientation of a device, and so forth. In WinForms development, event handlers in the code-behind of a Form or UserControl class handle this logic. As you will see later, XAML's data-binding capabilities, coupled with the Model-View-ViewModel (MVVM) design pattern, provide new and interesting ways to handle logic in the presentation layer.

Service Layer

The *service layer* acts as a gateway between the presentation layer and the domain layer. It's important to put some consideration into the application service layer's interfaces that you want to expose as part of your API. The design of the service layer will vary greatly, depending on your choice of the physical location of the service layer logic. For instance, the service layer interface design will be much different for services that are exposed via web service technologies than for a service layer that is meant to run on the same machine as the rest of the application.

Domain Layer

Next, the domain layer is the most important part of any application. The *domain layer* contains your domain model, which should reflect the business processes that belong to your problem domain. It's important that your domain layer be ignorant in regard to all other layers in your application. You don't want your domain layer to be dependent upon the user interface technology or the data access library that you are using because you need to be able to use your domain model in other implementations, such as web or mobile applications. By the same token, you don't want to have to change your domain layer to be able to introduce a new database system into your organization. Your design should ensure that the domain layer is pure and consists only of classes that represent the business domain in which you are modeling.

Infrastructure Layer

Finally, the *infrastructure layer* is the "low-level" code that you will find in most applications. This is where you keep the "plumbing" of the application. The infrastructure layer will contain data access, logging, exception handling, caching, MSMQ, performance metrics, code to send e-mails, and classes to support interaction with other software systems and API libraries. Code found in the infrastructure layer should support all of the mechanisms required that aren't specific to the business domain but *are* required in order for your application to function properly.

Once again, the domain layer shouldn't care about any other layer in the system. It should be completely self-sufficient.

The Layered architecture approach works great for separating your code into logical units that are related. One of the problems with this design is that if you need to make a change to the lower levels (which is often the case), then you may need to change the levels above to account for the dependencies on the lower levels. The Layered architecture's strict rules for layer access can prove to be problematic regarding changes in requirements. The *Hexagonal architecture*, also known as the *Ports and Adapters architecture*, provides a different way to view layers and solves the issues regarding extending existing applications.

■ **Note**   A common practice associated with layered architectures is that a layer can use any layer below it, but no layer can reference any layer above it. The only exception to this rule is the domain layer.

Design Patterns Used Throughout the Book

We will now review the design patterns that will be used throughout the reference application. The patterns covered include Repository, Adapter, Model-View-ViewModel, and Command.

The Repository Pattern

The *Repository pattern* is related to data access. When you use the Repository pattern, you create classes called *repositories*, which serve as abstractions to how your data is retrieved and stored in the database. To the user of the API, a repository is like an in-memory collection of domain entities. A repository class has no database-specific implementation details, which allows you to switch your database server easily, with no need to modify the repository's code. This also allows you to create special repository implementations for unit testing.

The test repository implementations allow you to write unit tests in which you can hard-code method-return values, which gives you complete control over the execution of your unit tests. This will ensure that your unit tests won't break because of a database server that's down or because of unexpected data in your database. In fact, when you create a test repository in which you hard-code method-return values, you remove the need for a database schema to exist, which allows a team to work on different parts of an application at the same time. Long gone are the days in which you had to wait for a database administrator (DBA) to create a database before you could proceed with development. By using the Repository pattern and Test-Driven Development (TDD), you can write code without any concern for unfinished dependencies. By definition, unit tests should be controlled, predictable, and fast. By removing the need to connect to a database to run your unit tests, the Repository pattern will assist you in writing unit tests that reflect these conditions (see Listing 4-1).

Listing 4-1. A Repository Used to Retrieve Product Entities from the Database

```csharp
using System;
using System.Collections.Generic;
using System.Linq;
using System.Text;
using System.Threading.Tasks;
using Ch4DesignPatterns.Entity;
using Ch4DesignPatterns.Repository.Interfaces;
using Ch4DesignPatterns.UnitOfWork.Interfaces;

namespace Ch4DesignPatterns.Repository
{
    //TODO consider adding repositories to the unit of work to
    //implement an entity framework Uow with DBSet<Product> collections.

    public class ProductRepository : IProductRepository
    {
        private IUnitOfWork _UnitOfWork;

        /// <summary>
        /// Constructor
        /// </summary>
        /// <param name="unitOfWork">
        /// Unit of work dependency which
        /// will be injected into the constructor.
        /// </param>
        public ProductRepository(IUnitOfWork unitOfWork)
        {
            if (unitOfWork == null)
                throw new ArgumentNullException("unitOfWork");

            _UnitOfWork = unitOfWork;
        }

        /// <summary>
        /// Retrieve all products from the db
        /// </summary>
        /// <returns>A collection of Product entities.</returns>
        public IEnumerable<Product> GetProducts()
        {
            if (_UnitOfWork == null)
                throw new NullReferenceException();

            return _UnitOfWork.Products;
        }

        /// <summary>
        /// Retrieve a product from the db by it's id
        /// </summary>
        /// <param name="id">The unique product identifier</param>
        /// <returns>A product with the specified id.</returns>
        public Product GetProduct(int id)
```

41

```
    {
        if (_UnitOfWork == null)
            throw new NullReferenceException();

        return
            _UnitOfWork.Products.Where(p => p.Id == id).FirstOrDefault();
    }

    /// <summary>
    /// Create a new Product instance
    /// and add it to the UnitOfWork.
    /// </summary>
    /// <param name="createInDatabase">
    /// If true, the new product will be saved
    /// to the database to receive an id.
    /// If false, return a new product instance.
    /// </param>
    /// <returns>A new Product entity.</returns>
    public Product NewProduct(bool createInDatabase)
    {
        var newProduct = new Product();

        if (createInDatabase)
            return _UnitOfWork.Save(newProduct);
        else
            _UnitOfWork.Add(newProduct);

        return newProduct;
    }

    /// <summary>
    /// Insert or Update a product to the db
    /// </summary>
    /// <param name="product">The product to save.</param>
    /// <returns>
    /// The product that was saved to the db.
    /// If the Product exists, an update is performed.
    /// If the Product is new, the retuned product will
    /// have a unique Id from the database system.
    /// </returns>
    public Product SaveProduct(Product product)
    {
        if (product == null)
            throw new ArgumentNullException("product");

        if (_UnitOfWork == null)
            throw new NullReferenceException();

        return _UnitOfWork.Save(product);
    }
  }
}
```

The Adapter Pattern

The *Adapter pattern* is a well-known pattern in the .NET Framework. If you've ever used ADO.NET to fill a DataSet, chances are that you've used an implementation of the Adapter pattern. Just as the name suggests, the Adapter pattern involves creating a class that serves as an adapter, which coordinates work between two objects with different interfaces.

To understand the Adapter pattern, it helps to imagine a real-world adapter. One author of this book enjoys recording music when not programming. The headphones that he uses in his studio as well as his laptop have a 1/8-inch connector that most computer sound cards support. The mixer has a 1/4-inch jack for headphones. Obviously, the 1/8-inch connector is too small to use with the 1/4-inch headphone jack on the mixer. Thus, should he buy a new pair of headphones to record? No, he simply needs to buy a 1/8-inch to 1/4-inch adapter. This allows him to plug his headphones into a 1/8-inch female port on one side of the adapter, which then converts the signal and has a 1/4-inch jack on the opposite side. This is exactly how the Adapter pattern works.

As mentioned previously, ADO.NET utilizes the adapter design pattern to coordinate the work between an IDbConnection interface and an IDbCommand interface to fill a DataSet with results from a query. Listing 4-2 shows an example.

Listing 4-2. Using a SqlDataAdapter to Fill a DataSet

```
using System;
using System.Collections.Generic;
using System.Data;
using System.Data.SqlClient;
using System.Linq;
using System.Text;
using System.Threading.Tasks;

namespace Ch4DesignPatterns.Adapter
{
    public class AdapterExample
    {
        public static DataSet GetDataset()
        {
            var connection = new SqlConnection("[cnn string]");

            var command = new SqlCommand("[SQL Query]", connection);
            command.CommandType = CommandType.Text;

            var adapter = new SqlDataAdapter(command);

            var dataSet = new DataSet();
            adapter.Fill(dataSet);

            return dataSet;
        }
    }
}
```

The MVVM Design Pattern

The *Model-View-ViewModel (MVVM)* design pattern is known as a User Interface design pattern. MVVM is based on the *Presentation Model (PM)* design pattern and was created specifically for XAML and WPF by John Gossman. The MVVM pattern allows you to separate your domain model's business logic (the model) from the user interface (the view) by adding a layer of abstraction that encapsulates all of the logic required by the user interface, and it processes requests from the user to perform actions on or retrieve data from the model.

When using MVVM, the view is represented by XAML. The view is directly dependent on the view model; however, the view model is view agnostic. You should not have any user interface elements or other dependencies related to the view in the view model. The view model's public interface should be well defined. Any changes to the view model's public interface will usually require that any views associated with the view model be changed as well.

The view model will work with the application service layer to modify or retrieve data from the model. The model consists of domain entities, which should only contain code that is relative to the business domain at hand. It's important not to allow any of the user interface–related code from the view or view model to "leak" its way into the domain model. The domain model should be isolated from any code that does not relate to the business domain. See Figure 4-2, which represents the communication between the different parts of the MVVM design pattern.

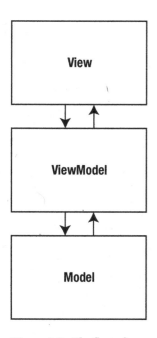

Figure 4-2. *The flow of communication when using the MVVM design pattern*

As you can see, the view will declaratively create an instance of the view model. The view model's properties will be data-bound to controls declared in the view. The data binding will allow for automatic updating of view control display values as well as to bind user interface control events and commands related to user interaction to methods and properties of the view model. The view model will respond to user interaction events to interact with the model. The view model will communicate with the model to make changes and report updates to the model. This allows a complete separation of the user interface, presentation layer logic, and domain model of your application.

Basic MVVM Implementation in WPF

In this section, we will show how to create a bare-bones MVVM implementation using WPF and C#. This example will illustrate the key concepts of the MVVM design pattern. The view will be represented as a WPF window. The view model will contain properties that provide data to display in the view using data binding. Notice that there is no code-behind needed, only XAML, the view model, and the model that represents a class called PersonModel. There will be more examples and explanations throughout the book. Listing 4-3 shows the WPF application markup.

Listing 4-3. The XAML for App.xaml

```
<Application x:Class="BasicMVVMWPF.App"
        xmlns="http://schemas.microsoft.com/winfx/2006/xaml/presentation"
        xmlns:x="http://schemas.microsoft.com/winfx/2006/xaml"
        StartupUri="MainWindow.xaml">
    <Application.Resources>

    </Application.Resources>
</Application>
```

As you can see, the Application class can hold application-level resources such as styles and templates. The main purpose for the Application class is to provide the main startup object of the application, which is specified in the StartupUri attribute. Next up is Listing 4-4, which shows the definition of MainWindow.xaml, which represents the view.

Listing 4-4. The XAML for MainWindow.xaml (the View)

```
<Window
    xmlns="http://schemas.microsoft.com/winfx/2006/xaml/presentation"
    xmlns:x="http://schemas.microsoft.com/winfx/2006/xaml"
    xmlns:d="http://schemas.microsoft.com/expression/blend/2008" xmlns:mc="http://schemas.
    openxmlformats.org/markup-compatibility/2006" mc:Ignorable="d" x:Class="BasicMVVMWPF.
    MainWindow"
    xmlns:vm="clr-namespace:BasicMVVMWPF"
    Title="MainWindow" Height="350" Width="525">
    <Window.Resources>
        <vm:MainWindowViewModel x:Key="viewModel" />
    </Window.Resources>
    <Grid>
        <Grid.RowDefinitions>
            <!--Header row-->
            <RowDefinition />
            <!--Content row-->
            <RowDefinition />
            <!--Footer row-->
            <RowDefinition />
        </Grid.RowDefinitions>
```

```xml
    <TextBox x:Name="txtInstructions"
            Text="This is the View of the application." FontSize="20" Grid.Row="0" />
    <Grid DataContext="{StaticResource ResourceKey=viewModel}" Height="236"
    VerticalAlignment="Top" Grid.RowSpan="3" Margin="0,54,0,0">
        <Grid.RowDefinitions>
            <RowDefinition Height="44*" />
            <RowDefinition Height="34*" />
            <RowDefinition Height="40*" />
            <RowDefinition Height="39*" />
            <RowDefinition Height="40*" />
            <RowDefinition Height="39*" />
        </Grid.RowDefinitions>
        <TextBlock x:Name="txtFullNameDescription" Text="The field below represents the
        person's full name"
            FontSize="20" Grid.Row="0" />
        <TextBlock x:Name="txtPersonFullName" Text="{Binding FullName}"
            FontSize="20" Grid.Row="1" />
        <TextBlock x:Name="txtFirstNameDescription" Text="The field below represents the
        person's first name"
            FontSize="20" Grid.Row="2" />
        <TextBox x:Name="txtFirstName"
            Text="{Binding FirstName}" FontSize="20" Grid.Row="3"  />
        <TextBlock x:Name="txtLastNameDescription" Text="The field below represents the
        person's last name"
            FontSize="20" Grid.Row="4" />
        <TextBox x:Name="txtLastName"
            Text="{Binding LastName}" FontSize="20" Grid.Row="5" />
    </Grid>
    </Grid>
</Window>
```

Here you have a WPF window with two Grid objects for controlling the layout of the TextBox and TextBlock elements. You add a new XML namespace (xmlns:vm), and instead of referencing a URI, you reference the namespace of the view model. Now you can access any class defined under that namespace in XAML. In the Window.Resources element, you add a resource to the view model, and you give the resource a key to "viewModel" so you can access the resource in XAML. You set DataContext equal to the viewModel resource. Now when you are using data binding on other controls in the Grid, the binding will reference a property on the view model by the same property name. Now let's take a look at Listing 4-5, which is the source code for the model class.

Listing 4-5. The C# Source Code for PersonModel.cs (the Model)

```csharp
using System;
using System.Collections.Generic;
using System.ComponentModel;
using System.Linq;
using System.Text;
using System.Threading.Tasks;

namespace BasicMVVMWPF
{
    public class PersonModel : INotifyPropertyChanged
```

```
{
    private string _FirstName;
    private string _LastName;

    public string FirstName
    {
        get { return _FirstName; }
        set
        {
            _FirstName = value;
            OnPropertyChanged("FirstName");
        }
    }

    public string LastName
    {
        get { return _LastName; }
        set
        {
            _LastName = value;
            OnPropertyChanged("LastName");
        }
    }

    public event PropertyChangedEventHandler PropertyChanged;

    public void OnPropertyChanged(string propertyName)
    {
        if (PropertyChanged != null)
            PropertyChanged(this, new PropertyChangedEventArgs(propertyName));

    }
}
}
```

As you can see, the model is simple. It represents a Person entity. There are two properties exposed: FirstName and LastName. The class implements the interface INotifyPropertyChanged, which allows the model to alert the view model of any property changes. Finally, Listing 4-6 shows the source code for the ViewModel class.

Listing 4-6. The C# Code for MainWindowViewModel.cs (the ViewModel)

```
using System;
using System.Collections.Generic;
using System.ComponentModel;
using System.Linq;
using System.Text;
using System.Threading.Tasks;
```

```
namespace BasicMVVMWPF
{
    public class MainWindowViewModel : INotifyPropertyChanged
    {
        private PersonModel _Model;
        private string _FullName;

        public MainWindowViewModel()
        {
            _Model = new PersonModel
            {
                FirstName = "Buddy",
                LastName = "James"
            };

            this.FullName =
                    string.Format("{0} {1}", _Model.FirstName, _Model.LastName);
        }

        public string FirstName
        {
            get { return _Model.FirstName; }
            set
            {
                _Model.FirstName = value;

              this.FullName =
                    string.Format("{0} {1}", _Model.FirstName, _Model.LastName);

                OnPropertyChanged("FirstName");
            }
        }

        public string LastName
        {
            get { return _Model.LastName; }
            set
            {
                _Model.LastName = value;
                this.FullName =
                    string.Format("{0} {1}", _Model.FirstName, _Model.LastName);

                OnPropertyChanged("LastName");
            }
        }
```

```
public string FullName
{
    get { return _FullName; }
    set
    {
        _FullName = value;
        OnPropertyChanged("FullName");
    }
}

public event PropertyChangedEventHandler PropertyChanged;

public void OnPropertyChanged(string propertyName)
{
    if (PropertyChanged != null)
        PropertyChanged(this,
                    new PropertyChangedEventArgs(propertyName));
    }
}
}
```

The view model's source applies the same techniques as the model. You implement the INotifyPropertyChanged interface to alert the view of changes to the properties (via data binding). You also include a new property named FullName, which will return the first and last names when either of those values changes. The first and last names are represented as TextBox controls in the view, so their values can be changed. The FullName property is represented by a TextBlock, which means that the user can't modify the value. However, because of the data binding to the view model, you can instantly see the FullName TextBlock's Text property value change when you modify either the first or last name TextBox.

ICommand: The Cure for the Common Event Handler

We will wrap up this chapter on design patterns by discussing Microsoft's implementation of the Command design pattern. At first glance, the ICommand interface seems simple, which it is. However, don't let the simplicity fool you. The way that the commands are used in XAML-based user interfaces provides a powerful alternative to adding event handlers in your view's code-behind file. Table 4-1 describes the ICommand interface members.

Table 4-1. *ICommand Interface Members*

Member Name	Description
CanExecute	The method that indicates whether the specified command's state is valid for execution. For example, WPF implements a command to support the Paste command when something is copied to the clipboard. This method will allow all user interface elements that are bound to the command to be enabled and disabled based on their return value. In the case of the Paste command, this means that any paste button element will be enabled or disabled based on the method's return value.
Execute	The method that contains the logic to execute when the command is triggered and the command's CanExecute method returns true.

49

The ICommand interface provides a test-friendly alternative to event handlers in your code-behind for handling user events. There are several controls that have properties called Command and CommandParameter. For this example, you will use a simple WPF button control. The CommandParameter property should be set before the Command property. This is because both the CanExecute method and the Execute method have a single parameter argument of type object. When the XAML parser processes the Command property, it will check the CanExecute method to determine whether the button should be enabled or disabled. If the parser processes the Command property before the CommandParameter property, the parameter argument of the CanExecute method will be null, which, depending on your implementation, will either throw an exception or, at the least, return false.

So, what value do you use for the CommandParameter property? This depends on the nature of your command; however, we typically use the same strategy for nearly all ICommand implementations. Ninety-nine percent of the time, we will store the view model that contains a property that represents the ICommand implementation in a window-level ResourceDictionary. Next, we will bind the view model reference to the CommandParameter attribute of the Button control. Next, we will bind the view model's ICommand property of interest to the Command attribute of the Button control. Then, in the CanExecute method, we will check the parameter argument for null. If it's null, then we return false. If not, we cast the object parameter as the view model type and store the view model in a private field in the ICommand implementation. Since both CanExecute and Execute have the same object parameter, we will add a null check for the parameter of the Execute method. If the parameter is null, we'll then check the private field that should already contain the view model by way of the CanExecute method for null. If they are both null, then there is a problem, and we throw an exception.

Otherwise, we have a valid reference to the view model to work with in the Execute method of the ICommand implementation. With the view model handy, we perform the expected command in the Execute method, which usually involves calling a method or changing properties on the view model reference. This will trigger the data-binding mechanism by way of the INotifyPropertyChanged interface in the view model, and any modified properties will then be updated in the view. Perhaps an example will clear up any confusion that you may have.

The following example is a WPF window with two TextBox controls and a Button control. Each TextBox is supposed to hold a number, and the Button will execute a command that will add the two numbers together and store the answer in a property called Sum. Sum is data-bound to a TextBlock, so when the command executes, the Sum property is updated, and this will update the view.

■ **Note** It may be helpful to set a breakpoint in the CanExecute method, as well as the Execute method in the ICommand implementation. We also suggest that you set a breakpoint in the view model's ICommand property implementation. This will give you some insight on how the ICommand bindings are used.

As you can see, Listing 4-7 illustrates a view that defines the user interface of the example. Listing 4-8 provides an ICommand implementation that provides the logic to add two numbers on the view model. The implementation will also provide change notification to all bound user interface controls. Finally, in Listing 4-9, you have a view model, which provides properties to be bound to the view. The "Add numbers" button is bound to the command implementation in the view model. The Command property of the button is bound to the AddNumbersCommand property of the view model. The CommandParameter property of the button is bound to the view model. This property will use the bound object as the parameter argument of the ICommand, CanExecute, and Execute methods. Figure 4-3 shows the running example.

Listing 4-7. CalculatorCommandExample.xaml View

```xml
<Window x:Class="BasicMVVMWPF.CalculatorCommandExample"
        xmlns="http://schemas.microsoft.com/winfx/2006/xaml/presentation"
        xmlns:x="http://schemas.microsoft.com/winfx/2006/xaml"
        xmlns:vm="clr-namespace:BasicMVVMWPF.ViewModel"
        Title="CalculatorCommandExample" Height="300" Width="300">
    <Window.Resources>
        <vm:CalculatorViewModel x:Key="viewModel" />
    </Window.Resources>
    <Grid DataContext="{StaticResource ResourceKey=viewModel}">
        <Grid.RowDefinitions>
            <!--Window instructions-->
            <RowDefinition />
            <!--First number-->
            <RowDefinition />
            <!--Second number-->
            <RowDefinition />
            <!--Sum of two numbers-->
            <RowDefinition />
            <!--Add button-->
            <RowDefinition />
        </Grid.RowDefinitions>
        <Grid.ColumnDefinitions>
            <ColumnDefinition />
            <ColumnDefinition />
        </Grid.ColumnDefinitions>

        <TextBlock Name="AppTitle" Text="Simple Calculator" Grid.Row="0"
                Grid.Column="0" Grid.ColumnSpan="2" />

        <TextBlock Name="FirstNumberTitle" Text="First number"
                Grid.Row="1" Grid.Column="0" />

        <TextBox Name="txtFirstNumber"
                Text="{Binding FirstNumber}" Grid.Row="1" Grid.Column="1" />

        <TextBlock Name="SecondNumberTitle" Text="Second number"
                Grid.Row="2" Grid.Column="0" />

        <TextBox Name="txtSecondtNumber"
                Text="{Binding SecondNumber}" Grid.Row="2" Grid.Column="1" />

        <TextBlock Name="AnswerTitle" Text="Sum of two numbers:"
                Grid.Row="3" Grid.Column="0" />

        <TextBox Name="txtSum"
                Text="{Binding Sum}" Grid.Row="3" Grid.Column="1" />
```

```
        <Button Name="btnAddNumbers" Content="Add numbers" Grid.Row="4"
            Grid.Column="0" Grid.ColumnSpan="2"
            CommandParameter="{StaticResource ResourceKey=viewModel}"
            Command="{Binding AddNumbersCommand}" />
    </Grid>
</Window>
```

Listing 4-8. ICommand Implementation (AddNumbersCommand.cs)

```csharp
using System;
using System.Collections.Generic;
using System.Linq;
using System.Text;
using System.Threading.Tasks;
using System.Windows.Input;
using BasicMVVMWPF.ViewModel;

namespace BasicMVVMWPF.Command
{
    public class AddNumbersCommand : ICommand
    {
        private CalculatorViewModel _ViewModel;

        public bool CanExecute(object parameter)
        {
            if (parameter == null)
                return false;
            else
            {
                _ViewModel = (CalculatorViewModel)parameter;
            }

            return true;
        }

        public event EventHandler CanExecuteChanged;

        public void Execute(object parameter)
        {
            if (parameter == null)
            {
                if (_ViewModel == null)
                    throw new ArgumentNullException("parameter");
            }
            else
            {
                _ViewModel = (CalculatorViewModel)parameter;
            }

            _ViewModel.Sum = _ViewModel.FirstNumber + _ViewModel.SecondNumber;
        }
    }
}
```

Listing 4-9. The View Model Used to Bind the Command and the TextBox Values

```
(CalculatorViewModel.cs)
using System;
using System.Collections.Generic;
using System.ComponentModel;
using System.Linq;
using System.Text;
using System.Threading.Tasks;
using System.Windows.Input;
using BasicMVVMWPF.Command;

namespace BasicMVVMWPF.ViewModel
{
    public class CalculatorViewModel : INotifyPropertyChanged
    {
        private int _FirstNumber;
        private int _SecondNumber;
        private int _Sum;
        private ICommand _AddNumbersCommand;

        public ICommand AddNumbersCommand
        {
            get { return _AddNumbersCommand; }
            set
            {
                _AddNumbersCommand = value;
                OnPropertyChanged("AddNumbersCommand");
            }
        }

        public int FirstNumber
        {
            get { return _FirstNumber; }
            set
            {
                _FirstNumber = value;
                OnPropertyChanged("FirstNumber");
            }
        }

        public int SecondNumber
        {
            get { return _SecondNumber; }
            set
            {
                _SecondNumber = value;
                OnPropertyChanged("SecondNumber");
            }
        }
```

```
        public int Sum
        {
            get { return _Sum; }
            set
            {
                _Sum = value;
                OnPropertyChanged("Sum");
            }
        }

        public CalculatorViewModel()
        {
            _AddNumbersCommand = new AddNumbersCommand();
        }

        public event PropertyChangedEventHandler PropertyChanged;

        public void OnPropertyChanged(string propertyName)
        {
            if (PropertyChanged != null)
                PropertyChanged(this, new PropertyChangedEventArgs(propertyName));
        }
    }
}
```

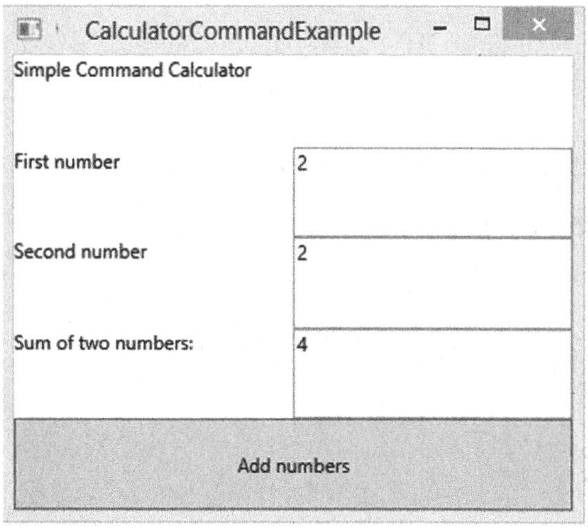

Figure 4-3. *Output of Listing 4-9*

■ **Note**   The XAML markup for Listing 4-7 has the CommandParameter attribute set before the Command attribute. This order is required. If you specify Command before CommandParameter, ICommand is bound before the view model is passed to the CanExecute and Execute methods.

Summary

Design patterns are extremely valuable to any software development team. The Repository pattern allows you to develop your data access code with no need to wait for the database to be created. You will use the Adapter pattern to create an architecture that will make changes to your application extremely easy to implement for years to come. We've covered the MVVM design pattern, which we consider to be a XAML application's bread and butter. You also learned how to use the ICommand interface to eliminate code-behind event handlers by creating Command classes that are extremely simple to unit test. In the following chapters, you will analyze a business problem and use what you've learned to create a complete, multiplatform line-of-business application using domain-driven design.

The next chapter will introduce you to unit testing. The chapter will cover popular unit testing frameworks and provide examples on testing the MVVM calculator example code.

■ ■ ■

CHAPTER 5

Unit Testing

In the history of software development, there has always been one adversary that has plagued the intrepid software developer. I'm talking about the archenemy known as the software *bug*. The bug has wreaked havoc in the careers of every programmer since software was developed on paper punch cards. They strike without warning. They feed on the time and budget of every project. They compromise the integrity of your data. They inspire angry support calls. These elusive creatures can pop up at any moment. Just as fast as they appear, they have the ability to hide deep within your source code, as if they never existed.

Have you ever heard anyone say, "It worked on my machine?" If not, you are lucky. We too have uttered these damning words. This is the phrase spoken by unfortunate developers and software testers when trying to reproduce a defect submitted by a customer. It's a difficult task to explain to a paying customer that you are unable to lure these horrific beasts out of hiding when you perform the exact steps that they've submitted in an angry e-mail or described in a support call.

Indeed, the software bug can vary in scope from an annoying session timeout straight through to a data trashing disaster. "But how can I defeat such a cunning and clever pest?" you ask. Just as in the real world, there is no silver bullet when it comes to debugging software.

■ **Note**   Admiral Grace Hopper made the term *debugging* popular in the 1940s at Harvard University. The story goes that a moth had been trapped inside a relay in a Mark II computer, which caused problems in its operation. When the moth was removed from the computer, she suggested that they "debugged" the system.

Debugging Strategies

The main strategies that have been used throughout the years to discover and destroy bugs in a software system are covered in the following sections.

Defensive Programming

Defensive programming should be part of every developers skill set. The following are some defensive programming basics:

- Defensive programming is the practice of designing all of the methods you create to try to anticipate all possible points of error and then writing code to handle such errors gracefully so that they don't cause problems for the end users of the application. This includes identifying all valid input argument values and writing code to test all of the inputs to handle any invalid values.

- In data entry applications, it's important to identify all sources of data that enter the system and to write code to protect the data at all costs. After all, you've probably heard the old saying, "Garbage in, garbage out."

- It's important to keep in mind that sources of data are not limited solely to human data entry. Many enterprise software applications communicate with other programs to send and receive data. These sources include systems such as web servers, imaging scanners, message queues, and one of the most common sources, database systems. You can write as much defensive code as you like; however, if your system shares a database with another application, you don't have control over the quality of data that is produced by these external systems. This is why it's imperative that you check all data, regardless of its origin, for potential issues.

- Bad data will find its way into your application; however, you can handle the error in such a way that the user experience won't be interrupted unless necessary. For instance, a well-designed application will handle the error and write a detailed description of the problem to a database, log file, or event log.

- It's also handy to include code that sends an e-mail to your support team to alert them of the issue. If you write code with the user in mind, errors that can be handled by the system should be invisible to the end user. Users panic when they encounter a cryptic, unhandled exception web page or message box. As a rule of thumb, try not to interrupt the user's workflow if at all possible.

- In the event that your application cannot recover from a "fatal" error, it's best to notify users with an apologetic, aesthetically pleasing, human-readable message to let them know that a problem was encountered. Always be sure to provide instructions to users as to what they should do next. If at all possible, try to restart the application after all of the relevant error details have been logged for later investigation.

System Testing

System testing is the practice of testing an application in its entirety. This is often the job of a quality assurance team. If your company is small and you don't have a QA team, however, this responsibility then falls on you, the developer.

It's best to create a collection of test cases so that testing is consistent from build to build. This approach, however, involves testing the same steps each time. Considering this drawback, it's good practice also to incorporate what we like to call *Break Challenge Testing*. What is Break Challenge Testing, you ask? It's when the tester of an application is challenged to break the system by any means necessary. (Of course, we mean by using absurd data inputs or clicking multiple toolbar buttons or menu items—not by beating the computer with a blunt object.)

It's important to think like a user. Oftentimes, as developers and testers, we know where the quirks exist, and we know how to avoid them. An enterprise system shouldn't allow you to compromise the data's integrity or crash the application.

Regression Testing

Regression testing involves testing a bug fix to make sure that the bug was eradicated and to make sure that no new bugs were created as a result of the code changes used to resolve the original bug. As you can imagine, this form of testing can be tricky because it's nearly impossible for you to keep up with all of the instances in which a unit of code could possibly affect another part of the system.

User Acceptance Testing

User acceptance testing is a critical point in any software development schedule. From iterative release schedules in which you deploy a build at the end of each iteration to legacy software development paradigms where the end user doesn't see the application until construction has been completed, you always need to let the client test the system in order to verify that the solution you've delivered serves its purpose. This is referred to as user *acceptance testing*.

The details of how acceptance testing is performed can vary from project to project. In some instances, the team will work closely with the client to establish a series of test cases. A *test case* is a series of steps performed by the client in order to verify that a particular feature works as expected. There are less formal acceptance testing practices, such as simply deploying the application and waiting for the client to report problems. Obviously, this method is far from optimal; however, it does occur in the field.

Unit Tests to the Rescue

Don't get me wrong; all of the methods that I've mentioned up to this point are important weapons in the fight against buggy software. Unit testing, when done correctly, can greatly improve the quality of the software solutions that you develop.

Unit testing is a time-tested paradigm founded in the 1970s by Kent Beck. If you are unfamiliar with this name, we suggest you search for it and educate yourself. Mr. Beck was coding in SmallTalk when he coined the term *unit testing*. The rest of this chapter explains what makes a good unit test as well as a few third-party products that will help you make the most of your unit testing efforts. We will also cover Test Driven Development (TDD), including the pros and cons of using this design methodology. Let's begin, shall we?

■ **Caution** It's important to understand that in order to utilize unit testing effectively, you need to invest a significant amount of time practicing if you want to take advantage of the benefits that this process offers. Furthermore, unit testing will add time to your project schedule. It's no easy task to convince management that unit testing is worth the investment; however, when implemented correctly, unit testing can easily pay for itself in maintenance cost alone.

It's important to understand that unit testing can cause more harm than good if you don't fully grasp the concepts and practices required. If you put in the time and effort to learn about unit testing, your code will benefit in terms of fewer bugs, instant bug detection, code that is easier to read, and loosely coupled components that can be reused across multiple applications. You will also gain confidence in deploying an application to a production environment, and you will feel safe when it comes time to make a change to your source code.

Test-Driven Development (TDD) is a software development method that allows you to drive your code's design by starting with unit tests to define the way that your classes will be used. If you are concerned only with the unit test, you don't have to think about the implementation of the methods that you are testing. You can concentrate on designing well-defined class interfaces first. When you add TDD to the mix, your class interfaces will improve, and you will actually reduce the amount of time you spend designing your classes and routines. TDD also helps increase the percentage of your code's test coverage as well as improve the quality of your source code because refactoring is a required step in the TDD process. Finally, TDD will help prevent *gold plating*, that is, when implemented correctly, you can rest assured that your class methods will have one single responsibility. Any code that doesn't support that single responsibility will be refactored out into its own class.

We firmly believe in the benefits of unit testing and TDD; however, we think that it would be irresponsible not to give you the whole story. So read on and try the examples to learn enough to make an educated decision about whether unit testing and TDD are the right solution for your project.

Unit Testing Basics

Enough with the disclaimers, let's learn about unit testing! A *unit test* is source code that is used to test a logical unit of code. A *logical unit of code* is any method or routine that contains logic instructions (if/else, switch statements, loops, and so forth) that are used to control the behavior of the system by setting the return value of a method or property. This type of testing allows you to test your source code at a much lower level than system or regression testing.

As long as you run your unit tests often, you will know exactly when a bug is introduced into the system, assuming that all of your classes and methods have proper test coverage. The moment that a unit test fails, you know that a bug has been discovered, and you also know which class and method are involved and why the test failed. No other type of software testing provides this level of contextual information regarding new bugs. These are just a few of the benefits to be gained when you consistently implement proper unit tests in your software solutions.

Characteristics of a Great Unit Test

As we stated in the disclaimer at the beginning of this chapter, improper unit tests can result in more harm than good. So, you might be asking, "Well then, Buddy, what makes a great unit test?"

Ask and you shall receive. The following sections are a checklist that you can use to assess the quality of your unit tests.

Automated Unit Test Execution

Can you automate the execution of your unit tests? If your tests must be executed manually by a mere mortal, there is a good chance that sooner or later you or someone on your team will be so busy working to meet a deadline that you just might hear that little voice in your head whispering, "You don't have to execute these tests with every little change; after all, it's nearly 5 p.m." Or "I'll run the tests after I complete just these two remaining features." From here on out, it's a slippery slope and, before you know it, you will lose the benefit of early bug detection, which will then make you question the effectiveness of the unit tests. What is the end result? Some team members will write unit tests, while others will abandon the practice.

The tests will become stale, and when you do decide to execute the unit tests, you can't be sure which changes to the system caused the bug that resulted in the failed unit test. This is why it's important to automate the execution of all unit tests after any code modification. Prime candidates include having the unit tests execute with each and every build or with every check-in to your source control system.

There are several options out there for source control systems that integrate with Visual Studio. My personal favorite is TFS 2013. All references to source control from this point forward will target Team Foundation Server. Nevertheless, the concepts are similar for most source control systems.

Unit Test Execution Speed

Continuous integration (CI) is a set of principles that pertain to the deployment of builds during the entire construction phase of a software development project. Continuous integration is most often implemented as a supplement to other agile methodologies. This is because of the iterative nature of agile development as well as the frequent build deployments of working software.

In agile development, teams implement features that add business value during every iteration throughout the entire project. Furthermore, the source code that contains the new features from the last iteration is compiled and deployed to the client's production environment.

This approach has several benefits. For instance, if you deliver a build that contains at least one complete feature that adds business value, then the client experiences the benefits of the product that they requested after the first iteration. This gives users the ability to provide constructive feedback, which will guarantee that the end result will be exactly what the client requested.

Deploying a build can go off without a hitch; however, problems are often discovered during deployment that no one knew existed prior to the deployment attempt. This is where CI and unit tests work together to make sure that deployments go smoothly. If problems still occur, then the developers shouldn't have any problem reverting to a previous build.

Here's an example of how you utilize CI, unit tests, and TFS source control. You use TFS to handle project planning, source control, issue tracking, automated builds, and automated unit test execution. You also use TDD so that you have plenty of unit tests. When you implement a new feature, you must make sure that all unit tests pass before you check any source files into source control. Otherwise, it's possible that you may have introduced a new bug into the system as a side effect of the changes that you made while resolving the original bug or implementing a new feature.

Obviously, you should only check in code that is bug free. Thanks to the tight integration between Visual Studio and TFS, you have the ability to create an automated build definition from within Visual Studio. Figure 5-1 illustrates the Builds option in Visual Studio's Team Explorer window.

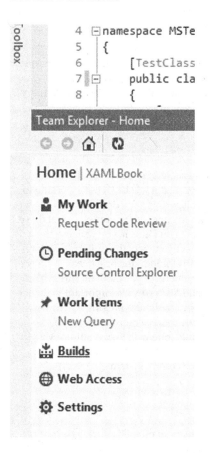

Figure 5-1. *Visual Studio 2012 TFS Team Explorer*

The Builds menu option allows users with proper permissions to create build definitions. There are several types of build definitions. However, the one in which you are interested is known as the *Gated Check-in* build definition type. The Gated Check-in build definition will first attempt to build your solution using the source code that you are trying to check into source control. If the build fails, the check-in is rejected, the user is notified, and a bug work item is created in TFS so that the issue is recorded and tracked. If the build succeeds, the automated build will then execute all unit tests.

If the build succeeds and all unit tests pass, then the source code is checked into source control. You can even configure the build definition to deploy the project's assemblies to a local folder or a network share. As you can imagine, this will greatly cut down on any deployment surprises. Depending on your needs, you can even configure Visual Studio to trigger unit test execution on every build attempt from every user. This way, you never have to worry about forgetting to run your unit tests.

Figure 5-2 shows how to configure a TFS build definition in Team Explorer. Here you can set up a Gated Check-in trigger to specify that check-ins should only be accepted if the submitted code changes build successfully.

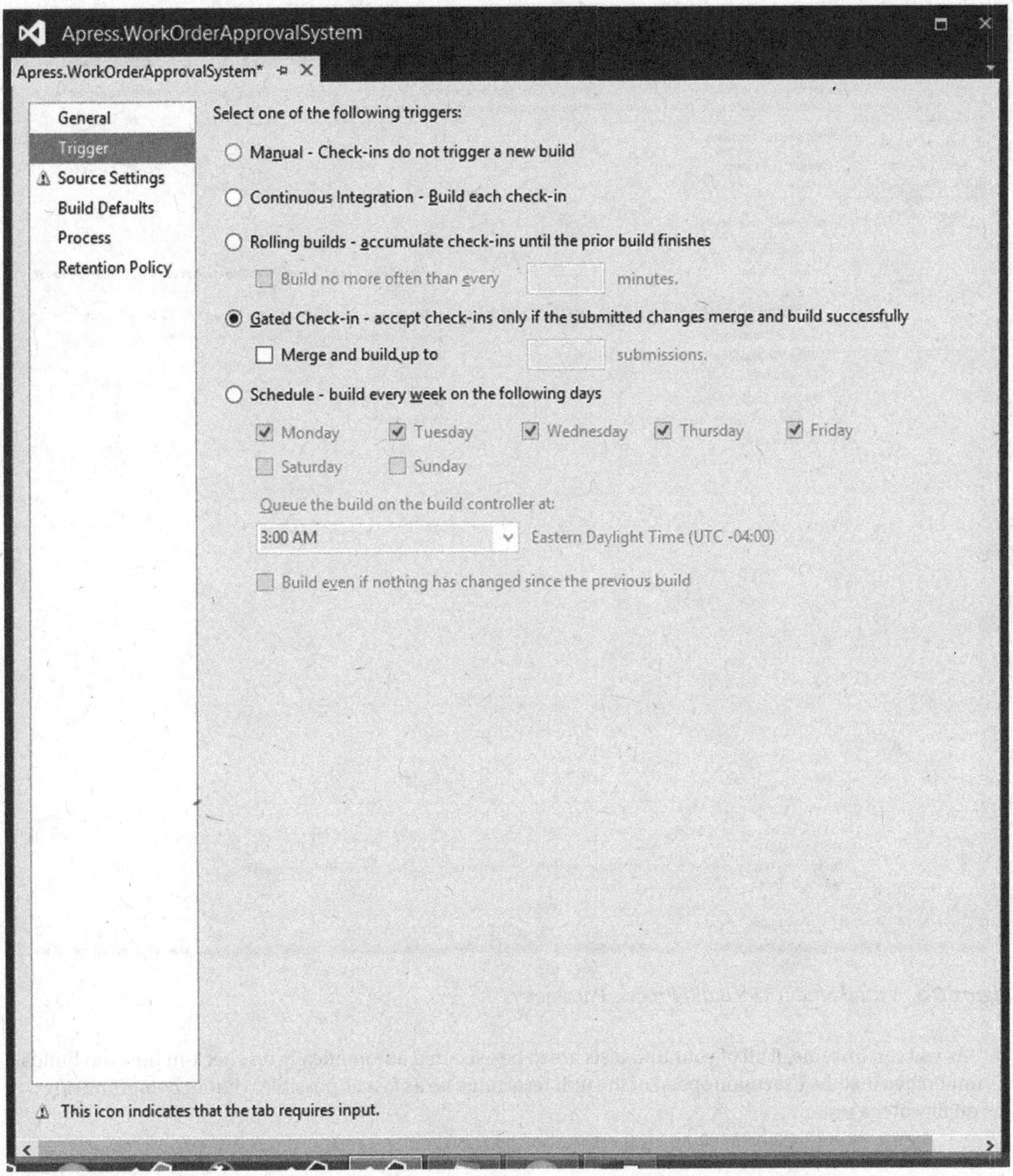

Figure 5-2. *Visual Studio TFS Build Definition Triggers*

Figure 5-3 shows how to configure automated unit test execution in a TFS build definition. The relevant settings can be found under the Build Process tab.

Figure 5-3. *Visual Studio TFS Build Process Parameters*

As you can imagine, if all of your unit tests are to be executed automatically on check-ins or even builds, it's imperative that the execution speed of the unit tests must be as fast as possible without compromising the quality of the tests.

K.I.S.S. Your Unit Tests

K.I.S.S is an infamous acronym that stands for "Keep It Simple, Stupid." Much like the design of your class interfaces and method implementations, it's important that you design your unit tests with simplicity in mind. This helps to keep the execution speed down while promoting unit tests that can easily be understood and modified by any member of your development team. If your unit tests don't execute quickly, you are less likely to run them, which defeats the purpose. If a team member has to ask questions of the author of a unit test in order to understand the implementation, you may need to refactor the unit test.

Finally, a clean and simple unit test makes it easier for a developer to see the interface of the class being tested or *class under test (CUT)* as well as to understand its intended use. A good unit test clearly demonstrates the use of the CUT as well as the expected result of the test.

All Team Members Should Be Able to Execute Unit Tests

It's not practical to rely on one team member to be in charge of unit tests or any other development process for that matter. Software developers often change jobs, so it's extremely important that all of the knowledge associated with a project be shared among all team members.

A good unit test should be easy to execute for all developers on the team. If at all possible, any member of the team should be able to execute all unit tests with a single click of the mouse.

Great Unit Tests Survive the Test of Time

A unit test should produce the same results two years after it was first written. This has just as much to do with the quality of the test that was written as maintaining each and every unit test to make sure that any changes to the software, which cause a unit test to fail, are also addressed in the unit test. If unit tests don't change along with major software design changes, then that clearly means the unit tests are not executed, and thus they become stale and useless. As long as a project builds, all of the associated unit tests should pass.

Unit Test Fixtures

A unit test fixture is a class in which the methods are unit tests or are helper methods that are used to prepare the unit tests. A test fixture should contain unit tests that are designed to test related features, often tests that reside in the same class or class library. One popular naming convention for a test fixture is the CUT name with *TestFixture* as a suffix. For example, if you were writing a test fixture class full of unit tests for a class called `Calculator`, you name the test fixture class `CalculatorTestFixture`.

Unit Testing Frameworks

There are several unit-testing frameworks for .NET. We will introduce you to two of them in this chapter. We will review the NUnit framework as well as the native Visual Studio unit testing project template.

NUnit

NUnit is an open source unit-testing framework that is based on Junit, which is a unit-testing framework for the Java programming language. NUnit is popular with open source advocates. The framework is a complete unit-testing tool, which includes the following:

- Easy installation via NuGet.

- Integration with Visual Studio.

- A command-line interface that you can use to execute your unit tests. This makes automated test execution when building your solution from the command line a breeze.

- A GUI interface that provides visual cues regarding the status of your testing efforts such as which test is executing, which tests have passed or failed, and which tests have yet to be run.

- Several test method attributes used to mark special test methods for purposes such as test setup, teardown, expected exceptions, and more. You can find a comprehensive list of attributes at http://nunit.org/index.php?p=documentation.

- The [TestFixture] attribute identifies a class whose purpose is to provide all unit test methods. The unit test methods are marked with the [Test] attribute.

- When writing unit tests, oftentimes you must write boilerplate code that is used to prepare dependencies and other related objects, which are used in multiple unit test methods. In honor of the DRY principle ("don't repeat yourself"), NUnit offers the [Setup] attribute that indicates that the specified method should be run before each test is executed. This allows you to initialize all of the related variables to a predefined state before running each test. This is a perfect place to create stubs and mock objects to be used in your unit tests.

- Much like the [Setup] attribute, the [TearDown] attribute designates a method to be used in disposing of any unmanaged resources that aren't handled by the .NET CLR garbage collector. A few examples of such resources include database connections, web service references, file system objects, and so on. This is also a prime candidate for setting all object references to null and deleting any files created as part of your unit tests. If your test creates any objects in memory or any other type of resource that should be disposed, this is the attribute to use.

- A plethora of methods that allow you to assert that your code is executing as expected. You can find all of the assertion methods in the official NUnit documentation at http://nunit.org/index.php?p=documentation.

As you can see in Figure 5-4, the NUnit framework can be installed using the NuGet package manager in Visual Studio.

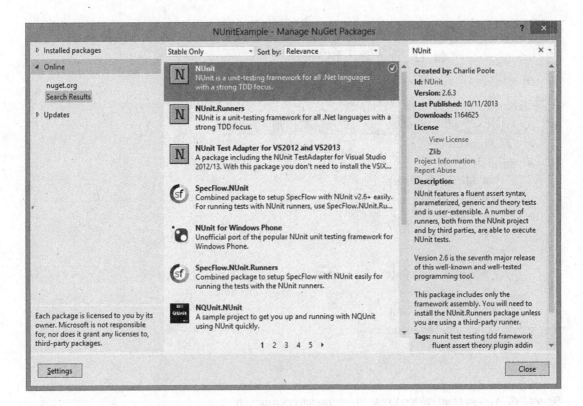

Figure 5-4. *NUnit installed from the NuGet package manager*

By installing NUnit from the NuGet package manager in Visual Studio, the nunit.framework reference will be added to your project's references automatically. Observe the project references in Figure 5-5.

Figure 5-5. A project that references the NUnit framework assembly

NUnit is more than a unit-testing library. NUnit provides command line support for executing your unit tests. This is useful for automated test execution. If you'd like to see the results of your tests, you can use the NUnit test runner GUI, as shown in Figure 5-6.

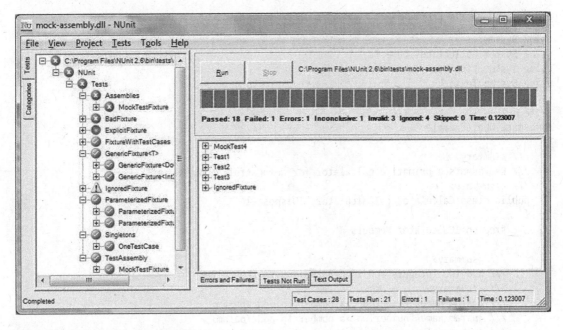

Figure 5-6. *NUnit Test Runner GUI*

As you can see, the NUnit unit-testing framework is a comprehensive testing suite, and best of all, it is open source (and free). Now that we've covered NUnit, I'll provide an example of a unit test and the class under test. Listing 5-1 shows an `interface` for a calculator class. There are methods for Add, Subtract, Divide, and Multiply.

Listing 5-1. *ICalculator.cs Code*

```csharp
using System;
using System.Collections.Generic;
using System.Linq;
using System.Text;

namespace NUnitExample
{
    public interface ICalculator : IDisposable
    {
        int Add(int numberOne, int numberTwo);
        int Subtract(int numberOne, int numberTwo);
        int Divide(int numberOne, int numberTwo);
        int Multiply(int numberOne, int numberTwo);

    }
}
```

Listing 5-2 shows the implementation of the Calculator class. The Calculator class implements the ICalculator interface.

Listing 5-2. Calculator.cs Code

```
using System;
using System.Collections.Generic;
using System.Linq;
using System.Text;
using System.Threading.Tasks;

namespace NUnitExample
{
    /// <summary>
    /// Represents a primative calculator for demonstration purposes
    /// </summary>
    public class Calculator : ICalculator, IDisposable
    {
        #region ICalculator Members

        /// <summary>
        /// Add two integers and return the sum to the caller
        /// </summary>
        /// <param name="numberOne">a number to add</param>
        /// <param name="numberTwo">a number to add</param>
        /// <returns>The sum of the two input arguments</returns>
        public int Add(int numberOne, int numberTwo)
        {
            return numberOne + numberTwo;
        }

        /// <summary>
        /// Subtract two integers and return the difference to the caller
        /// </summary>
        /// <param name="numberOne">a number to subtract</param>
        /// <param name="numberTwo">a number to subtract</param>
        /// <returns>The difference between the two input arguments</returns>
        public int Subtract(int numberOne, int numberTwo)
        {
            return numberOne - numberTwo;
        }

        /// <summary>
        /// Divide two numbers
        /// </summary>
        /// <param name="numberOne">A number that should be divided by the second
        argument</param>
        /// <param name="numberTwo">A number to use to divide the first argument</param>
        /// <returns>The result of the division</returns>
        /// <remarks>Generally, you should always check for a DivideByZero exception,
        however, we are leaving this out to demonstrate how to test for expected
        exceptions in unit tests.</remarks>
```

```
public int Divide(int numberOne, int numberTwo)
{
    return numberOne / numberTwo;
}


/// <summary>
/// Multiply two integers and return the product to the caller
/// </summary>
/// <param name="numberOne">a number to multiply</param>
/// <param name="numberTwo">a number to multiply</param>
/// <returns>The product of the multiplication between the two numbers</returns>
public int Multiply(int numberOne, int numberTwo)
{
    return numberOne * numberTwo;
}

#endregion

#region IDisposable Members

/// <summary>
/// if we had any unmanaged resources, we would free the associated
/// resources here.
/// </summary>
public void Dispose()
{
    Console.WriteLine("Clean as a whistle.");
}

#endregion
    }
}
```

Listing 5-3 shows a unit test fixture class called CalculatorTestFixture. As you can see, the class is decorated with the TestFixture attribute. This marks the class as a unit test class. We use the Setup attribute on Initialize_Test to specify the method that should be executed before any tests are run. This can be used to initialize your test class and its dependencies. The TearDown attribute is used to specify a method to be executed after all tests have run. This method can be used to release any references that you may have to external resources. In this example, I implemented the IDisposable interface in the Calculator class. We use the TearDown_Test method to dispose of the class under test. Finally, we have four methods marked with the Test attribute. These are our unit tests.

Listing 5-3. CalculatorTestFixture.cs Code

```
using System;
using System.Collections.Generic;
using System.Linq;
using System.Text;
using System.Threading.Tasks;
using NUnit.Framework;
```

```csharp
namespace NUnitExample
{
    [TestFixture]
    public class CalculatorTestFixture
    {
        private ICalculator _Calculator;

        [SetUp]
        public void Initialize_Test()
        {
            //Create a new instance of the calculator class for each test.
            _Calculator = new Calculator();
        }

        [Test]
        public void When_Adding_Two_Integers_The_Method_Should_Return_The_Sum()
        {
            var numberOne = 2;
            var numberTwo = 8;

            Assert.AreEqual(10, _Calculator.Add(numberOne, numberTwo));
        }

        [Test]
        public void When_Subtracting_Two_Integers_The_Method_Should_Return_The_Difference()
        {
            var numberOne = 10;
            var numberTwo = 2;

            Assert.AreEqual(8, _Calculator.Subtract(numberOne, numberTwo));
        }

        [Test]
        public void When_Multiplying_Two_Integers_The_Method_Should_Return_The_Product()
        {
            var numberOne = 2;
            var numberTwo = 2;

            Assert.AreEqual(4, _Calculator.Multiply(numberOne, numberTwo));
        }


        [Test]
        [ExpectedException("System.DivideByZeroException")]
        public void When_Dividing_A_Number_By_Zero_The_Method_Should_Throw_A_
        DivideByZeroException()
        {
            var numberOne = 0;
            var numberTwo = 0;

            _Calculator.Divide(numberOne, numberTwo);
        }
```

```
    [TearDown]
    public void TearDown_Test()
    {
        //perform any necessary clean up
        _Calculator.Dispose();
    }


}
}
```

Microsoft Unit Testing Project Template

Don't get us wrong, we think NUnit is a great product; however, our unit-testing framework of choice is *Microsoft Unit Testing Project Template*. It is a unit-testing framework with native support built in to Visual Studio. To create a new Microsoft unit test project, simply right-click in your Solution Explorer and select Add New. Next, choose the Test category and select Unit Test Project. Figure 5-7 shows how to add a new Unit Test Project in Visual Studio.

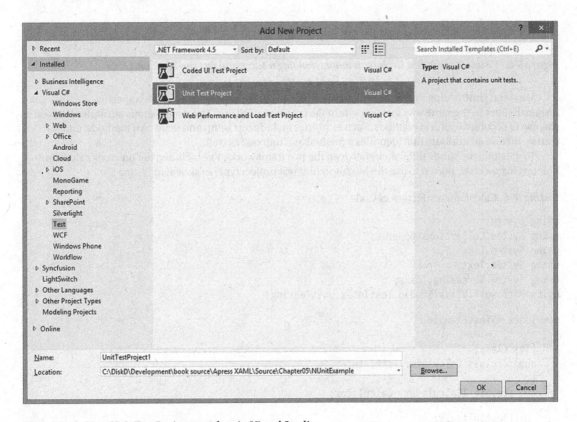

Figure 5-7. *New Unit Test Project template in Visual Studio*

Visual Studio's Test Explorer window makes it easy to execute one or all unit tests with a single click of the mouse. The Test Explorer window is also used to view the status of the execution of your unit tests (see Figure 5-8).

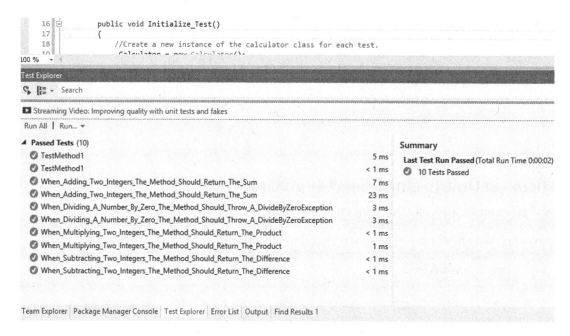

Figure 5-8. *Visual Studio's Test Explorer window showing a successful test run of all unit tests*

Microsoft Unit Testing Project Template has attributes that give your test methods specific responsibilities in the same way that you saw in the coverage of NUnit. There are various attributes that you can use to decorate your test methods. Such attributes include test setup and teardown methods, and, of course, there is an attribute that identifies a method as a unit test as well.

To illustrate the subtle differences between the two frameworks, I've included the previous calculator unit test fixture class, ported to use the Microsoft unit test project type, as shown in Listing 5-4.

Listing 5-4. CalculatorTestFixture.cs Code

```
using System;
using System.Collections.Generic;
using System.Linq;
using System.Text;
using System.Threading.Tasks;
using Microsoft.VisualStudio.TestTools.UnitTesting;

namespace MSTestExample
{
    [TestClass]
    public class CalculatorTestFixture
    {
        private ICalculator _Calculator;

        [TestInitialize]
        public void Initialize_Test()
        {
            //Create a new instance of the calculator class for each test.
            _Calculator = new Calculator();
        }
```

```
[TestMethod]
public void When_Adding_Two_Integers_The_Method_Should_Return_The_Sum()
{
    var numberOne = 2;
    var numberTwo = 8;

    Assert.AreEqual(10, _Calculator.Add(numberOne, numberTwo));
}

[TestMethod]
public void When_Subtracting_Two_Integers_The_Method_Should_Return_The_Difference()
{
    var numberOne = 10;
    var numberTwo = 2;

    Assert.AreEqual(8, _Calculator.Subtract(numberOne, numberTwo));
}

[TestMethod]
public void When_Multiplying_Two_Integers_The_Method_Should_Return_The_Product()
{
    var numberOne = 2;
    var numberTwo = 2;

    Assert.AreEqual(4, _Calculator.Multiply(numberOne, numberTwo));
}

[TestMethod]
[ExpectedException(typeof(System.DivideByZeroException))]
public void When_Dividing_A_Number_By_Zero_The_Method_Should_Throw_A_
DivideByZeroException()
{
    var numberOne = 0;
    var numberTwo = 0;

    _Calculator.Divide(numberOne, numberTwo);
}

[TestCleanup]
public void TearDown_Test()
{
    //perform any necessary clean up
    _Calculator.Dispose();
}
    }
}
```

As you can see in Listing 5-4, the code is nearly identical to the NUnit example shown in Listing 5-1. This proves that your choice in a unit-testing framework is purely a personal preference. We like the Microsoft framework for the simple fact that you don't have to download any packages or assemblies. Everything that you need to unit test your code can be achieved using the same workflow as any other project created within Visual Studio.

Summary

In this chapter, we covered the basics of using various testing methods and programming techniques to minimize the time and money wasted on finding, fixing, and retesting software as a result of bugs. When implemented properly, automated unit tests can dramatically reduce the amount of bugs as well as the impact of finding and fixing them. We gave you the "whole story" regarding unit tests as well as the damage that they can produce if implemented incorrectly.

It's important that your class interface designs promote the creation of objects that are easy to read, understand, modify, and maintain. TDD, when implemented correctly, can help you do just that, and, at the same time, it will improve your code's test coverage because you don't write any code without writing a test for it first.

We provided a list of criteria that you can use to assess the quality of your unit tests. We also discussed the importance of automating the execution of unit tests so that you will know about any bugs introduced into your source code at the moment that a unit test fails. The CUT in the test fixture that contains the failing unit test will eliminates the guessing game associated with finding the source of the bug that caused your test to fail.

We introduced you to two popular unit-testing frameworks: NUnit and Microsoft's Unit Test Project template. We also provided a simple example of how to write a basic test fixture class using each framework.

In Chapter 6, we will explore some of the advanced aspects of unit testing such as stubs, fakes, and mock objects. We will also cover Test-Driven Development, which is a software design methodology that allows you to design your classes and methods by writing tests for your code before the code is written. This introduces a layer of abstraction that helps you to ignore the implementation details of each method and allows you to design your class interfaces based on how you intend to use the class.

CHAPTER 6

■ ■ ■

Advanced Unit Testing and Test-Driven Development

If unit testing is a practice that you choose to utilize in your projects, chances are that once you get the hang of writing effective unit tests, you will write a lot of them. It's important to remember that a unit test fixture is a class, and as such, you should take advantage of the benefits offered by object-oriented design.

Test Fixtures Are Classes Too

When writing your unit tests, be sure to keep your eyes open for any chance to reduce complexity. Since your test fixtures are usually centered on the same domain, you will find yourself creating instances of entities to be used throughout all of your test classes. If you find that you are writing the same code in several methods or test classes, you should remember to adhere to the DRY principle: don't repeat yourself. Inheritance is obviously a great tool to use in this case.

Use Inheritance to Avoid Duplicate Code

The business domain that you are modeling in your application's design is based on creating and taking quizzes to assist the user in studying for official exams. As we've previously discussed, there is a root entity called Quiz. A Quiz is a collection of Question instances, and a Question is a collection of Answer instances.

You will generally create a unit test library for each layer of your application. To test each layer of the application, it's safe to assume that you will need routines to create instances of the Quiz root entity as well as all of the Quiz properties. Instead of duplicating all of the boilerplate code used to create these test classes, you can create a base class with methods to create all of the test entities that you will need throughout your unit test classes. All unit test classes can inherit from this base class and take advantage of inheritance to eliminate duplicated code.

Consider the base class shown in Listing 6-1.

Listing 6-1. QuizTestBase.cs

```csharp
using System.Collections.Generic;
using QuizIt.Domain;

namespace MoqExample
{
    /// <summary>
    /// Base class for all quiz related unit testing classes
    /// </summary>
    public abstract class QuizTestBase
    {
        private int _IdCounter = 0;

        /// <summary>
        /// Create a quiz object to be used in unit tests.
        /// </summary>
        /// <returns>A Quiz object to use for testing.</returns>
        protected virtual Quiz PrepareTestQuiz()
        {
            var testQuiz = new Quiz
            {
                Id = _IdCounter++,
                Name = string.Format("Test Quiz #{0}", _IdCounter),
            };

            testQuiz.Questions = PrepareQuizQuestions();

            return testQuiz;
        }

        /// <summary>
        /// Create a collection of quiz question objects for testing
        /// </summary>
        /// <returns>A collection of question objects.</returns>
        protected virtual IEnumerable<Question> PrepareQuizQuestions()
        {
            var quizQuestions = new List<Question>
            {
                PrepareQuestion(),
                PrepareQuestion(),
                PrepareQuestion()
            };

            return quizQuestions;
        }
```

```csharp
/// <summary>
/// Create a question for testing
/// </summary>
/// <returns>A question object.</returns>
protected virtual Question PrepareQuestion()
{
    return new Question
    {
        Id = _IdCounter++,
        DisplayText = string.Format("Question # '{0}'.", _IdCounter++),
        Points = 10,
        Answers = PrepareAnswers()
    };
}

/// <summary>
/// Create a collection of question answers for testing
/// </summary>
/// <returns>A collection of answer objects.</returns>
protected virtual IEnumerable<Answer> PrepareAnswers()
{
    return new List<Answer>
    {
        PrepareAnswer("Incorrect Answer 1.", false),
        PrepareAnswer("Incorrect Answer 2.", false),
        PrepareAnswer("Correct Answer.", true),
        PrepareAnswer("Incorrect Answer 3.", false)
    };
}

/// <summary>
/// Create an answer for testing
/// </summary>
/// <returns>An answer object.</returns>
protected Answer PrepareAnswer(string displayText, bool isCorrect)
{
    return new Answer
    {
        Id = _IdCounter++,
        DisplayText = displayText,
        IsCorrect = isCorrect
    };
}

/// <summary>
/// Create a collection of Quizes for testing
/// </summary>
/// <returns>A collection of quiz objects.</returns>
protected virtual IEnumerable<Quiz> PrepareTestQuizCollection()
{
    return new List<Quiz>
```

```
        {
            this.PrepareTestQuiz(),
            this.PrepareTestQuiz(),
            this.PrepareTestQuiz()
        };
    }
  }
}
```

As you can see, this class provides methods to create instances of any entity that you will need while unit testing the layers of your application.

Unit Testing Classes That Have Dependencies

As we've discussed in previous chapters, dependency injection and inversion of control are two ways to design code that is open to change and closed to modifications (also known as the *open/closed principle*). If you design your classes with this open/closed principle in mind, you can greatly reduce the costs associated with a project's maintenance after the solution has been deployed.

Dealing with Dependencies

Unit testing and Test-Driven Development can be great tools to use to design and develop loosely coupled components that are open to change and easy to reuse in other projects with a minimum amount of code modification. To test a specific class effectively, you need a way to deal with the dependencies of the class in which you can't control or predict the behavior.

Some examples of such dependencies include objects that interact with a database, the file system, or any third-party dependency in which you don't have access to the source code. For instance, suppose you are testing a web service or an implementation of the repository design pattern. In either case, you need to write tests that produce the same results on every test run.

If you are unit testing a domain service class that has a dependency on a web service, how can you control the speed in which packets of information are transmitted across the network to and from the web service? Remember, one of the requirements of a good unit test is that it needs to run fast. Suppose the developer's workstation that is running the unit test loses its connection to the Internet. How can you control or predict the return value from a method call on a dependency class if it's possible that an exception could be thrown?

You run into the same issues when unit testing a class that depends on a database connection. Let's pretend that your DBA's only two weaknesses are kryptonite and schema changes. Super DBA can guarantee that the database server will never lose its connectivity, and it has created indexes that result in SELECT statements that are faster than a speeding bullet.

For argument's sake, connection issues and speed of execution aren't your problem. There are still many issues that you will face if you try to write unit tests for a class that has a dependency on the super database. First you will need a database that is dedicated to unit testing. After all, you can't write tests against a database unless you can guarantee the state of the data and the values that will be returned with every query.

To achieve this, you will need to develop the unit test with a considerable amount of setup and teardown logic to prepare the tables that you plan to use. In a situation like this, you will need to make sure that the test table is in the correct state before each test, populate the table with the return values that you expect, and reset the table to the initial state after each test is run.

Even with a dedicated database, what happens if two developers execute the same unit test at the same time? What about three, four, or twenty developers? I think you can see where I'm going with this. If your unit test causes any INSERT statements to execute on the super server while another developer executes a test that will SELECT data, then chances are that someone will end up with an unexpected return value, which could fail the test.

You can't rely on these types of dependencies. So, how do you unit test classes with dependencies that you can't control? To begin with, it's important to keep these issues in mind when designing your classes. This is one of the many benefits of Test-Driven Development. If you write your tests before you write your code, your code will be open to change as a side effect of designing classes that can be effectively unit tested.

Another important design decision that will help you manage dependencies in unit testing is to utilize interfaces to create classes that are open to change without modification. If you utilize polymorphism through interface references when designing your classes, then you can easily change the implementation of the dependencies used in your unit tests. You simply create different implementations of the dependencies used by the class under test. If you can easily switch the implementation of an interface reference, you can then create a class that will always behave exactly as the assertions in your test methods expect them to behave. The only requirement is that each class implementation must adhere to the contract defined by the interface. These special test class implementations are called *stubs*.

For example, let's say you've created a data access class with an implementation that is tightly coupled to the SQL Server–specific ADO.NET data access classes, which are baked into the .NET Framework class library. Listing 6-2 provides some example code.

Listing 6-2. A Data Access Class That Deals Directly with a Database Connection Using ADO.NET

```
using System;
using System.Collections.Generic;
using System.Configuration;
using System.Data;
using System.Data.SqlClient;
using DataAccess.Interfaces;
using QuizIt.Domain;

namespace DataAccess.Sql
{
    /// <summary>
    /// Provides methods to load and save quiz related data to the database
    /// using ADO.NET and SQL.
    /// </summary>
    public class QuizSqlDataAccess : IQuizDataAccess
    {
        #region "private members"

        private string _DbConnectionString;
        private SqlConnection _DbConnection;
        private IDbCommand _DbCommand;

        #endregion

        #region "constructor(s)"

        /// <summary>
        /// Default constructor
        /// </summary>
```

```csharp
        public QuizSqlDataAccess()
        {
            _SetConnectionString();
        }

        #endregion

        #region IQuizSqlDataAccess Members

        /// <summary>
        /// Retrieve all quiz objects from the database.
        /// </summary>
        /// <returns>A collection of quizes.</returns>
        public IEnumerable<Quiz> GetAllQuizesFromDatabase()
        {
            throw new NotImplementedException();
        }

        /// <summary>
        /// Retrieve all quiz objects from the database.
        /// </summary>
        /// <param name="id">
        /// The primary key associated
        /// with the quiz to be
        /// retrieved.
        /// </param>
        /// <returns>
        /// The quiz associated with
        /// the specified id.
        /// </returns>
        public Quiz GetQuizById(int id)
        {
            if (id <= 0)
                throw new ArgumentOutOfRangeException("id");

            var quizDataReader = _GetQuizDataReaderById(id);

            if (quizDataReader == null)
                throw new NullReferenceException("error reading quiz data.");

            return _LoadQuizFromDataReader(quizDataReader);
        }

        #endregion

        #region "private helpers"
```

```csharp
private IDataReader _GetQuizDataReaderById(int id)
{
    //TODO consider moving the creation of the connection and object
    //into the using statements to gaurantee the IDisposable Dispose() method is
    called to close the connections
    if (_DbConnection == null)
        _DbConnection = new SqlConnection(_DbConnectionString);

    var getQuizStoredProc = "usp_GetQuizById";

    _DbCommand = new SqlCommand(getQuizStoredProc, _DbConnection);

    _DbCommand.CommandType = CommandType.StoredProcedure;

    var storedProcParam = new SqlParameter("@id", id);

    if (_DbConnection.State != ConnectionState.Open)
        _DbConnection.Open();

    var quizDataReader = _DbCommand.ExecuteReader();

    return quizDataReader;
}

private Quiz _LoadQuizFromDataReader(IDataReader dr)
{
    if (dr == null)
        throw new ArgumentNullException("dr");

    var quiz = new Quiz();

    using (_DbConnection)
    {
        using (_DbCommand)
        {
            using (dr)
            {
                while (dr.Read())
                {
                    quiz.Id = (int)dr["Id"];
                    quiz.Name = (string)dr["Name"];
                    quiz.Questions = _LoadQuestionsFromDataReader(dr);
                }

                dr.Close();
            }
        }
```

```csharp
            _DbConnection.Close();
        }

        return quiz;
    }

    private IEnumerable<Question> _LoadQuestionsFromDataReader(IDataReader dr)
    {
        if (dr == null)
            throw new ArgumentNullException("dr");

        var questions = new List<Question>();

        while (dr.Read())
        {
            var question = new Question();
            question.Id = (int)dr["QuestionId"];
            question.DisplayText = (string)dr["QuestionDisplayText"];
            question.Points = (int)dr["QuestionPoints"];
            question.Answers = _LoadAnswersFromDataReader(dr);
            questions.Add(question);
        }

        return questions;
    }

    private IEnumerable<Answer> _LoadAnswersFromDataReader(IDataReader dr)
    {
        if (dr == null)
            throw new ArgumentNullException("dr");

        var answers = new List<Answer>();

        while (dr.Read())
        {
            var answer = new Answer();
            answer.Id = (int)dr["AnswerId"];
            answer.DisplayText = (string)dr["AnswerDisplayText"];
            answer.IsCorrect = (bool)dr["AnswerPoints"];

            answers.Add(answer);
        }

        return answers;
    }

    private void _SetConnectionString()
    {
        if (ConfigurationManager.ConnectionStrings["DbCnnString"] == null)
            throw new NullReferenceException("Null DbCnnString.");

        _DbConnectionString =
            ConfigurationManager.ConnectionStrings["DbCnnString"].ConnectionString;
```

```
        if (string.IsNullOrEmpty(_DbConnectionString))
            throw new NullReferenceException("null connection string");

        _DbConnection = new SqlConnection(_DbConnectionString);
    }

    #endregion
}
}
```

The first thing to note is that the class implements the IQuizDataAccess interface. Listing 6-3 shows the interface definition.

Listing 6-3. IQuizDataAccess.cs

```
using System.Collections.Generic;
using QuizIt.Domain;

namespace DataAccess.Interfaces
{
    /// <summary>
    /// Provides a contract for classes
    /// used to read and write quiz data.
    /// </summary>
    public interface IQuizDataAccess
    {
        Quiz GetQuizById(int id);
        IEnumerable<Quiz> GetAllQuizesFromDatabase();
    }
}
```

As you can see, the QuizSqlDataAccess class requires a valid connection to a SQL Server database in order to load quiz data to return to the caller. Now you could use the data access object directly in your domain service classes; however, what happens when you need to support a different database system? If your domain services directly reference the ADO.NET-specific implementation of the IQuizDataAccess interface, you would need to create an implementation of the interface that is designed to work with the new database technology. You will also need to modify every class in the entire project, as well as any other project that uses the QuizSqlDataAccess class. If you apply object-oriented design principles, you would write your classes so that they can be reused in other applications. (If you don't, then shame on you.) This can be a big problem, depending on how many different applications share your data access class. If only there were a design pattern that you could use to abstract the data access technology away from the code that uses it. Well, you're in luck! You can use the repository pattern to achieve the level of abstraction that you desire.

Repository Pattern

This is the problem that the repository pattern was created to solve. As discussed in Chapter 4, the *repository pattern* is designed to provide a level of abstraction between the database access logic and the caller of that logic. The repository is meant to act as an in-memory collection of all objects stored in the database. This provides a level of abstraction that removes the complexity of dealing with the database and places it in a class that is dedicated to one specific data access technology. This also allows the developer to switch to any database system easily without making any modification to the repository. If a new database technology is created, all that is required is for a developer to create a new implementation of the IQuizDataAccess interface. The dependency injection pattern and inversion of control principle allow you to change an interface's class implementation in only one place. This is great. However, you still need a way to test the repository in your unit tests without relying on the database. This is where you can apply stubs and mock objects.

Stubs

One way to deal with dependencies in unit testing is by creating stub classes. Before we discuss stubs, we need to talk about interfaces. We're sure that you know the importance of interfaces in relation to basic object-oriented programming and design. Interfaces are essential in leveraging polymorphism in C#.

When you create an interface reference, your code's design makes it easier to replace the implementation of an interface by dynamically creating an instance of the appropriate class and then passing that object as an interface reference.

If you utilize interfaces and polymorphism when designing your dependencies, then you can create an implementation that is used only for unit testing purposes. This is known as a *stub*. Let's take a look at the example shown in Listing 6-4.

Listing 6-4. QuizSqlDataAccessStub.cs

```
using System.Collections.Generic;
using DataAccess.Interfaces;
using QuizIt.Domain;

namespace MoqExample.Data.Stub
{
    /// <summary>
    /// A stub implementation of
    /// IQuizDataAccess. This
    /// implementation is for testing
    /// only.
    /// </summary>
    public class QuizSqlDataAccessStub : QuizTestBase, IQuizDataAccess
    {
        #region IQuizDataAccess Members

        /// <summary>
        /// Return a test quiz object.
        /// </summary>
        /// <param name="id">
        /// The id of the quiz.
        /// </param>
        /// <returns>
        /// A test quiz object with the specified id.
        /// </returns>
        public Quiz GetQuizById(int id)
        {
            var quiz = this.PrepareTestQuiz();
            quiz.Id = id;

            return quiz;
        }
```

```
/// <summary>
/// Return a collection of test quizzes
/// </summary>
/// <returns>
/// A collection of quizzes for unit testing.
/// </returns>
public IEnumerable<Quiz> GetAllQuizesFromDatabase()
{
    return PrepareTestQuizCollection();
}

#endregion
    }
}
```

As you can see, the Stub class implements the IQuizDataAccess interface as well as inherits the functionality of the QuizTestBase base class created at the beginning of the chapter. The sole purpose of the Stub class is to provide an implementation of the IQuizDataAccess interface that removes the dependency on the database-specific logic, and therefore it guarantees that the methods will return the same results on every call. This allows you to achieve your goal of writing predictable unit tests that execute quickly. Stub objects are great for simple dependencies. Sometimes the dependencies are complex, however, and you find that you are writing a stub that needs unit tests. If you find yourself in this position, then Stub classes may not be the best tool for the job. If you are dealing with complex dependencies, there is another option to help you to write effective unit tests, known as *mock objects*.

Mock Objects

Stub classes are extremely useful when you need to create an implementation of a dependency in order to dictate the return value of a method or property. Sometimes, though, you need more control over the dependencies of the class under test. For instance, you may need to verify that a dependency's methods are called in a specific order. When you need this type of control over the dependencies that you deal with in your unit tests, you don't need a stub—you need a mock object.

Since you use mock objects for complex dependencies, their design and implementation are more complex than stubs. As such, there are existing open source frameworks that can save you time and effort when creating mock dependency objects. We will deal with only one mock framework in this chapter.

The mock framework that you will use is called Moq. You can easily install the framework using the NuGet package manager. You can also download the full source code for the framework from https://github.com/Moq/moq4.

Using the Moq Framework

We will provide an overview of some of the essential tasks that you will use the most when utilizing the Moq framework to enhance your unit tests. Don't fret, the Moq project has a nice overview on the GitHub project site mentioned earlier. We'll also provide other URLs that will come in handy as you learn to use this awesome Mock framework.

- The official Moq framework's documentation is at www.nudoq.org/- !/Projects/Moq.

- The Moq framework tutorial is at https://github.com/Moq/moq4/wiki/Quickstart.

Using the Mock Class to Set Up Your Dependencies

The first step in using the Moq framework is to create an instance of the Mock class.

Create an Instance of the Mock Class

You start by creating an instance of the Mock<T> class. The Mock<T> class is a generic type where T represents the type that you want to mock. In this instance, you are mocking a class that implements the IQuizDataAccess interface:

```
var mock = new Mock<IQuizDataAccess>();
```

As you can see, the Mock class makes use of generics to specify the type of mocked instance that you want to create. The next step is to set up the behavior of the method or property that you want to use in your unit test.

Set Up the Behavior of the Mock Dependency Object

When you set up the behavior of the Mock dependency object, you use the framework to specify which member you plan to work with and the return value of that member. Moq allows you to do this using LINQ expressions, which will give you IntelliSense and enforce type safety.

In this example, you want to test the GetAllQuizesFromDatabase method of the data access object. The QuizTestBase class defines the PrepareTestQuizCollection method that will return a collection of Quiz objects. You will use this method to create a collection of Quiz objects to use to set up the return value of the Mock object's GetAllQuizesFromDatabase method. Listing 6-5 shows an example.

Listing 6-5. Set Up the Mock Object to Return a Collection of Quiz Objects When Calling the GetAllQuizesFromDatabase Method

```
var returnQuizList = PrepareTestQuizCollection();

//Setup the mock object to return a collection of quiz objects
//when calling the GetAllQuizesFromDatabase method
mock
    .Setup<IEnumerable<Quiz>>(q => q.GetAllQuizesFromDatabase())
    .Returns(returnQuizList);

//Set the quiz sql data access to the mocked object reference
//The IQuizDataAccess reference will return the Quiz list
//that we've configured above. This allows us to test
//the repository without depending on the database which
//can't be relied on.
IQuizDataAccess mockedDataAccess = _MockingService.Object;
```

As you can see, Moq is flexible in that it allows you to set up a dependency without the need to create a class by hand. This is only one of the benefits associated with the Moq framework. You can also use the Moq framework to determine whether a method has been called or a property has been accessed or had its value set in the unit test.

A Complete Example

To complete the coverage of how to deal with dependencies in unit testing, we will provide an example of two unit test fixtures. Both of the classes inherit the functionality defined in the QuizTestBase base class. The first unit test class demonstrates the use of a Stub class. The other unit test class demonstrates the use of the Moq framework to create a mock dependency. Review the example shown in Listing 6-6.

Listing 6-6. QuizRepositoryStubFixture.cs

```
using DataAccess.Interfaces;
using DataAccess.Repositories;
using Microsoft.VisualStudio.TestTools.UnitTesting;
using MoqExample.Data.Stub;

namespace MoqExample
{
    /// <summary>
    /// This class contains unit tests that
    /// test the methods of a specific IQuizRepository
    /// interface implementation
    /// </summary>
    [TestClass]
    public class QuizRepositoryStubFixture : QuizTestBase
    {
        #region "private fields"

        private IQuizRepository _QuizRepository;
        private IQuizDataAccess _QuizSqlDataAccess;
        private int _IdCounter;
        private QuizSqlDataAccessStub _DataAccessStub;

        #endregion

        /// <summary>
        /// Initialize all test dependencies
        /// </summary>
        [TestInitialize]
        public void TestInitialize()
        {
            _IdCounter = 1;
            _QuizRepository = _PrepareQuizRepositoryForTesting();
        }

        #region "unit tests"

        [TestMethod]
        public void When_Calling_GetById_Then_Return_A_Quiz_With_Stub()
        {
            Assert.IsNotNull(_QuizRepository, "The QuizRepository is null.");

            var quiz = _QuizRepository.GetById(1);
```

```csharp
        Assert.IsNotNull(quiz, "QuizRepository.GetById returned null.");
        Assert.AreEqual(1, quiz.Id, "The id should be 1.");
    }

    #endregion

    #region "private helper methods"

    /// <summary>
    /// This method will create an instance of an
    /// IQuizRepository implementation.
    /// </summary>
    /// <returns>
    /// A reference to an IQuizRepository
    /// implementation.
    /// </returns>
    private IQuizRepository _PrepareQuizRepositoryForTesting()
    {
        var dataAccessStub = _GetQuizDataAccessStub();

        //Inject the dependency via constructor injection
        _QuizRepository = new QuizRepository(dataAccessStub);

        return _QuizRepository;
    }

    private IQuizDataAccess _GetQuizDataAccessStub()
    {
        return new QuizSqlDataAccessStub();
    }

    #endregion
    }
}
```

Listing 6-7 shows the unit test fixture for the IQuizRespository using the Moq framework. The Moq framework is used to mock the SQL-specific data access service that is used by the repository.

Listing 6-7. QuizRepositoryMoqFixture.cs

```csharp
using System;
using System.Collections.Generic;
using DataAccess.Interfaces;
using DataAccess.Repositories;
using Microsoft.VisualStudio.TestTools.UnitTesting;
using Moq;
using QuizIt.Domain;
```

```csharp
namespace MoqExample
{
    /// <summary>
    /// This class contains unit tests that
    /// test the methods of a specific IQuizRepository
    /// interface implementation
    /// </summary>
    [TestClass]
    public class QuizRepositoryMoqFixture : QuizTestBase
    {
        #region "private fields"

        private IQuizRepository _QuizRepository;
        private IQuizDataAccess _QuizSqlDataAccess;
        private int _IdCounter;
        private Mock<IQuizDataAccess> _MockingService;

        #endregion

        /// <summary>
        /// Initialize all test dependencies
        /// </summary>
        [TestInitialize]
        public void TestInitialize()
        {
            _IdCounter = 1;
            _QuizRepository = _PrepareQuizRepositoryForTesting();
        }

        #region "unit tests"

        [TestMethod]
        public void When_Calling_GetAll_Then_Return_A_List_Of_Quizes_With_Moq()
        {
            Assert.IsNotNull(_QuizRepository, "The QuizRepository is null.");

            var quizes = _QuizRepository.GetAll();

            Assert.IsNotNull(quizes, "QuizRepository.GetAll returned null.");

            var quizCount = ((List<Quiz>)quizes).Count;

            if (_MockingService == null)
                throw new NullReferenceException("Moq colaborator is null.");

            //Make sure that the method was called on
            //the mock object and that the expected
            //value was returned.
            _MockingService
                .Verify(q => q.GetAllQuizesFromDatabase());
```

```csharp
        Assert.AreEqual(3, quizCount,
            string.Format("Expected 3. Actual count is {0}.", quizCount));
    }

    #endregion

    #region "private helper methods"

    /// <summary>
    /// This method will create an instance of an
    /// IQuizRepository implementation.
    /// </summary>
    /// <returns>
    /// A reference to an IQuizRepository
    /// implementation.
    /// </returns>
    private IQuizRepository _PrepareQuizRepositoryForTesting()
    {
        _PrepareMockedQuizDataAccess();

        //Inject the dependency via constructor injection
        _QuizRepository = new QuizRepository(_QuizSqlDataAccess);

        return _QuizRepository;
    }

    private void _PrepareMockedQuizDataAccess()
    {
        //prepare the repository's db dependency using the moq framework
        _MockingService = new Mock<IQuizDataAccess>();

        var returnQuizList = PrepareTestQuizCollection();

        //Setup the mock object to return a collection of quiz objects
        //when calling the GetAllQuizesFromDatabase method
        _MockingService
            .Setup<IEnumerable<Quiz>>(q => q.GetAllQuizesFromDatabase())
            .Returns(returnQuizList);

        //Set the quiz sql data access to the mocked object reference
        //The IQuizDataAccess reference will return the Quiz list
        //that we've configured above. This allows us to test
        //the repository without depending on the database which
        //can't be relied on.
        _QuizSqlDataAccess = _MockingService.Object;
    }

    #endregion
    }
}
```

Now that we've covered some of the more advanced concepts involved in writing unit tests, we will explain the basics of a powerful design methodology that, when used correctly, can help you to design loosely coupled classes that are open to change, closed to modification, and have proper unit test coverage. The design methodology that we're referring to is *Test-Driven Development* (TDD).

Design by Testing: Test-Driven Development

Test-Driven Development is an iterative process. There are three basic steps required when implementing TDD. The steps are easy to understand; however, they can be difficult to implement correctly without discipline, which can be gained only with a lot of practice. The steps involved are covered in the following sections.

Step 1: All Unit Tests Should Fail on the First Test Run

When you use TDD, you start by writing one unit test to validate the expected result of the class under testing. You may simply need to verify that a method returns the correct value or that an object's property contains the expected value after a sequence of method calls.

Keep in mind, however, that when you begin writing a unit test, the class in which you are testing should not even exist. Once you have finished writing the unit test, your first goal is to run the test so that it fails. You might be asking yourself, "Why would I want a unit test to fail?" For a unit test to fail, you must be able to run the test. To run a unit test, your solution must be buildable. So, your first step will be to create the class definition of the class under test.

■ **Caution**   It is extremely important to write the smallest amount of code possible in order for your unit test to build.

This means that you should write enough code to make the test build. If you are testing a method that returns a value, you shouldn't worry about writing any code that is related to the logic of the routine. You simply define the method signature and throw a new System.NotImplementedException instead of leaving the method's body empty. Otherwise, the method body will be empty, and since the method signature specifies a return data type, the project will not build unless there is a return statement or you throw an exception that specifies that the method has not yet been implemented. This exception will allow the project to build without implementing the specified method. Once you have defined any class, interface, method, or property that is used in your unit test, you should be able to build your unit test project. Once the project is in a buildable state, you are ready for the first step.

You simply run the unit test using your framework of choice and verify that the test fails as expected. Remember, up until this point, your class does not have any implementation details. However, you have created a test, and at the same time, you have created an interface for the class under test that is designed with the use of the class's interface in mind. This provides a layer of abstraction, which allows you to focus on the high-level design of how the class is used while encapsulating the gory implementation details, allowing you to ignore the complexities of how the class's members are implemented. To put it simply, you first define how the class is used, and then you iteratively define what makes the class work.

This will help you to write tests that clearly document how the CUT is meant to be used and, just as important, how it should not be used. If a new developer joins the team, they can simply review a test fixture to understand the intended use of a specific class, method, or property.

The first test run fails because the class under test GetAll method currently does not have an implementation. The method throws a System.NotImplemented exception, which allows the solution to build. You can see the failed test in the Visual Studio test runner in Figure 6-1.

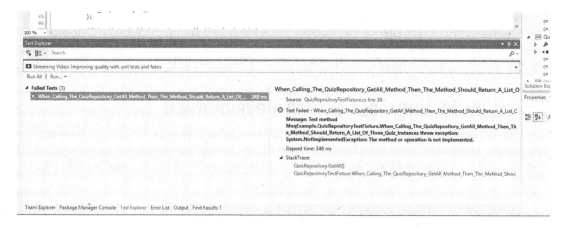

Figure 6-1. *Failed unit test in Visual Studio*

One of the keys to understanding and mastering TDD is to make sure that you make small iterative modifications when implementing a method in order to make your test pass.

Step 2: Add Only Enough Code to Pass the Test and No More

At this point, you've written a unit test to define how to use the class under testing. You've created an empty class definition, along with any class members that are used in the unit test. The next step is to implement any method that you call in the unit test so that the test passes.

■ **Caution** Remember to add only enough code to make the test pass and nothing more. This is important because it keeps your methods simple, and it promotes the design of tightly cohesive methods. In other words, the method will do one thing and only one thing. Any extra code that you add at this stage adds complexity. Complexity increases the potential for bugs, as well as diverting attention away from the intent of the method. You should follow the KISS principle: keep it simple, stupid.

Now that you've implemented the method, the unit test should now pass. Figure 6-2 shows the test pass in the Visual Studio test runner.

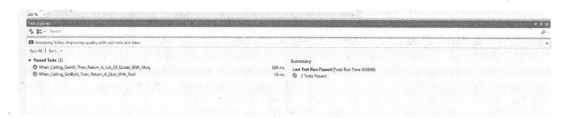

Figure 6-2. *Passed test in Visual Studio*

Step 3: Tighten Up Your Code by Refactoring

So now you've created a unit test to define how the class will be used, and you implemented the logic required to make the unit test pass (and *only* enough code to make it pass). At this point, you can look at the implementation of the method that you've created to identify ways to improve the readability of your code as well as to add any defense programming–related input checks. The term for improving the internal design of a routine without modifying the external interface in which the method or routine is called is referred to as *refactoring*. You should always remember that all TDD steps should be performed in small iterative steps. With each iteration, it's mandatory that you execute all unit tests. This will guarantee that any modifications that you made in the previous iteration haven't caused a side effect that introduced a bug of which you aren't aware. Once you've used refactoring to clean up the code that you've written and all of your unit tests pass, you can start the process over again and start a new unit test.

■ **Caution**   I can't stress enough the importance of sticking to the steps of fail, pass, and refactor. It's also extremely important that you make modifications in small increments. As we've said, this requires a great amount of discipline that can be learned only through lots of practice.

Summary

We covered a lot of information in this chapter. Test-Driven Development can be an effective tool when implemented properly. It can be a terrible waste of time when done incorrectly. One great way to practice TDD is a method that is borrowed from martial artists: katas. Katas involve writing lines of code over and over again to learn the iterative approach and other disciplines required to utilize TDD effectively. Here is a URL to a website by Roy Osherove, which is full of resources to help you to learn how to implement TDD properly: `http://osherove.com/tdd-kata-1/`.

Next up in Chapter 7, we will cover exception handling and logging using the Microsoft Enterprise Library Exception Handling Application Block.

CHAPTER 7

■ ■ ■

Exception Handling and Logging

In a perfect world, we would all develop quality, bug-free applications that are worthy of high honors, praise, and accolades. Unfortunately, we don't live in a perfect world, and sometimes, bad things happen to good people. Make sure that your application is not one of those bad things. You need to design your application to handle all situations that it may encounter through user interaction—the good, the bad, and the ugly.

Exception handling is a necessity in any application to ensure application stability and to prevent users from experiencing an unexpected crash. You also need to thwart exceptions that will display cryptic error messages containing stack traces and sensitive information, which in turn may expose weaknesses in your application. For example, an unhandled database exception may display an error message to the user containing the full, uncensored details of your application, including sensitive data such as database connection strings, stored procedure calls, and SQL queries. That's an open invitation for hackers to exploit these weaknesses for their own benefit.

Along with ensuring that your application handles errors gracefully, you need a way to trace, troubleshoot, and resolve any issues that arise when the application is in production. Application logging allows you to monitor and track issues in real time by writing information to a file, to a database, or to the cloud.

Let's take a look at some of the options available for exception handling and logging when developing WPF, Windows Store, and Windows Phone applications.

Enterprise Library Exception Handling Application Block

How often have you seen empty try/catch blocks within application code? Better yet, how often were you the one who authored that empty try/catch block? We've all been there, no doubt. Writing exception handling logic is repetitive and frankly boring. That's likely why so many developers include it sparingly within their code. At some point, I'm sure you've thought to yourself, "There must be a better way." Well, there is! It's called the *Enterprise Library Exception Handling Application Block.*

The Enterprise Library Exception Handling Application Block is available for use within Windows Desktop applications, web applications, and WCF services. It is not supported in Windows Phone or Windows Store applications. We will cover alternatives to exception handling and logging for Windows Phone and Windows Store applications in the section "Logging Options for Windows Device Apps" later in this chapter.

This Application Block encapsulates exception handling logic within a separate library and makes it possible for you to design the approach that your application will take when handling exceptions.

The Enterprise Library Exception Handling Application Block allows you to include error handling easily within your application without the need to pollute your code with `try`/`catch` blocks. It allows you to do the following:

- Define one or more policies for handling exceptions

- Decide on one or more exception types that will be managed by each policy

- Configure the action that will occur when exceptions of a specific type are caught or whether the same action will apply to all exception types

The exception handling approach that you define is stored within the application's configuration file. Therefore, you can change its behavior at any time without having to recompile the application for the changes to take effect.

An additional helper library, the Enterprise Library Exception Handling Logging Handler, is available. It allows you easily to incorporate logging within your application.

Now let's walk through the steps that you need to take to include the Exception Handling Application Block and its respective Logging Handler in a WPF application.

Installing the Exception Handling Application Block

Launch Visual Studio and create a new WPF application. Once the application is loaded, you will need to include the Exception Handling Application Block and its respective logging handler in the application. This is accomplished through Nuget Package Manager.

Launch Nuget Package Manager and select Online ➤ nuget.org in the left pane. In the Search field, enter the term **exception handling** and press Enter, as shown in Figure 7-1.

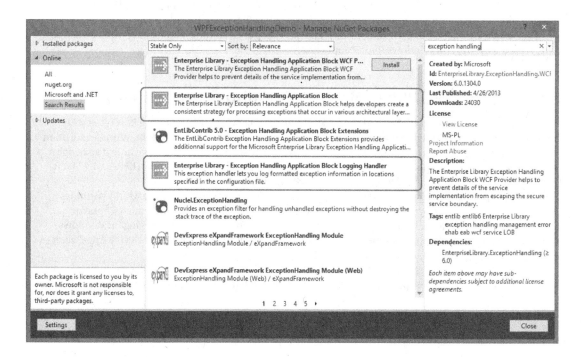

***Figure 7-1.** Installing Exception Handling Application Block using Nuget*

Select the Enterprise Library - Exception Handling Application Block Logging Handler, and click Install to add it to the application.

■ **Tip** By installing the Exception Handling Application Block Logging Handler first, the Exception Handling Application Block is installed automatically since the Logging Handler has a dependency on that library.

With the necessary libraries installed, you can now define how your application will manage exceptions and which exceptions will be logged. As mentioned earlier, the configuration is defined within the application's configuration file. There are two ways to modify this file to include your exception handling and logging configuration: manually or through the Enterprise Configuration Console.

Manual modification is error prone, and it requires in-depth knowledge of the XML elements, attributes, and values that are needed to define your exception handling policies, types, and handlers. It is our opinion that this is worse than writing repetitive exception handling code within the application—thanks, but no thanks.

The Enterprise Configuration Console provides a nice user interface that makes it easy for you to configure the Enterprise Library Application Blocks to suit the needs of your application. It then generates the XML configuration automatically. Perhaps you have a different perspective, but we would rather not spend a lot of time handwriting XML for the fun of it. Let's go with the second approach.

Installing the Enterprise Configuration Console

The Enterprise Configuration Console is available as an extension for Visual Studio 2010 and Visual Studio 2012. It isn't available for Visual Studio 2013, but it is easy enough to tweak the original extension so that it can be installed in Visual Studio 2013 and Visual Studio 2015. The steps to accomplish this are as follows:

1. Download the Enterprise Library 6 Configuration Console extension from the Microsoft Downloads page.

    a. Navigate to the Microsoft site, http://microsoft.com, and then click the Downloads link.

    b. Search for *Microsoft Enterprise Library 6*.

    c. Select the option Download Enterprise Library 6 and then click the Download button.

    d. Select the Microsoft.Practices.EnterpriseLibrary.ConfigConsoleV6.vsix entry from the list and click Next to download.

2. Open Windows File Explorer to the directory where you downloaded the extension. Rename the file, changing the .vsix file extension to .zip. When prompted with a warning about changing the extension, confirm the action and continue.

3. Right-click the .zip file in Windows File Explorer and select the option to extract the file contents to a folder.

4. Open the extension.vsixmanifest file in a text editor, such as Notepad.

5. Replace the SupportedProducts XML element with the following:

```xml
<SupportedProducts>
  <VisualStudio Version="11.0">
    <Edition>Ultimate</Edition>
    <Edition>Premium</Edition>
    <Edition>Pro</Edition>
  </VisualStudio>
  <VisualStudio Version="12.0"> <!-- VS2013 -->
    <Edition>Ultimate</Edition>
    <Edition>Premium</Edition>
    <Edition>Pro</Edition>
  </VisualStudio>
  <VisualStudio Version="14.0"> <!-- VS2015 -->
    <Edition>Ultimate</Edition>
    <Edition>Premium</Edition>
    <Edition>Pro</Edition>
  </VisualStudio>
</SupportedProducts>
```

6. Save the file and close the text editor.

Right-click the Microsoft.Practices.EnterpriseLibrary.ConfigConsoleV6 folder containing the modified file and select Send to ➤ Compressed (zipped) folder.

7. Rename the file to use its original name with the .vsix extension.

Make sure that all instances of Visual Studio are closed and then double-click the modified .vsix file to install the Enterprise Library Configuration Console Extension.

Configuring Policies, Exception Types, and Handlers

Now it's time to edit the App.config file to include exception handling and logging within the application. Right-click the App.config file in Solution Explorer and select "Edit configuration file v6," as shown in Figure 7-2, to open the Configuration Console.

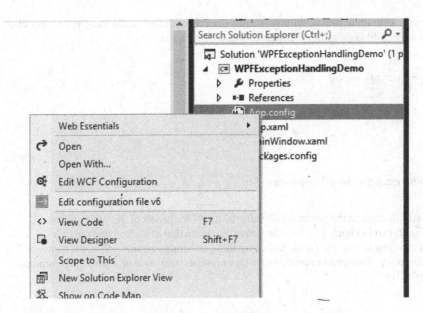

Figure 7-2. *Opening the Enterprise Library Configuration Console Extension*

In the Console menu, select Blocks ➤ Add Exception Handling Settings, as shown in Figure 7-3.

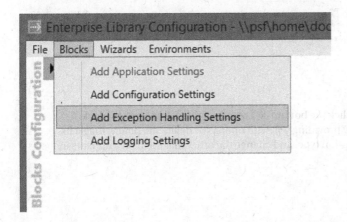

Figure 7-3. *Adding exception handling settings to App.config*

This action adds an Exception Handling Settings section within the console, which creates a policy and an associated exception type by default. These can be thought of as two of the many available building blocks for creating an exception handling solution for your application.

Policy

A *policy* allows you to configure the manner in which one or more exception types will be handled within your application.

You can define one or more policies, provide unique names for policies, delete existing policies, and change the ordering of policies in your configuration file.

101

To add policies to your exception handling settings, simply click the + button at the top-right corner of the Policies section; then select Add Policy from the menu, as shown in Figure 7-4.

Figure 7-4. *Adding multiple exception handling policies*

To rename a policy, simply expand the policy by clicking the arrow to the left of the policy name to reveal the Name field, as shown in Figure 7-5. You can provide a name that describes this policy's configuration so that you can refer to it in your code later. Providing an intuitive name will make it easy to identify the purpose of the policy when you or another developer revisits your code at a later time. Rename the default policy to FilePolicy.

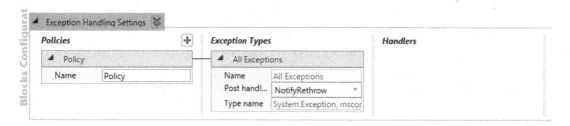

Figure 7-5. *Renaming a policy*

To manage an existing policy, simply click the bottom-left corner of the defined policy block. As illustrated in Figure 7-6, a menu will display providing you with options to delete the policy, toggle its properties, validate the policy, add an exception type, and change the order that the policy appears in the list if there is more than one defined policy.

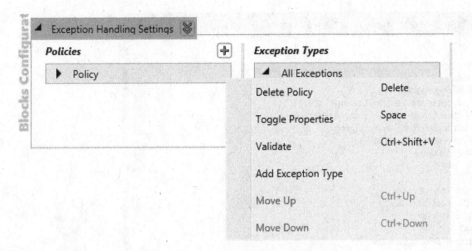

Figure 7-6. *Managing policies and adding exception types*

A policy isn't useful on its own. It simply is a named grouping where you will define the application's exception handling logic for one or more exception types. Even though you have an exception type that was created by default, let's create one that references a single, specific exception type. Go ahead and select the Add Exception Type option for this policy.

You will be presented with a dialog that lists all of the loaded assemblies, which contain objects that are derived from exceptions within your application, similar to what is shown in Figure 7-7.

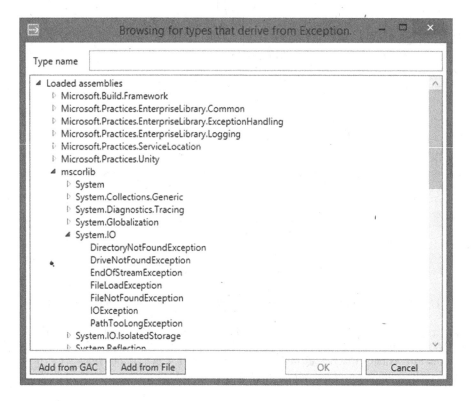

Figure 7-7. *Selecting an exception type*

Within this dialog, you can do the following:

- Filter the list by entering part of an exception type name in the field provided at the top of the dialog

- Drill down through the list of assemblies and their namespaces to find the desired exception type

- Add an assembly from the GAC, or file system, to the list so that you can drill down to select an exception type

For this example, select the FileNotFoundException type from the System.IO namespace within mscorlib, as shown in Figure 7-8, and then click OK.

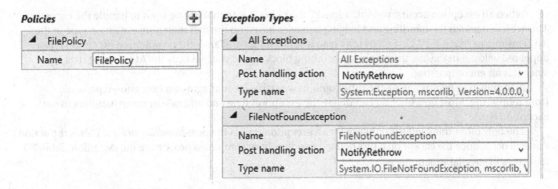

Figure 7-8. *FileNotFoundException type added to FilePolicy*

Now that you have added an exception type to `FilePolicy`, you will need to make some changes to ensure it is set up properly and that it will be processed when that exception type is raised within the application.

Exception Type

An exception type within a policy represents the exception that will be processed by the exception handling block.

As mentioned earlier, an exception type of `All Exceptions` is added when a policy is created by default. You can add multiple exception types per policy and order them in the console. The ordering of exception types is important in the configuration file because the exception handling settings are processed in the order that they appear. Also, when the exception type of `All Exceptions` is processed, any other exception types that follow will not be processed. Therefore, if you are including that exception type, you want to be sure that it appears last in the list.

Click the bottom-right corner of the `FileNotException` section and select Move Up in the pop-up menu, as shown in Figure 7-9.

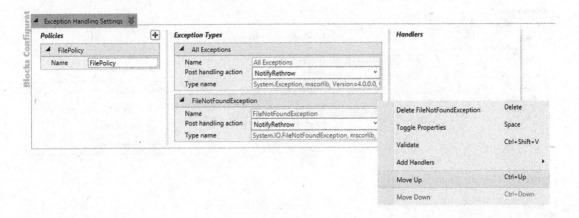

Figure 7-9. *Reordering exception types*

When an exception occurs, you must specify the policy name that will be used to handle the exception. This will then match the handling and logging behavior based on the first matching exception type in the list. This means that if the All Exceptions type was listed first and any other configured exception types appeared below it in the list, the exception handling block would process only the All Exceptions type since it is all-encompassing.

Also shown in Figure 7-9 are the other options available for managing an exception type, aside from reordering. Most notably, you can delete the exception type and add one or more handlers to each exception type.

The only other thing left to configure for an exception type is the *post-handling action*. This is the action that will occur once the exception type's defined handlers have completed processing the exception. Table 7-1 describes the available actions.

Table 7-1. *Post-Handling Actions*

Action	Description
None	Once the handler has processed the exception, no other action will be taken.
NotifyRethrow	This signals the exception handling method to rethrow the exception.
ThrowNewException	This allows you to wrap the current exception within a new exception or replace it with a new exception. This exception is thrown after the handler has completed processing exceptions.

Handler

A *handler* encapsulates the necessary logic for processing an exception. This could include actions such as logging, sending e-mail notifications, or posting exceptions to a web service so that they can be logged on a remote server. Those are just a few examples of the most common ways that exceptions are handled.

To add a handler to an exception type, click the bottom-right corner of a specific exception type and then select Add Handlers from the menu, as shown in Figure 7-10.

Figure 7-10. *Adding handlers*

You can define your own custom implementation of an exception handler, or you can use one of the readily available implementations included in the Enterprise Library Exception Handling Application Block. Table 7-2 lists the exception handlers that you can use when configuring your exception handling policy, along with a brief explanation on when to make use of them.

Table 7-2. *Exception Handlers Usage*

Handler	When to Use This Handler
Custom exception	Use this handler when a custom exception handler implementation will be used to process the exception that was thrown.
Logging exception	Use this handler when it is desirable to add entries to the application log whenever the particular exception type has been thrown in the application. Log entries may include details about the exception as well as information about the current machine, app domain, process, and thread information.
Replace	Use this handler when you want to replace the exception type with a new exception and do not want to preserve information from the original exception.
Wrap	Use this handler when you want to raise a new exception, but you also want to preserve information from the original exception. The original exception will then be contained in the InnerException of the new exception.

You can associate multiple handlers with an exception type and configure the order in which the exception types are processed. For example, if you choose to add a replace exception handler and then a logging exception handler, in that order, the following actions will occur:

- The original exception will be replaced with a new exception. Details from the original exception will be lost.

- The new exception will be logged to the application log.

In looking at the order of operations here, would it make more sense to log the original exception and then replace it with a new exception? It depends. Each application is different, and the way in which you manage application exceptions is completely configurable. You may want to leave the order as is, and that's perfectly fine. The point is that it is important to understand when and how the exception is processed and that ultimately the exception handling and logging behavior that you configure works as expected.

Wrap Handler

Now that you know how to add a handler to an exception type, go ahead and add a wrap handler to the FileNotFound exception type. Set the "Post handling action" setting in the FileNotFound exception type to ThrowNewException. In the Exception Message field within the wrap handler, enter some text so that you can identify which handler is being processed from within the application, as illustrated in Figure 7-11. For example, enter **Original exception wrapped. Check inner exception.**

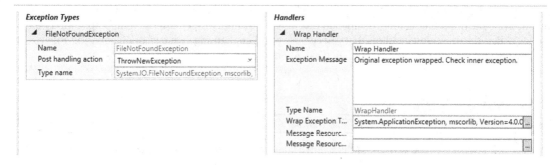

Figure 7-11. *Adding a wrap handler to the FileNotFound exception type*

Replace Handler

Next, add a replace handler to the All Exceptions exception type and set its message to something unique as well, as shown in Figure 7-12. For example, enter **Original exception replaced.** Set the "Post handling action" field within the All Exceptions exception type to ThrowNewException as well.

Figure 7-12. *Replacing the handler added to AllExceptions exception type*

Custom Exception Handler

For the most part, you should be able to leverage the logging exception, wrap, and replace handlers to cover the most common scenarios in your exception handling approach. However, there may be instances where you will need to write your own custom exception handler.

To achieve this, you must create a class that implements the IExceptionHandler interface. You must in turn implement the interface method HandleException(Exception exception, Guid handlingInstanceId). This method will contain your custom processing logic and the exception you want to return to the exception handling block, which will pass it along to any other configured handlers in the exception handling chain for processing. Finally, you must mark up your class to denote that it is a custom exception handler using the attribute ConfigurationElementType passing in the type CustomHandlerData. Note that this requires you to add the System.Configuration library as a reference in your project. Listing 7-1 depicts an example of a custom exception handler class.

Listing 7-1. Sample Custom Exception Handler Class

```
[ConfigurationElementType(typeof(CustomHandlerData))]
public class MyCustomExceptionHandler : IExceptionHandler
{
    public Exception HandleException(Exception exception, Guid handlingInstanceId)
    {
        //You can perform any custom logic here that makes sense for your application
        //Finally, you may then return the same exception that was passed in, or
        //return a new exception, which will then be further processed along the
        //exception handling chain.
    }
}
```

You can learn more about custom exception handlers, as well as the multitude of ways that you can configure the Exception Handling Application Block, from the MSDN site. Navigate to https://msdn.microsoft.com and search for *Enterprise Library 6*. Within the results list, click the link Enterprise Library 6 – April 2013. Next, within the left treeview pane, select the link 3 - Error Management Made Exceptionally Easy: Using the Exception Handling Application Block. Alternatively, you can use this short URL to access the article directly: http://bitly.com/EL6ExceptionBlock.

Modifying the Code

Once you have completed adding both handlers within the console, select File ➤ Save from the menu. You can leave the console open to use as a reference as you are working within your app.

Within Visual Studio, in your WPF demo project, open the MainWindow.xaml file. Add two buttons and a text box to the page. The first button will inevitably launch a FileNotFoundException in code. The second button will launch a NullReferenceException. You can do this by dragging and dropping WPF controls from the toolbox to the designer or by modifying the markup. Listing 7-2 shows the resulting XAML markup.

Listing 7-2. MainWindow with Two Buttons and a Text Box

```
<Window x:Class="WpfLoggingDemo.MainWindow"
        xmlns="http://schemas.microsoft.com/winfx/2006/xaml/presentation"
        xmlns:x="http://schemas.microsoft.com/winfx/2006/xaml"
        Title="MainWindow" Height="350" Width="500">
    <Grid>
        <Grid.RowDefinitions>
            <RowDefinition Height="Auto" />
            <RowDefinition Height="*" />
        </Grid.RowDefinitions>
        <StackPanel Orientation="Horizontal">
            <Button Content="Throw FileNotFound Exception"
                    HorizontalAlignment="Left"
                    Margin="10"
                    Click="FileNotFoundExceptionButton_Click" />
            <Button Content="Throw Null Reference Exception"
                    HorizontalAlignment="Left"
                    Margin="10"
                    Click="NullReferenceExceptionButton_Click" />
        </StackPanel>
        <TextBox HorizontalAlignment="Left"
```

```
            x:Name="ExceptionOutputTextBox"
            Margin="10"
            Grid.Row="1"
            TextWrapping="Wrap"
            Width="450"/>

    </Grid>
</Window>
```

We will explore the XAML elements depicted within Listing 7-2 in Chapter 8. One thing to point out here is that the markup also illustrates the button's Click events being wired up. You will add these events to the code behind them as you progress through the remainder of this walkthrough.

For now, you need to modify the code to ensure that the application leverages the exception handling configuration settings that you created. Open the MainWindow code behind MainWindow.xaml.cs and add the following using directives:

```
using System.IO;
using Microsoft.Practices.EnterpriseLibrary.ExceptionHandling;
```

Next you will make sure that the application loads the exception handling configuration provided in the App.config file. The Enterprise Library Exception Handling Application Block makes it easy for you to do this by using its ExceptionPolicyFactory.

The ExceptionPolicyFactory is an object that will create an instance of an ExceptionManager object, loaded with all of the current policies, exception types, and handlers that are defined in the App.config file. When the ExceptionManager object is required to process an exception using a named policy, it will search for a matching policy name in its list of loaded policies. If it finds a matching policy, it will handle the exception according to the policy's configuration.

To initialize the ExceptionManager object when the MainWindow is created, add the code shown in Listing 7-3 within the MainWindow partial class in the code-behind file.

Listing 7-3. Initializing an Instance of ExceptionManager

```
private ExceptionManager exceptionManager;

private void InitializeExceptionManager()
{
    ExceptionPolicyFactory exceptionFactory = new ExceptionPolicyFactory();
    exceptionManager = exceptionFactory.CreateManager();
}

public MainWindow()
{
    InitializeComponent();
    InitializeExceptionManager();
}
```

The next steps will be to create a couple of methods that will be called when the buttons are clicked in the MainWindow, as shown in Listing 7-4. The OpenFile method will simply try to open a file that doesn't exist. The GetFileByte method will attempt to read from a FileStream that has not been created.

Listing 7-4. *The ExceptionManager Will Process Exceptions Raised Within These Methods*

```
private FileStream fs;

private void OpenFile(string fileName)
{
    exceptionManager.Process(() => fs = File.Open(fileName, FileMode.Open,
    FileAccess.Read),
        "FilePolicy");
}

private int GetFileByte()
{
    int fileByte = 0;

    exceptionManager.Process(() => fileByte = fs.ReadByte(),
        "FilePolicy");
    return fileByte;
}
```

In both cases, the ExceptionManager will be responsible for handling any exceptions.

Next, add the two-button Click event handlers that will call their respective method, as shown in Listing 7-5.

Listing 7-5. *The Click Events Will Catch Any Unhandled Exceptions*

```
private void FileNotFoundExceptionButton_Click(object sender, RoutedEventArgs e)
{
    try
    {
        OpenFile("myfakefile.txt");
    }
    catch (Exception ex)
    {
        //the original exception should be wrapped
        HandleMyException("FileNotFoundExceptionButton_Click", ex);
    }
}

private void NullReferenceExceptionButton_Click(object sender, RoutedEventArgs e)
{
    try
    {
        int fileByte = GetFileByte();
        MessageBox.Show(fileByte.ToString());
    }
    catch (Exception ex)
    {
        //the original exception should be replaced
        HandleMyException("NullReferenceExceptionButton_Click", ex);
    }
}
```

111

```
private void HandleMyException(string exceptionPrefix, Exception ex)
{
    string exceptionDetails = string.Format("{0} Exception: {1} {2}",
        exceptionPrefix,
        ex.Message,
        System.Environment.NewLine);

    if (ex.InnerException != null)
    {
        exceptionDetails += string.Format("{0} Inner Exception: {1} {2}",
            exceptionPrefix,
            ex.InnerException.Message,
            System.Environment.NewLine);

    }

    ExceptionOutputTextBox.Text += exceptionDetails;
}
```

At this point, you might be thinking, "Why are there try/catch blocks here? I thought you said I wouldn't need to riddle the code with try/catch blocks." Those are good questions. Now let's explore what this means.

Take a moment to refer to Table 7-1 in the "Exception Type" section. Recall that there are three post-handling actions that can be set: None, NotifyRethrow, and ThrowNewException. If the post-handling action on the exception types is configured to None, the ExceptionManager will process the exception, and the application will continue as normal. However, because you configured the post-handling action on both the FileNotFound and AllExceptions exception types to ThrowNewException, you will need to account for handling that exception in some way. For this example, you will handle it with a try/catch block and display the error message within the text box.

Now that the code is in place, you can build and run the application to test it. Click each of the buttons. What do you notice about the output?

■ **Tip** When the ExceptionManager.Process method experiences an error while running in Debug mode, execution will halt indicating that the application experienced an unhandled error. Simply click F5 to continue processing. If you're not interested in stepping through the code, you can use the key combination Ctrl+F5 to launch the application without debugging in order to focus on the application's behavior and output.

Experiment with changing the post-handling actions for each exception type, saving the file, and launching the application. What do you notice when the post-handling action is set to None or NotifyRethrow?

Configuring the Logging Exception Handler

Select Add Logging Exception Handler from the submenu that appears within the Add Handlers menu option. Look at Figure 7-13. What do you notice?

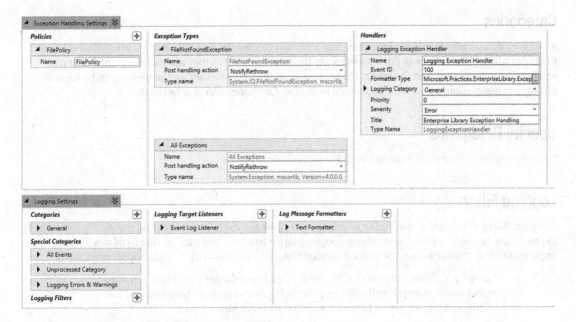

Figure 7-13. *Configuring the logging exception handler*

You added the logging exception handler, and the Logging Settings Application Block was automatically added along with it, as shown in Figure 7-14.

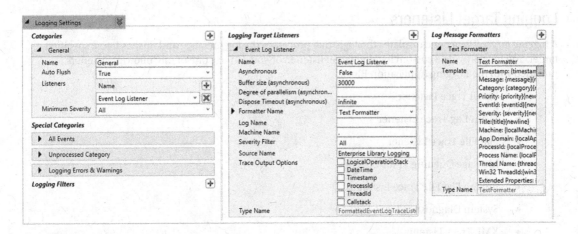

Figure 7-14. *Configuring the logging settings*

The logging exception handler will use the General category logging configuration to log any messages. Let's take a look what is included in the Logging Application Block to make sure that it is set up according to your application's needs.

Categories

A *category* defines how log messages will be handled. You can specify a unique category name, whether or not the configured listeners will flush messages to the target as soon as they are received, which listeners will process the message, and the minimum severity level that must be met for the message to be logged. Multiple categories can be added and ordered in the list. Categories can also be deleted.

Special Categories

Special categories are ones that cannot be deleted or reordered in the list.

Logging Filters

A *logging filter* can be used to determine which action to take against log messages and potentially filter which log messages can be passed to the configured logging target listeners. You can provide a custom filtering implementation, or you can use one of the following filters provided with the Logging Application Block:

- *Category*: Defines which action to take against log messages based on each message's associated category. It will allow or prevent log messages from being passed to the configured logging target listeners based on its Filter Mode value.

- *Logging Enabled*: Turns logging actions on or off through a single setting.

- *Priority*: Allows or prevents log messages from being passed to the configured logging target listeners based on the priority specified in the log message.

Logging Target Listeners

A *logging target listener* encapsulates the logic that processes the log message and flushes it to a specified target. You may provide a custom logging target listener, or you can use one of the following listeners provided with the Logging Application Block:

- Email Trace Listener

- Event Log Trace Listener

- Flat File Trace Listener

- Message Queuing Trace Listener

- Rolling Flat File Trace Listener

- System Diagnostics Trace Listener

- XML Trace Listener

Logging Message Formatters

A *logging message formatter* allows you to configure the format of the log message before it is sent to a target, such as an e-mail message, flat-file log, or Windows Event Log. You can provide a custom log message formatter, or you can use one of the following formatters provided with the Logging Application Block:

- *Binary:* Generates log message in binary format. Use this formatter with the Message Queuing trace listener.

- *JSON*: Generates the log message in JSON format. Use this formatter with a file-based trace listener or a custom trace listener that submits the output to a web service for logging on a server.

- *Text*: Generates the log message in a text format. Use this formatter with a Flat File Trace Listener, an Email Trace Listener, or an Event Log Trace Listener.

For this demo, add a basic Flat File Trace Listener and have it use the default Text Formatter that is already created. Add the Flat File Trace Listener to the General category. Figure 7-15 illustrates this configuration.

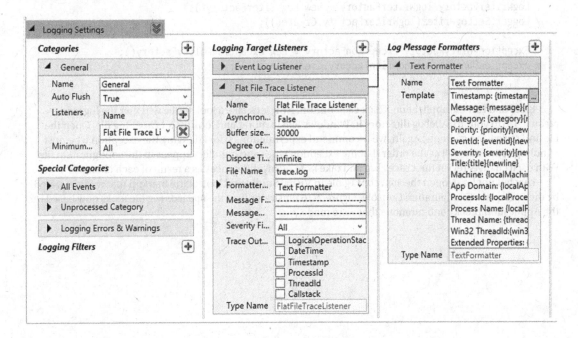

Figure 7-15. *Logging to a flat file*

Once you have the configuration defined for the Logging Application Block, save your changes. The Logging Application Block will request its LogWriter to be initialized before attempting to instantiate the ExceptionManager.

Go back into the MainWindow.xaml.cs file and add the following using directive:

```
using Microsoft.Practices.EnterpriseLibrary.Logging;
```

Next modify the InitializeExceptionManager method to initialize the LogWriter for the Logging Application Block prior to creating a new instance of the ExceptionManager, as shown in Listing 7-6. Failing to do so will result in an InvalidOperationException at runtime when the call to the CreateManager() method is executed.

Listing 7-6. Initializing LogWriter for the Logging Application Block

```
private ExceptionManager exceptionManager;

private void InitializeExceptionManager()
{
    LogWriterFactory logWriterFactory = new LogWriterFactory();
    Logger.SetLogWriter(logWriterFactory.Create());

    ExceptionPolicyFactory exceptionFactory = new ExceptionPolicyFactory();
    exceptionManager = exceptionFactory.CreateManager();
}
```

Build and run the application. Click each button. Now let's take a look to see whether the log was created. Go to your bin\Debug directory in Windows File Explorer and look for a trace.log file. Open the file and review the contents. Again, we recommend experimenting with changing the exception type post-handling actions as well as the order that the exception types and handlers appear in the configuration file. With each change, revisit the trace.log and take note of any differences as a result of each change.

Last but not least, open the App.config file in Visual Studio and look at the markup that was generated by the Enterprise Configuration Console. Figure 7-16 illustrates how the App.config file looks now based on the Application Block configurations that were made.

```
App.config  ⇉ ✕  App.xaml.cs        MainWindow.xaml       MainWindow.xaml.cs
  <?xml version="1.0" encoding="utf-8" ?>
  <configuration>
    <configSections>
      <section name="loggingConfiguration" type="Microsoft.Practices.EnterpriseLibr
      <section name="exceptionHandling" type="Microsoft.Practices.EnterpriseLibrary
    </configSections>
    <loggingConfiguration name="" tracingEnabled="true" defaultCategory="General">
      <listeners>
        <add name="Event Log Listener" type="Microsoft.Practices.EnterpriseLibrar
            listenerDataType="Microsoft.Practices.EnterpriseLibrary.Logging.Confi
            source="Enterprise Library Logging" formatter="Text Formatter"
            log="MyWpfDemo" machineName="." traceOutputOptions="None" />
        <add name="Flat File Trace Listener" type="Microsoft.Practices.Enterprise
            listenerDataType="Microsoft.Practices.EnterpriseLibrary.Logging.Confi
            fileName="trace.log" header="------------------------------------"
            footer="------------------------------------" formatter="Text Format
      </listeners>
      <formatters>
        <add type="Microsoft.Practices.EnterpriseLibrary.Logging.Formatters.TextF
            template="Timestamp: {timestamp}{newline}&#xA;Message: {message}{newl
            name="Text Formatter" />
      </formatters>
      <categorySources>
100 %  ▾
```

Figure 7-16. *App.config exception handling and logging configuration markup*

As you scroll through the App.config file to view all of the markup that was added by the Enterprise Configuration Console, think about how tedious and error prone the process would have been if you had to write this XML from scratch!

Logging Options for Windows Device Apps

As we mentioned in the first section within this chapter, the Enterprise Library Application Blocks are available for a variety of .NET applications. Unfortunately, Windows Store and Windows Phone apps are not among them. So, you will need to devise an exception handling approach that works for your application, which means handling it the old-fashioned way. And by this we mean putting in those try/catch blocks that you've been desperately attempting to avoid at all costs.

The following are some options that you can use to handle logging within Windows Store and Windows Phone applications:

- *Custom logging library*: Create your own portable class library to write messages to a log file, SQLite database, or Azure SQL database, or to your own web service endpoint.

- *MetroLog*: This is an open source project available on GitHub, https://github.com/mbrit/MetroLog, which allows you easily to implement logging based on NLog.

- *Visual Studio Application Insights*: This is a client library for an Azure service that allows you easily to incorporate tracing, logging, and analytics within your Windows Phone and Windows Store applications.

Visual Studio Application Insights

Application Insights requires that you have a Microsoft Azure account. If you do not have one, visit http://azure.microsoft.com/en-us/ to create a free trial for the purpose of this example. At the time of this writing, Application Insights is in preview, so it is free to use.

In Visual Studio, initiate the process to create a new Windows Store app. In the New Project dialog, select the Blank App template and then select the Add Application Insights to Project checkbox, as shown in Figure 7-17.

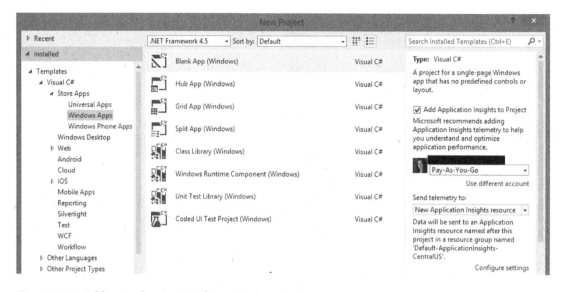

Figure 7-17. *Adding Application Insights to Windows Store app*

At this point, you will be prompted to log in with your Azure account credentials using your Microsoft Live ID. Once you have been authenticated, your Azure account information will display, including your avatar, Microsoft Live e-mail address, and subscription type.

Leave the "Send telemetry to" drop-down value set to New Application Insights resource. This will create a new Application Insights resource in Azure for the current application. Click OK to create the project and load it in Visual Studio.

Drill down into the MainPage code behind MainPage.xaml.cs and add the following using directives:

```
using Microsoft.ApplicationInsights;
using Microsoft.ApplicationInsights.Extensibility;
```

Next you will need to initialize a custom TelemetryClient. The TelemetryClient object provides multiple methods to enable logging custom messages to Application Insights. Table 7-3 lists the methods available.

Table 7-3. *Application Insights Telemetry Client Methods*

Method	Description	Parameters
TrackEvent	Logs custom events or user actions	Event name or EventTelemetry object
TrackException	Logs exceptions	Exception object or ExceptionTelemetry object
TrackMetric	Logs custom metrics	MetricTelemetry object or name and value
TrackPageView	Logs page, screen, or blade views	Name of item viewed or PageViewTelemetry object
TrackRequest	Logs the frequency and duration of server requests for performance analysis	RequestTelemetry object or name, timestamp, duration, response code, and success flag
TrackTrace	Logs diagnostic messages	TraceTelemetry object or message name and/or severity level or message name and/ or properties dictionary

To initialize the TelemetryClient, simply add the following variable:

```
private TelemetryClient client = new TelemetryClient();
```

The TelemetryClient is initialized and associated with your Application Insights account using the InstrumentationKey value within the ApplicationInsights.config file.

Next add the code shown in Listing 7-7, which will use the TelemetryClient to log a basic event when the application launches, force an exception to be thrown, and log the exception.

Listing 7-7. Simple Event and Exception Logging with TelemetryClient

```
private TelemetryClient client = new TelemetryClient();

public MainPage()
{
    this.InitializeComponent();
    LogAppEvent("Application launched");
}

private void LogAppEvent(string message)
{
    try
    {
        client.TrackEvent("Application launched");
        throw new Exception("My custom exception");
    }
    catch (Exception ex)
    {
        client.TrackException(ex);
    }
}
```

Now it's time to test it! When creating a Windows Store app in Visual Studio, you have the option to run the application on your local machine or within the simulator, which replicates the application running on a Windows desktop while allowing you to remain in Desktop mode. The simulator also provides options to configure the screen size and resolution to use when testing the applications as well as simulate custom touch and rotation events, geolocation coordinates, and network connection properties. For this reason, we recommend testing the application in the simulator.

Build and run the application to see how Application Insights is used to track and log user actions. Once the code to log Application Insights is executed for the first time, you will notice a notification popup, as shown in Figure 7-18.

Your first Application Insights events have been sent!   ✕

To see them in real time, click the Application Insights button.

Open Application Insights

Figure 7-18. Application Insights Events notification

Click the Open Application Insights link, which will take you to your Application Insights resource in the Azure portal. The first thing you will notice is the Application Health section, which displays details on the number of users, sessions, page views, and crashes, as shown in Figure 7-19.

Figure 7-19. *Custom event logged to Application Insights on Azure*

Notice that the Usage section shows your custom event along with the number of times it was called. Run the application a few more times and then refresh the Azure Portal to see this number increase.

Scroll down in the Azure portal and select the Diagnostic search tile, as shown in Figure 7-20.

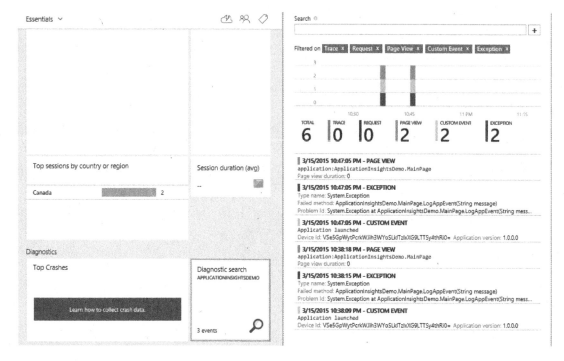

Figure 7-20. *Application Insights diagnostics*

Here you can view more details about the information the application has logged, including traces, requests, page views, and exceptions.

Although this example is simple, you can easily see the power behind using Application Insights to monitor your applications in real time. Although we demonstrated using Application Insights within a Windows Store application, you can follow the same steps to include it within a Windows Phone application.

Summary

Devising a strategy for exception handling and logging within your application is an important requirement that should never be overlooked. Regardless of the approach you take, it is your responsibility to ensure that your application does not crash unexpectedly and that it does not expose sensitive information through unhandled error messages that may inadvertently be displayed to your end users.

Remember that logging is in place to enable members of your Development or DevOps team to track down and troubleshoot issues. However, there is a fine line between what information is appropriate to include in the log messages and what information must be excluded. As a basic rule of thumb, never store sensitive information in the application's logs, such as a user's credentials, credit card numbers, personal information, or anything else that puts your end users at risk.

For continued maintenance of your application, a proper logging strategy will make all the difference in helping your team track down and resolve issues that arise.

Now that you have a solid understanding of how to implement exception handling and logging within your application to ensure that your application functions as expected, we will switch gears in the next chapter to focus on designing the Windows Presentation Foundation user interface.

■ ■ ■

PART III

Completing the User Interface Layer

CHAPTER 8

■ ■ ■

The WPF User Interface

Windows Presentation Foundation (WPF) is a graphical system that was first made available in the .NET 3.0 Framework. It supports the creation of sophisticated user interfaces in Windows applications using Extensible Application Markup Language (XAML), as discussed in Chapter 1. XAML enables an abstraction of the visual elements within an application from the main business logic. Designers have fine-grained control over the look and feel of the application without requiring any coding knowledge. In turn, developers can focus on working on the main functionality of the application without getting bogged down in the UI design details.

Although this chapter focuses on the WPF user interface, the majority of the concepts discussed here are applicable when developing other XAML-based applications, such as Silverlight, Windows Store, and Windows Phone applications.

The Basics

There are some basic points to understand when developing XAML-based applications. In this section, we will take a look at the basic structure of a WPF application and discuss some common controls that will serve as the basis for each view that you design within your application.

Application Class

The starting point for a WPF application is the Application class, which determines the window that will be loaded on startup. It also contains shared resources and properties, and it allows you to override application life-cycle events, which enables custom behavior to be handled during application launch, activation, deactivation, and exit. Table 8-1 lists the events that are raised for each of those application states along with information about when they are triggered and when it may be useful to consider overriding the events to include custom code.

Table 8-1. *Application Events*

Life-Cycle Event	Triggered When...	Override This Method When...
Startup	The Application.Run() method is called.	You need to process command-line arguments, initialize application resources and properties, or instantiate one or more windows.
Activated	The application becomes the foreground application. This occurs when the application loads its first window or when the user forcibly brings the application window to the foreground by returning the focus to the application when switching between application windows on the desktop.	You want to perform custom actions, such as updating and displaying any notifications that the user might have missed while the application was deactivated.
Deactivated	The application window loses focus because the user has switched to an alternate application in the desktop.	You want to store the application's state.
SessionEnding	The user ends the Windows session by logging off or shutting down the operating system.	You want to store the application's state or data changes before the application exits.
Exit	The Application.Shutdown() method is called or when a Windows session is ended by logging off or shutting down the operating system.	You want to store the application's state or data changes before the application exits.
DispatcherUnhandled Exception	An exception is thrown by the application that is not handled.	You want to deal gracefully with unhandled exceptions or raise a user-friendly error message before the application shuts down. This would also be a good opportunity to log unexpected crashes in the application to assist with troubleshooting when the application is in production.

The application within a markup file is named App.xaml, and it also includes a code-behind file named App.xaml.cs. For more information about the code-behind file, refer to the section "The Code-Behind File" later this chapter.

Listing 8-1 shows an example of the App.xaml markup that is automatically generated when you first create a WPF project.

Listing 8-1. App.xaml Markup

```
<Application x:Class="WpfDemo.App"
             xmlns="http://schemas.microsoft.com/winfx/2006/xaml/presentation"
             xmlns:x="http://schemas.microsoft.com/winfx/2006/xaml"
             StartupUri="MainWindow.xaml">
    <Application.Resources>

    </Application.Resources>
</Application>
```

The first attribute, x:Class, contains the fully qualified name of the class in the application's code-behind.

The next attribute, xmlns, defines the main namespace for the application. This is the WPF core classes namespace, and it must be included in the root element of every WPF view in the project.

The third attribute, xmlns:x, is the XAML namespace declaration, and it also must be included in the root element of every WPF view.

The last attribute, StartupUri, indicates the window that will be displayed when the application first loads.

Windows, Pages, and User Controls

A single view within a WPF application consists of a markup file ending with the extension .xaml. At a minimum, the markup file will consist of the following:

- The root element that represents the view, such as a Window, NavigationWindow, Page, or UserControl. For the remainder of the book, when we refer to view, it refers to any of these element types.

- The WPF core classes namespace declaration: xmlns="http://schemas.microsoft. com/winfx/2006/xaml/presentation".

- The XAML namespace declaration: xmlns:x="http://schemas.microsoft.com/ winfx/2006/xaml".

- One or more visual elements that will be displayed within the view at runtime. Each visual element may have custom markup that defines its appearance and behavior. We will discuss this in depth in the section "Resources and Styles" later in this chapter.

Listing 8-2 shows the default markup that is generated when a window is added to a WPF project.

Listing 8-2. MainWindow Markup

```
<Window x:Class="WpfDemo.MainWindow"
        xmlns="http://schemas.microsoft.com/winfx/2006/xaml/presentation"
        xmlns:x="http://schemas.microsoft.com/winfx/2006/xaml"
        Title="MainWindow" Height="350" Width="525">

</Window>
```

By default, a title along with a default height and width are defined. These are properties of the window. You can change the values of these properties directly in the markup file or in the code-behind file. Alternatively, you can choose to provide default values for other properties of the window right within the markup as well.

The Code-Behind File

So far, you have learned that each view is defined using a markup file. The markup file defines how the view is going to look. However, if you would like the view to respond to user actions or perform additional functions, you will need a class that allows you to tie in code that interacts with the view.

This is known as a *code-behind file*. This is the location where you will provide code to react to user events, such as a button click or list item selection, as well as to load and/or save data to a backing data store. However, it is best to keep code-behind files as lightweight as possible and to encapsulate business logic within a separate class. This is accomplished using the *Model-View-ViewModel (MVVM) pattern*, along with data binding. If you are unfamiliar with the MVVM pattern, refer to the section "The MVVM Design Pattern" in Chapter 1. We will discuss the details of data binding in the "Data Binding" section later in this chapter.

The code-behind file must be given the same name as its associated markup file, including the .xaml extension followed with the extension of the target programming language of the application. For example, a window in WPF named MainWindow.xaml must contain a code-behind file named MainWindow.xaml.cs in your C# project. By convention, the class is also named to match its given file name. The class must inherit from the same class that is defined in the markup file. Listing 8-3 shows the code-behind for MainWindow. You can see that it inherits from Window, which aligns with its defined markup in Listing 8-2.

Listing 8-3. MainWindow Code-Behind

```
/// <summary> ·
/// Interaction logic for MainWindow.xaml
/// </summary>
public partial class MainWindow : Window
{
    public MainWindow()
    {
        InitializeComponent();
    }
}
```

If you wanted to change MainWindow to a NavigationWindow, you would need to change the markup element from <Window></Window> to <NavigationWindow></NavigationWindow> in the XAML. Then you would need to change the class definition to inherit from NavigationWindow in the code-behind; otherwise, you will receive compilation errors when trying to build and run the application.

Additionally, you can dynamically create controls and add them to the view from the code-behind, as well as modify various properties of existing controls. To access a control that is defined in your view's markup, you simply need to provide a unique name within the control's Name attribute in the markup, which you can then reference in your code-behind, as depicted in Listing 8-4 and Listing 8-5.

Listing 8-4. Set the Control's Name Attribute in Markup to Access It from the Code-Behind

```
<Window x:Class="WpfDemo.MainWindow"
        xmlns="http://schemas.microsoft.com/winfx/2006/xaml/presentation"
        xmlns:x="http://schemas.microsoft.com/winfx/2006/xaml"
        Title="MainWindow">
```

```
<Grid>
    <TextBlock x:Name="MyTextBlock" />
</Grid>
</Window>
```

Listing 8-5. Modifying the Named Control's Properties from the Code-Behind

```
public partial class MainWindow : Window
{
    public MainWindow()
    {
        InitializeComponent();

        MyTextBlock.Text = "This was set from code-behind.";
        MyTextBlock.FontSize = 24;
        MyTextBlock.TextAlignment = TextAlignment.Center;
    }
}
```

First Look

Let's create a WPF project and start experimenting with XAML. Launch Visual Studio and create a new project. Select the WPF Application template within the New Project dialog, as shown in Figure 8-1. Give the project the name, WpfDemo, and then click OK.

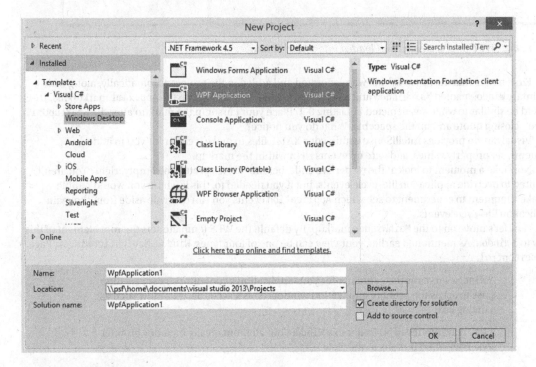

Figure 8-1. *Creating a new WPF application*

Once the project loads into Visual Studio, the `MainWindow` markup file should be displayed in the view, as shown in Figure 8-2.

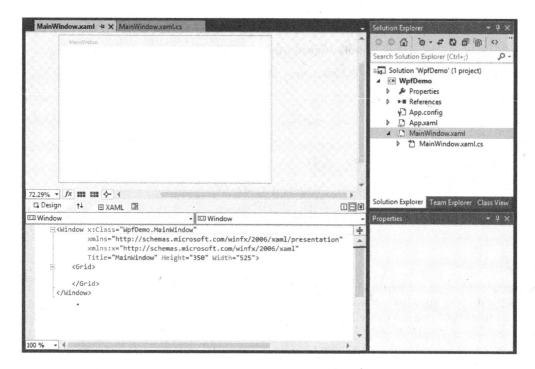

Figure 8-2. *WPF project created and loaded into Visual Studio*

First, notice that the `App.xaml` file was generated and added to the project automatically, along with a primary `Window` named `MainWindow` and an `App.config` file. Drill down into the `App.xaml` markup file. It should be similar to what was depicted in Listing 8-1. Place your cursor in the markup after the `StartupUri` value's closing quote and hit the spacebar. What do you notice?

Visual Studio provides IntelliSense within your XAML files to make it easier for you to add new elements, set property values, and wire up events right within the markup.

Now take a moment to look at the respective code-behind file. It's pretty well empty, right? You aren't required to override application life-cycle events, but if you needed to, this is where you would handle it. Take a moment to experiment to see which `Application` events you can override aside from the main application life-cycle events.

Now let's move on to the `MainWindow` markup. By default, the WPF template sets the root element of this view to a `Window`. As mentioned earlier, your view can be one of four types: `Window`, `NavigationWindow`, `Page`, or `UserControl`.

> A `Window` serves as the container for your application's content. You can use this class to act as the primary application window or as a secondary window such as a dialog box.

> A `NavigationWindow` is similar to a `Window`, but it automatically includes browser-style navigation buttons in the view.

A Page is used to package content, and it may be contained or dynamically loaded within a Window or NavigationWindow. It is ideal to design your application such that a single window serves as the main host container whose content is dynamically changed based on user actions. Designing separate pages that can be swapped in and out at runtime simplifies this task a great deal.

A UserControl is a custom, reusable control that can be added to one or more content pages.

XAML Designer

With the MainWindow.xaml file loaded into Visual Studio, you can see that you have the option to view and modify the XAML directly, or you can drag and drop controls from your Toolbox onto the window in the XAML Designer. You can choose to view the markup only, to view the XAML Designer only, or to have both the markup and the XAML Designer displayed at the same time. When you make a change to the window's markup, the resulting change is immediately rendered in the Designer and vice versa.

Within the XAML Designer, you can also select a control and modify its properties through the Properties pane in Visual Studio. Notice that as you change property values within the Properties pane, the selected control's markup is updated to reflect these changes, as shown in Figure 8-3.

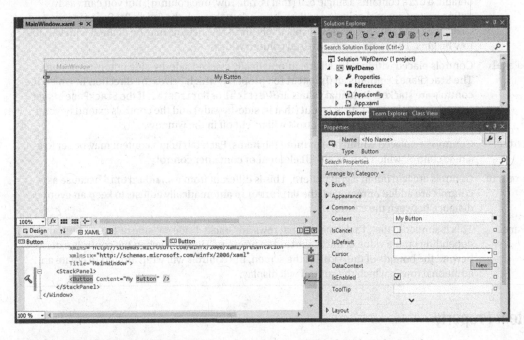

Figure 8-3. *The XAML Designer displays the Properties pane for the selected control*

Container Controls

A view consists of one or more UI controls. This is accomplished by setting its Content property, which can be any Common Language Runtime object, except for a Window or NavigationWindow. However, the Content property can be set to only a single object.

This works just fine if your view contains a single control or element, such as a string, button, or image; however, that makes the view pretty useless. Most often, your view will be comprised of a set of controls that allow the user to perform meaningful actions, such as logging into the application, navigating to another screen, and saving changes to data.

To create a view with a purpose, you can set its Content property to a container control, which in turn serves as the host to one or more UI controls.

Windows Presentation Foundation includes a variety of container controls that you can use within your views, as listed in Table 8-2.

Table 8-2. *WPF Container Controls*

Container	Description
Canvas	You place controls within this container using absolute positioning using an offset from any corner of the container. It is the least flexible of all container controls.
DockPanel	You place controls within this container that you want easily to dock to a specific side: Top, Bottom, Left, or Right. It also allows you to configure the last child element to fill the remaining available space in the container.
Grid	You place controls within cells in a tablelike layout with defined rows and columns. By default, a Grid contains a single cell (that is, one row, one column), but you can easily define more rows and columns within the markup through the Grid's RowDefinitions and ColumnDefinitions properties, respectively. Grid row heights may be defined with varying row heights. The same applies to Grid column widths.
StackPanel	Controls placed within this cell are automatically stacked side-by-side or top-to-bottom. The StackPanel contains an Orientation property, which drives the direction in which the controls are stacked. Potential values are Vertical or Horizontal. If the StackPanel is set to stack controls in a vertical layout (that is, side-by-side) and the controls extend beyond the bounds of the screen, the controls will be cut off in the window.
TabControl	Controls are placed within one or more tab items. Each tab item's content may be set to a single control, which can be any UI element or container control.
UniformGrid	Controls are laid out in a grid pattern. This is different from a standard Grid because as controls are added or removed, the UniformGrid automatically adjusts to keep an even distance between the controls.
WrapPanel	This is similar to the StackPanel in that rows are stacked side-by-side or top-to-bottom, depending on the value of the Orientation property. However, when the controls extend beyond the bounds of the width of the screen, the controls will wrap around to create an additional row in which the control will display.

Content Property

The Content property of a view can be defined in markup or in the code-behind. A view is a type of ContentControl. The Content property is the default property on a ContentControl. Within your XAML, if you place a control between the start and end element tags of your view, it is set as the Content of that control. Alternatively, you can explicitly include the View.Content start and end element tags that will contain the desired control.

For example, the XAML depicted in Listing 8-6 and Listing 8-7 provide the same end result. That is, an empty Grid is set as the content of the Window.

Listing 8-6. Set the Window's Content to a Grid

```
<Window x:Class="WpfDemo.MainWindow"
        xmlns="http://schemas.microsoft.com/winfx/2006/xaml/presentation"
        xmlns:x="http://schemas.microsoft.com/winfx/2006/xaml"
        Title="MainWindow">
    <Grid>
    </Grid>
</Window>
```

Listing 8-7. Explicitly Set the Window's Content to a Grid

```
<Window x:Class="WpfDemo.MainWindow"
        xmlns="http://schemas.microsoft.com/winfx/2006/xaml/presentation"
        xmlns:x="http://schemas.microsoft.com/winfx/2006/xaml"
        Title="MainWindow">
    <Window.Content>
        <Grid></Grid>
    </Window.Content>
</Window>
```

Controls that expose a Content property are derived from ContentControl. Some common examples of ContentControl include Button, CheckBox, Expander, Frame, GroupBox, ListBoxItem, NavigationWindow, RadioButton, Page, TabItem, and Window.

Attached Properties

Attached properties are essentially a global set of properties that can be set by any element. A common use of an attached property is to enable a child element to define unique values for properties that are part of its parent control but affect its own presentation within the view.

For example, a Canvas arranges its child elements based on a defined offset of its boundaries. The Canvas exposes the following attached properties for this purpose: Top, Left, Right, and Bottom. Each child element must indicate where its placement should be within the Canvas by defining values for these offsets. Although the properties belong to the Canvas, the child element has access to setting them because they affect the child's placement within the container. To use an attached property in markup, you must use the format AttachedPropertyProvider.PropertyName.

Listing 8-8 illustrates the approach of adding multiple controls to a Canvas control and defining their placement within the container using the Canvas's attached properties.

Listing 8-8. Buttons Using Attached Properties to Configure Their Placement Within the Canvas

```
<Canvas>
    <Button Content="My Button" Canvas.Left="80" />
    <Button Content="My Second Button" Canvas.Top="20" Canvas.Left="120" />
</Canvas>
```

Layouts

Proper UI design can make or break an application. A good UI needs to provide the user with the ability to view or modify data without overwhelming them with a wall of controls plastered across the application's window from top to bottom.

Using tab or expander controls helps to segregate the data and thus makes it easier for users to drill down to sections of data they are seeking. Historically, applications oftentimes show or hide controls based on a user's selection. However, whenever one or more controls were hidden, you would see a glaring void in the window, with large gaps of empty space being wasted. To circumvent this ugliness, developers chose to disable controls instead of hiding them, which was a bit better. These are just a few examples of the design challenges developers faced in the past.

Fixed vs. Dynamic Layouts

If you have ever developed Windows Forms applications, you will understand the struggles encountered when dealing with resizable forms and the coding involved in repositioning and resizing controls accordingly. Within Windows Forms applications, you were constricted to fixed layouts. Every form and control within Windows Forms applications was required to define its width and height. This was a painstaking process, especially as changes were made to accommodate new controls or to reorganize the layout of existing controls.

XAML has solved that problem by supporting dynamic layouts, which automatically handle the sizing of controls based on the control's content and the view's dimensions. You are still free to use fixed layouts if you so choose, but once you master the art of UI design using XAML, you may find that fixed layouts will be a thing of the past or used only sparingly at best.

Managing Layouts with Container Controls

Let's take a look at how container controls handle their child elements by default so that you have a better understanding of when to use each container control to achieve your intended UI layout.

Canvas

The Canvas is used for fixed positioning of controls. Child controls do not expand to fill the space of the Canvas. A control that is added to a Canvas is sized according to just the height and width that it needs to display its own content. The child control is placed within a Canvas using offsets of the Canvas boundaries: Top, Left, Right, and Bottom. Figure 8-4 depicts the placement of multiple button controls within a Canvas.

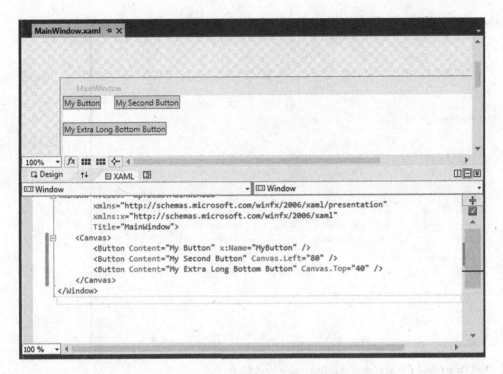

Figure 8-4. *The Canvas arranges its child elements using an offset of its bounds*

When a control is added to the Canvas without defining an offset, it is simply placed in the top-left corner (that is, its Top and Left offsets are zero). If multiple child controls do not list an offset value to configure their placement within the Canvas, they will automatically be positioned in the top-left corner. The end result is that all controls are stacked on top of each other. When adding multiple controls to the Canvas, make sure that you specify offset values either from the Top or Bottom or from the Left or Right of the Canvas.

DockPanel

The DockPanel is used to dock child controls to a specific side of the container: Top, Left, Right, or Bottom. Child controls must use the DockPanel's attached property Dock to indicate on which side of the container it should be placed. If a value for the Dock property isn't specified, the control is docked to the left of its container, and it expands vertically to match the height of its parent control. Figure 8-5 illustrates the difference in how controls are displayed when using a DockPanel.

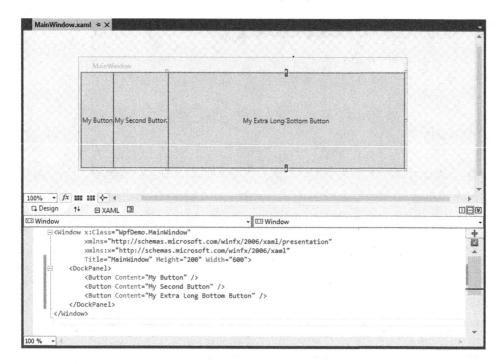

Figure 8-5. *DockPanel docks child elements side-by-side by default*

When multiple controls are docked to the same side, they do not overlap. Instead, they are docked side-by-side for controls that are docked left or right. They are docked top-to-bottom for controls that are docked at the top and are docked bottom-to-top for controls that are docked at the bottom. You can see an example of this behavior in Figure 8-6.

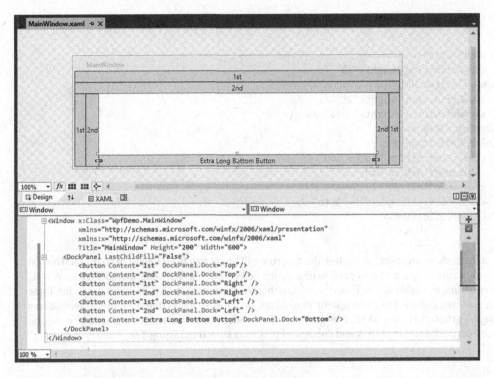

Figure 8-6. *Docking behavior with multiple child controls*

Grid

The Grid is used to organize controls within a table layout. You can define the number of rows and columns within the Grid using the Grid's RowDefinitions and ColumnDefinitions properties, respectively. If the markup doesn't include definitions for rows and columns, the Grid will contain a single cell by default.

Within a single row definition, you can choose to specify a row's height using the Height attribute. Similarly, you can specify a column's width using the Width attribute. The Height and Width attributes accept one of three potential value types.

- *Double value*: Representing the height or width of a row. A unit of measure may also be specified with the value, such as pixels (px), inches (in), centimeters (cm), or points (pt). If a unit of measure is not indicated, then the default unit of measure applied is pixels.

- *Auto*: Literal value indicating that the row's height will automatically adjust to fit the tallest control that is placed in the row.

- *Asterisk (*)*: Known as star sizing, which results in the row taking up the available remaining space. The asterisk can also be preceded by a number, which indicates the weight of available space that the row will take up in relation to the other available rows. If a value for Height is not specified on a row, it automatically applies star sizing. The same applies for columns where Width is not specified.

Listing 8-9 depicts an example of the use of each of these value types within a Grid.

Listing 8-9. Specifying Height and Width Values for a Grid's Rows and Columns

```
<Grid>
    <Grid.RowDefinitions>
            <RowDefinition Height="80" />
        <RowDefinition Height="*" />
            <RowDefinition Height="2*" />
            <RowDefinition Height="Auto" />
    </Grid.RowDefinitions>
    <Grid.ColumnDefinitions>
            <ColumnDefinition Width="100" />
            <ColumnDefinition Width="*" />
            <ColumnDefinition Width="2*" />
            <ColumnDefinition Width="Auto" />
    </Grid.ColumnDefinitions>
</Grid>
```

Based on the code example in Listing 8-9, the first row will be set to a fixed height of 80 pixels. The last row will use only as much space as is needed to display the cell's contents. The second and third rows will take up the remaining available space. However, notice that the third row's height includes a weighted star size value. In this case, the third row will take up double the available space as that used by the second row. Figure 8-7 displays the Grid in the XAML Designer, which provides rulers that show the rows and columns available based on the RowDefinitions and ColumnDefinitions shown in Listing 8-9.

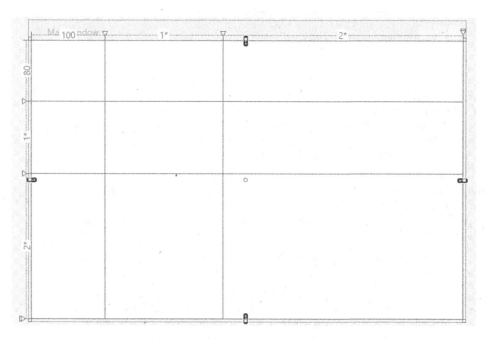

Figure 8-7. The effects of various sizing approaches on Grid rows and columns

Take another look at the Grid in Figure 8-7. Do you notice anything missing? We defined four rows and four columns, but the figure shows only three rows and three columns. Why is that?

As mentioned earlier, the row that is autosized will only take up the space needed to fit the contents of its cells. Since there are no controls in the row, the autosized row is collapsed. The same applies for the autosized column. As controls are added to the Grid, you will notice a change in the layout. Not only will there be the expected number of columns and rows visible, but the height and width of the star-sized rows and columns will shrink. The remaining amount of available space will be reduced based on how much space the autosized row and column requires.

Just as with the Canvas, you can define the row and column in which each control will be placed by specifying a value for the Grid's attached properties within the control's markup, as shown in Listing 8-10. If a control does not specify the row within which it should be placed, it is placed within the Grid's first row by default. Rows are referenced through a zero-based index. Therefore, the Grid's first row is referenced as row 0. The same concept applies to a Grid's column.

Listing 8-10. Arranging Controls Within the Grid's Rows and Columns

```
<Grid>
    <Grid.RowDefinitions>
        <RowDefinition Height="80" />
        <RowDefinition Height="*" />
        <RowDefinition Height="2*" />
        <RowDefinition Height="Auto" />
    </Grid.RowDefinitions>
    <Grid.ColumnDefinitions>
        <ColumnDefinition Width="100" />
        <ColumnDefinition Width="*" />
        <ColumnDefinition Width="2*" />
        <ColumnDefinition Width="Auto" />
    </Grid.ColumnDefinitions>
    <Button Content="Button" />
    <Button Content="Button" Grid.Column="1" />
    <Button Content="Button" Grid.Column="2"/>
    <Button Content="This is my extra long button" Grid.Column="3"/>
    <Button Content="This button spans across columns" Grid.Row="1" Grid.ColumnSpan="4"/>
</Grid>
```

In Listing 8-10, notice that the Grid.Row and Grid.Column attached properties are used to specify within which cell a button will be placed. Buttons that do not specify a Grid.Row value are placed in the first row by default.

The Grid.ColumnSpan attached property is used to enable a control to utilize the space across multiple columns. In the same respect, you can use the Grid.RowSpan attached property to configure a control to span multiple rows, as illustrated in Figure 8-8.

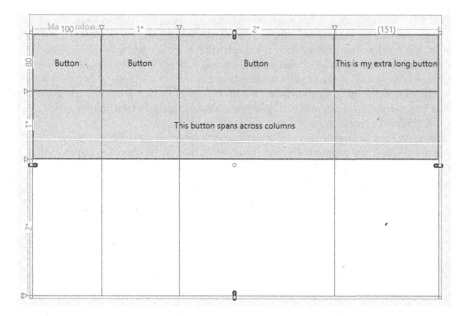

Figure 8-8. *An example of how to use the Grid's attached properties to place controls within the Grid*

StackPanel

The StackPanel is used to stack controls vertically or horizontally. The StackPanel contains an Orientation property, which drives the direction in which controls are stacked. The Orientation property's value may be set to Vertical or Horizontal. If an Orientation value isn't provided, the default orientation is set to vertical. Listing 8-11 shows an example of StackPanel markup, and Figure 8-9 depicts the result.

Listing 8-11. Using a StackPanel to Arrange Controls from Top-to-Bottom

```
<StackPanel Orientation="Vertical">
    <Button Content="Button A" />
    <Button Content="Button B" />
    <Button Content="Button C" />
    <Button Content="This is my extra long button" />
</StackPanel>
```

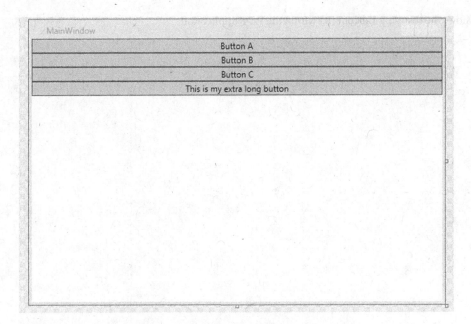

Figure 8-9. *Child control placement within a vertical StackPanel*

TabControl

A TabControl is used to group controls within one or more tab items. A TabControl defines the tabs it will contain through the Items property. Each TabItem within the collection may specify a Header, which will be displayed in the item's tab strip. The TabControl may be configured to display the tab strip at the Top, Left, Right, or Bottom. This is accomplished by setting the TabStripPlacement attribute on the TabControl. If a TabStripPlacement value isn't specified, the default placement of the tab strip is set to Top.

A TabItem may contain a single control or a container control, which in turn may host multiple controls, as shown in Listing 8-12.

Listing 8-12. *Configuring a TabControl in XAML*

```
<TabControl TabStripPlacement="Top">
    <TabControl.Items>
        <TabItem Header="First Tab">
            <StackPanel>
                <TextBlock Text="Do you like this example?"></TextBlock>
                <CheckBox Content="Yes"></CheckBox>
                <CheckBox Content="No"></CheckBox>
            </StackPanel>
        </TabItem>
        <TabItem Header="Second Tab">
        </TabItem>
        <TabItem Header="Third Tab">
        </TabItem>
    </TabControl.Items>
</TabControl>
```

Figure 8-10 shows the resulting TabControl within the WPF application.

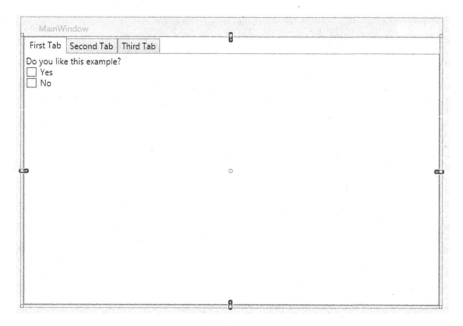

Figure 8-10. *A TabControl is used to separate child elements into logical sections*

UniformGrid

A UniformGrid is similar to the Grid in that controls are arranged within cells in a gridlike layout using rows and columns. However, this differs from a standard Grid because, as controls are added, the UniformGrid automatically generates rows and columns needed while maintaining an even distance between the controls. Listing 8-13 shows the sample markup for a UniformGrid within XAML. Figure 8-11 illustrates the resulting view that is displayed.

Listing 8-13. UniformGrid Automatically Arranges Controls in a Grid Pattern

```
<UniformGrid>
    <Button Content="A" />
    <Button Content="B" />
    <Button Content="C" />
    <Button Content="D" />
    <Button Content="E" />
    <Button Content="F" />
    <Button Content="G" />
    <Button Content="H" />
    <Button Content="I" />
</UniformGrid>
```

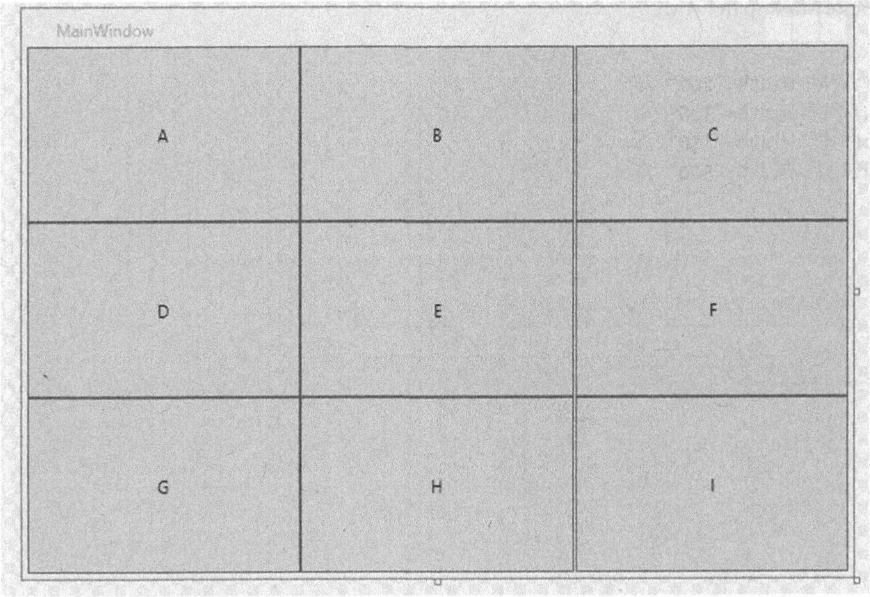

Figure 8-11. *A UniformGrid maintains equal distance between its child controls*

Alternatively, you can specify that a UniformGrid has a fixed number of rows and columns by specifying values for the Rows and Columns attributes, respectively, as shown in Listing 8-14.

Listing 8-14. Specifying a Fixed Number of Rows and Columns for the UniformGrid

```
<UniformGrid Rows="5" Columns="4">
    <Button Content="A" />
    <Button Content="B" />
    <Button Content="C" />
    <Button Content="D" />
    <Button Content="E" />
    <Button Content="F" />
    <Button Content="G" />
    <Button Content="H" />
    <Button Content="I" />
</UniformGrid>
```

If the number of rows and columns that you specify generates more cells than controls that are available to fill the grid, the remaining cells will simply contain whitespace. However, if the number of controls within the grid outnumber the cells available, because you set the rows and columns values too low, the remaining controls will be cut off.

WrapPanel

A WrapPanel is similar to the StackPanel in that rows are stacked side-by-side or top-to-bottom depending on the value of the Orientation property. However, when the controls extend beyond the bounds of the width of the screen, the controls will wrap around to create an additional row in which the control will display. Listing 8-15 shows sample markup using a WrapPanel, and the resulting view is depicted in Figure 8-12.

Listing 8-15. WrapPanel Markup in XAML

```xaml
<WrapPanel>
    <Button Content="A" Width="200" />
    <Button Content="B" Width="300" />
    <Button Content="C" Width="150" />
    <Button Content="D" Width="500" />
</WrapPanel>
```

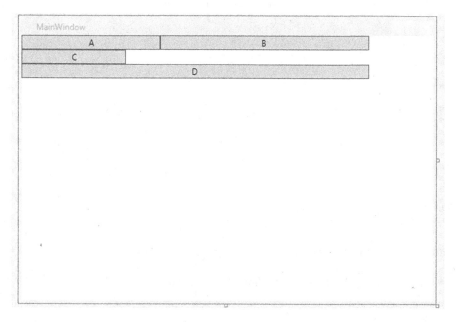

Figure 8-12. *WrapPanel automatically moves a control to the next row if it will extend beyond the bounds of the screen*

Margins and Padding

Up until now, you may have noticed that the controls do not provide proper spacing when added to the view. This is ideal to ensure that controls aren't squeezed together and there is adequate spacing between controls. To achieve this, you can set the Margin property on any UI control to configure the amount of space to include around the exterior rectangle of a control.

The Margin property is defined as a *thickness* structure. When defined in XAML, a margin is configured using a string, which may include one, two, or four comma-separated double values. The string value supplied for the Margin property in XAML is converted to the thickness structure's values for the Left, Top, Right, and Bottom sides of a rectangle, as detailed in Table 8-3.

Table 8-3. *Effects of Setting Margin on an Object in XAML*

Approach	Result	Example
Margin="left"	The specified unit of measure is applied to all sides of an object.	Margin="10"
Margin="left,top"	The first unit of measure specified is applied to the left and right sides of an object. The second unit of measure is applied to the top and bottom sides of an object.	Margin="10,20"
Margin="left,top, right,bottom"	Each specified unit of measure is applied only to its corresponding side: left, top, right, and bottom.	Margin="10,20,10,15"

Padding is used to configure the amount of space between the control's boundaries and its contents, such as the text within a button (for example, interior spacing). Similar to Margin, the Padding property is defined as a thickness structure, and it can be set in a similar manner as detailed in Table 8-3.

The code depicted in Listing 8-16 shows an example of using the Margin and Padding properties on a TextBox.

Listing 8-16. Using Margin to Provide Space Around the Exterior of the Control

```
<StackPanel>
        <TextBox Padding="10,20"
                TextWrapping="Wrap"
                Text="Lorem ipsum dolor sit amet, consectetur adipiscing elit. Integer eget
                consequat nulla. Sed vehicula posuere quam eu lobortis." />
        <TextBox Margin="10,20"
                TextWrapping="Wrap"
                Text="Lorem ipsum dolor sit amet, consectetur adipiscing elit. Integer eget
                consequat nulla. Sed vehicula posuere quam eu lobortis." />
</StackPanel>
```

Figure 8-13 illustrates the effects of setting the Margin and Padding properties on a TextBox.

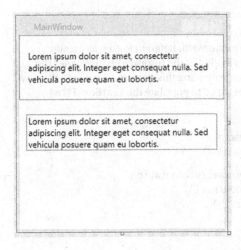

Figure 8-13. *Comparing the effects of margin and padding on a TextBox*

Resources and Styles

Now that you have a good handle on how to arrange your controls and how to provide adequate spacing between controls, the next step is to understand how to apply custom styles and theming within your WPF application.

Resources

A *resource* is an object that can be used throughout your WPF application, depending on where it is defined. The most common uses of resources include styles, templates, and color brushes. You can also use a single value or array of values as resources. A collection of resources can be defined at the application, view, or container level. Listing 8-17 illustrates how to define a resource that consists of an array of string values for a window within your application.

Listing 8-17. Defining a String Array as a Resource

```
<Window x:Class="WpfDemo.MainWindow"
        xmlns="http://schemas.microsoft.com/winfx/2006/xaml/presentation"
        xmlns:x="http://schemas.microsoft.com/winfx/2006/xaml"
        xmlns:sys="clr-namespace:System;assembly=mscorlib"
        Title="MainWindow">
    <Window.Resources>
        <x:Array x:Key="MyListItems" Type="sys:String">
            <sys:String>Apples</sys:String>
            <sys:String>Bananas</sys:String>
            <sys:String>Cherries</sys:String>
        </x:Array>
     </Window.Resources>
    <ListBox ItemsSource="{StaticResource MyListItems}" />
</Window>
```

Resources can be referenced as static or dynamic resources.

Static

A *static resource* is referenced using the StaticResource markup extension. Referencing a static resource will result in the resource being retrieved only once the XAML is loaded. If the resource changes after the initial load, the changes will not be reflected in the UI for any controls using this resource. Listing 8-18 shows an example of referencing the MyListItems array as a StaticResource to populate the ListBox Items collection.

Listing 8-18. Setting the ListBox Items Collection to a Static Resource

```
<Window x:Class="WpfDemo.MainWindow"
        xmlns="http://schemas.microsoft.com/winfx/2006/xaml/presentation"
        xmlns:x="http://schemas.microsoft.com/winfx/2006/xaml"
        xmlns:sys="clr-namespace:System;assembly=mscorlib"
        Title="MainWindow">
```

```
    <Window.Resources>
        <x:Array x:Key="MyListItems" Type="sys:String">
            <sys:String>Apples</sys:String>
            <sys:String>Bananas</sys:String>
            <sys:String>Cherries</sys:String>
        </x:Array>
    </Window.Resources>
    <ListBox ItemsSource="{StaticResource MyListItems}" />
</Window>
```

Dynamic

A *dynamic resource* is referenced using the DynamicResource markup extension. Doing so will result in the resource being retrieved when the XAML is loaded and at subsequent times whenever the resource changes. Reference a resource as a DynamicResource when you expect that the resource will change during its lifetime in the application and you want to have these changes reflected in the UI or, alternatively, if the resource will not exist at design time but will be added from the code-behind when the application runs. Listing 8-19 illustrates setting the TextBlockLabel resource as a DynamicResource on the TextBlock.

Listing 8-19. Setting the TextBlock to a Dynamic Resource in XAML

```
<Window x:Class="WpfDemo.MainWindow"
        xmlns="http://schemas.microsoft.com/winfx/2006/xaml/presentation"
        xmlns:x="http://schemas.microsoft.com/winfx/2006/xaml"
        xmlns:sys="clr-namespace:System;assembly=mscorlib"
        Title="MainWindow" Width="200">
    <Window.Resources>
        <sys:String x:Key="TextBlockLabel">Not Clicked</sys:String>
    </Window.Resources>
    <StackPanel>
        <Button Content="Click Me!" Click="AddItemButton_OnClick" />
        <TextBlock Text="{DynamicResource TextBlockLabel}" HorizontalAlignment="Center" />
    </StackPanel>
</Window>
```

Notice there is also a Button within the XAML whose Click event is wired up to the AddItemButton_OnClick event in the code-behind file. Every time the button is clicked, the TextBlockLabel resource will be updated, as shown in Listing 8-20.

Listing 8-20. Updating the TextBlockLabel Resource in the Code-Behind

```
public partial class MainWindow : Window
{
    private int clickedCount = 0;

    public MainWindow()
    {
        InitializeComponent();
    }
```

```
private void AddItemButton_OnClick(object sender, RoutedEventArgs e)
{
    this.Resources["TextBlockLabel"] = string.Format("Clicked {0} time(s)",
    ++clickedCount);

}
}
```

Run the application and click the button a few times. What do you notice? Do you experience the same result as shown in Figure 8-14?

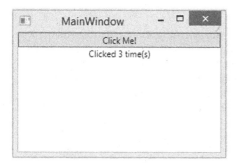

Figure 8-14. *The TextBlock text is updated when the resource is updated*

In the Window's XAML, change the TextBlock Text property's reference to indicate StaticResource instead of DynamicResource. Run the application again, and click the button a few times. Do you notice anything different?

You should notice that no matter how many times the button is clicked, the TextBlock's Text always indicates "Not Clicked."

It is important to understand the distinction between static and dynamic resources as well as the implications of using them within your XAML.

Styles

Each XAML UI control comes with a default look and feel, defined as a *style*. However, you can easily override the default style for any object in WPF using the Style property. A major benefit of defining a Style is the ability to define it once within your application and apply that style to all controls of a specific type or only to those controls that are explicitly configured to use it. You also have the flexibility to define a custom style, which will apply only to controls within a single view or to a single control.

To define a Style for an object, you must set its TargetType property to the desired object type. Once the TargetType is set, you will be able to define property values that are applicable to that object type using Setter elements within the Style.

Each Setter element must have a value set for its Property and Value attributes. The Property attribute specifies which property on the control to set. The Value attribute specifies the value that will be applied to the property, as shown in Listing 8-21.

Listing 8-21. Defining a TextBox Style

```
<Style TargetType="TextBox">
    <Setter Property="Margin" Value="10" />
    <Setter Property="Padding" Value="5" />
    <Setter Property="FontFamily" Value="Segoe UI" />
    <Setter Property="FontSize" Value="14" />
</Style>
```

Now that you know how to define a Style, you are probably wondering where to include this markup. A Style can be defined at the application, view, container, or control level.

Application-Level Styles

To avoid having to define the same style individually whenever a control is used within your application, you can choose to define a Style at the application level, which will apply to all controls of a common type. This enables you to define the style in one place so that if you decide to change the theme of your application, you need to change the style definitions in only one location.

To define a Style that applies to all controls of a specific type across your application, you must include the Style definition as part of the Application.Resources collection within the App.xaml file. Listing 8-22 depicts a TextBox Style, which configures default values for its Margin, Padding, FontFamily, and FontSize properties.

Listing 8-22. Defining a TextBox Style as an Application Resource

```
<Application.Resources>
    <Style TargetType="TextBox">
        <Setter Property="Margin" Value="10" />
        <Setter Property="Padding" Value="5" />
        <Setter Property="FontFamily" Value="Segoe UI" />
        <Setter Property="FontSize" Value="14" />
    </Style>
</Application.Resources>
```

View-Level Styles

Similarly, you can define a Style within a single view by including it within the view's resources collection. In this case, the Style defined in the application's main window for a specific object will overrule an application-level style definition for the same control. The example shown in Listing 8-23 depicts a TextBox Style defined within the main windows of a WPF application. This Style will take precedence over the application-level TextBox Style definition. Any TextBox added to the window will have a font size of 12 pixels with red font. It will not include any of the Margin or Padding property values defined in the application-level Style definition.

Listing 8-23. Defining a TextBox Style as a Window Resource

```
<Window.Resources>
    <Style TargetType="TextBox">
        <Setter Property="Foreground" Value="Red" />
        <Setter Property="FontSize" Value="12" />
    </Style>
</Window.Resources>
```

If you want to combine the Style definitions from both the application and view resources, you can simply specify that Style is based on the control's default style by setting its BasedOn attribute within the Window.Resources Style definition as follows:

```
<Style TargetType="TextBox" BasedOn="{StaticResource {x:Type TextBox}}">
```

In this way, the Style defined for the TextBox at the application level will be applied to the control first, and then the Style defined for the TextBox in the window will be applied next. The following property values will be applied to all TextBox controls that are added to the window:

- Left Margin = 10 pixels
- Top Margin = 10 pixels
- Right Margin = 10 pixels
- Bottom Margin = 10 pixels
- Left Padding = 5 pixels
- Top Padding = 5 pixels
- Right Padding = 5 pixels
- Bottom Padding = 5 pixels
- Font Family = Segoe UI
- Font Size = 12
- Font Text = Red

Container-Level Styles

Similarly, you can define a Style as part of a container's Resources collection, as shown in Listing 8-24. Any controls within that container that have a Style defined as a container's resource will have the custom Style applied to it. Remember that the Style will override any styles defined at the application or view level, unless the BasedOn attribute is used, as discussed in the "View-Level Styles" section, earlier in this chapter.

Listing 8-24. Including a Style Definition as a Grid Resource

```
<Grid>
    <Grid.Resources>
        <Style TargetType="TextBox">
            <Setter Property="TextAlignment" Value="Center" />
            <Setter Property="FontWeight" Value="Bold" />
        </Style>
    </Grid.Resources>
    <TextBox Text="Learning all about XAML styles" />
</Grid>
```

Control-Level Styles

Additionally, you can define a Style for a single control by setting the control's Style property directly, as shown in Listing 8-25.

Listing 8-25. Defining a Style for a Single Control Instance

```
<TextBox Text="Learning all about XAML styles">
    <TextBox.Style>
        <Style TargetType="TextBox">
            <Setter Property="FontSize" Value="16" />
            <Setter Property="FontWeight" Value="SemiBold" />
            <Setter Property="TextAlignment" Value="Center" />
        </Style>
    </TextBox.Style>
</TextBox>
```

Alternatively, you can provide a Key for a Style definition within the application or view resources collection in order to apply the Style to specific controls. This is accomplished by setting the Style property on a control to a StaticResource referencing the Style definition by its Key value, as shown in Listing 8-26.

Listing 8-26. Applying Style Definition as a Named Reference

```
<Window x:Class="WpfDemo.MainWindow"
        xmlns="http://schemas.microsoft.com/winfx/2006/xaml/presentation"
        xmlns:x="http://schemas.microsoft.com/winfx/2006/xaml"
        Title="MainWindow">
    <Window.Resources>
        <Style TargetType="TextBox" BasedOn="{StaticResource {x:Type TextBox}}">
            <Setter Property="Foreground" Value="Red"></Setter>
        </Style>
        <Style x:Key="MyCustomTextBoxStyle" TargetType="TextBox">
            <Setter Property="FontSize" Value="16" />
            <Setter Property="FontWeight" Value="Bold" />
            <Setter Property="TextAlignment" Value="Center" />
        </Style>
    </Window.Resources>
    <StackPanel>
        <TextBox Style="{StaticResource MyCustomTextBoxStyle}"
                 Text="This TextBox will have the MyCustomTextBoxStyle applied." />
        <TextBox Text="This TextBox will have the BasedOn TextBox Style applied." />
    </StackPanel>
</Window>
```

Data Binding

Data binding is the mechanism that manages the flow of data between the application's UI and a data provider. It involves a target and a source. The target is the object that will receive the data. The target is generally the property on a control in the view, such as the Text property of a TextBox. The source is the object that serves as the data provider. When configuring data binding for a target object, you can specify the manner in which data will flow, known as the Mode. Table 8-4 describes each Mode.

Table 8-4. *Direction of Data Flow*

Mode	Description
OneWay	When the source property changes, the target property is automatically updated. Changes to the target property do not affect the source property. This is the default behavior when no Mode is specified.
OneWayToSource	When the target property changes, the source property is automatically updated. Changes to the source property do not affect the target property.
OneTime	The source property changes the target property when it is first initialized. Any subsequent changes to the source property are not propagated to the target.
TwoWay	Changes to the source property are automatically propagated to the target property. Also, changes to the target property are propagated to the source property.

XAML Markup

Data binding can be set on an element's property within XAML or in the code-behind. You can configure the property to receive data from a data provider or from another element within the view.

To configure data binding for a property on a control when the data is coming from another element's property, use the following syntax:

```
<object Property="{ElementName=NameOfElement, Path=ElementPropertyName}" />
```

As an example, Listing 8-27 shows how to enable or disable a TextBox based on whether a CheckBox in the view is selected.

Listing 8-27. TextBox Is Enabled When the CheckBox Is Checked

```
<Window x:Class="WpfDemo.MainWindow"
        xmlns="http://schemas.microsoft.com/winfx/2006/xaml/presentation"
        xmlns:x="http://schemas.microsoft.com/winfx/2006/xaml"
        Title="MainWindow">
    <StackPanel>
        <CheckBox x:Name="DetailsCheckBox" Content="Enter details?"></CheckBox>
        <TextBox IsEnabled="{Binding ElementName=DetailsCheckBox, Path=IsChecked}" />
    </StackPanel>
</Window>
```

If you run the sample code in Listing 8-27 within a WPF application, you will notice that the TextBox is disabled when the MainWindow loads. Select the CheckBox and notice that the TextBox becomes enabled. This is accomplished through the data binding service. You did not need to write any code in the code-behind to manage this behavior.

To configure data binding for a property on a control when the data is coming in from an exposed property on a data provider, use the following syntax:

```
<object Property="{Binding Path=SourcePropertyName}" />
```

For example, to set the Text property on a TextBlock to display the value of a StatusMessage string property from a ViewModel class, use the following syntax:

```
<TextBlock Text="{Binding Path=StatusMessage}" />
```

If you add this TextBlock markup to the MainWindow markup in Listing 8-27, what will happen? Well, nothing of course. The CheckBox and TextBox will continue to function as expected, but the TextBlock will remain empty. The reason for this is that you do not have a data provider that exposes a StatusMessage property, nor have you told the view the source of the data, otherwise known as the DataContext. Let's get a data provider in place first.

ViewModel and INotifyPropertyChanged

As discussed in Chapter 1, it is best to implement the Model-View-ViewModel pattern in your WPF applications to encapsulate your business logic within a separate class. The ViewModel class will serve as the data provider to the view. The ViewModel may retrieve data from one or more sources, such as a database or a web service.

For this example, create a folder named ViewModels. Within that folder, add a simple view model, named MainViewModel, to the WPF application that you were working with from the section "XAML Markup," previously in this chapter. Set the namespace of this class to WpfDemo.ViewModels. The MainViewModel will expose a single public string property named StatusMessage.

For the view to receive notifications of property changes from the view model, the view model must implement the INotifyPropertyChanged interface. This simply requires declaring and managing the PropertyChanged event within the view model, as shown in Listing 8-28.

Listing 8-28. Implement INotifyPropertyChanged in the ViewModel

```
public class MainViewModel : INotifyPropertyChanged
{
    public event PropertyChangedEventHandler PropertyChanged;

    public void OnPropertyChanged([CallerMemberName]string propertyName = null)
    {
        if (PropertyChanged != null)
        {
            PropertyChanged(this, new PropertyChangedEventArgs(propertyName));
        }
    }
}
```

Each property that will participate in data binding within a view must raise the PropertyChanged event in the property's setter, as shown in Listing 8-29. In this way, whenever the property within the view model changes, the WPF system will automatically send a notification to view, causing any controls that are affected by the change to refresh.

Listing 8-29. Raise the OnPropertyChanged Event from the Property's Setter

```
public class MainViewModel : INotifyPropertyChanged
{
    private string _statusMessage;
    public string StatusMessage
    {
        get { return _statusMessage; }
        set
```

```
        {
            if (_statusMessage != value)
            {
                _statusMessage = value;
                OnPropertyChanged();
            }
        }
    }
}

    public event PropertyChangedEventHandler PropertyChanged;

    public void OnPropertyChanged([CallerMemberName]string propertyName = null)
    {
        if (PropertyChanged != null)
        {
            PropertyChanged(this, new PropertyChangedEventArgs(propertyName));
        }
    }
}
}
```

The majority of the code needed for data binding is now in place. The final piece of the puzzle is to specify a DataContext in the view.

DataContext

The view's DataContext provides a handle to the data provider that will feed data to the UI. The DataContext can be set in the view's code-behind, as shown in Listing 8-30. This sets the DataContext to the view. All controls within the view will use the DataContext of its parent by default, unless the controls specify an alternate DataContext.

Listing 8-30. Set the DataContext in the Window's Code-Behind to the MainViewModel

```
public partial class MainWindow : Window
{
    private MainViewModel _viewModel = new MainViewModel();

    public MainWindow()
    {
        InitializeComponent();
        DataContext = _viewModel;
    }
}
```

Alternatively, you may set the DataContext within the view's markup by defining the MainViewModel as a resource in the window and then setting the container control's DataContext to the MainViewModel resource, as shown in Listing 8-31. A child control within the StackPanel will automatically have its DataContext set to the DataContext of its parent, unless it is explicitly configured to use an alternate DataContext.

Listing 8-31. Set the DataContext in XAML

```xml
<Window x:Class="WpfDemo.MainWindow"
        xmlns="http://schemas.microsoft.com/winfx/2006/xaml/presentation"
        xmlns:x="http://schemas.microsoft.com/winfx/2006/xaml"
        xmlns:vm="clr-namespace:WpfDemo.ViewModels"
        Title="MainWindow">
    <Window.Resources>
        <vm:MainViewModel x:Key="MainViewModel" />
    </Window.Resources>
    <StackPanel DataContext="{StaticResource MainViewModel}">
        <CheckBox x:Name="DetailsCheckBox" Content="Enter details?"></CheckBox>
        <TextBox IsEnabled="{Binding ElementName=DetailsCheckBox, Path=IsChecked}"
                 Text="{Binding StatusMessage, Mode=TwoWay}" />
        <TextBlock Text="{Binding StatusMessage, Mode=OneWay}" />
    </StackPanel>
</Window>
```

The code in Listing 8-31 is configured to update the StatusMessage property in the view model with the contents of the TextBox's Text property. Notice that its binding mode is set to TwoWay binding. This will cause any changes in the TextBox to be propagated to the StatusMessage property in the view model. The update to the StatusMessage property will cause the PropertyChanged event to be fired. The TextBlock's Text property is configured to receive updates from the StatusMessage property. Notice that its binding mode is set to OneWay. Once the StatusMessage property fires the PropertyChanged event, the TextBlock's Text property will be updated to reflect the new value.

Run the application to test it. Select the CheckBox to enable the TextBox. Enter a message in the TextBox and then hit the Tab key to ensure that focus is moved from the TextBox. The result should be that the TextBlock is updated to display the message that was entered in the TextBox, as illustrated in Figure 8-15.

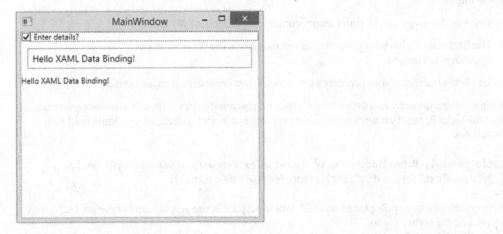

Figure 8-15. *Using data binding to display and update a property value between the view and its view model*

As shown in this simple example, data binding removes the need to set explicitly the state of a control from the code-behind file. The larger the application grows, the easier it will be to maintain as long as you adhere to the MVVM pattern.

Dependency Properties

As mentioned earlier, data binding involves a target and a source, where the target is the object that will receive the data. The target is generally the property on a control in the view. For a property to be eligible to participate in data binding, a DependencyProperty must back it. The purpose of a DependencyProperty is to enable the modification of a property's value through external inputs, such as data binding.

Within your WPF application, if you peek at the TextBox definition, you will see that it has a handful of dependency properties defined, as shown in Figure 8-16.

```
namespace System.Windows.Controls
{
    [ContentProperty("Text")]
    [Localizability(LocalizationCategory.Text)]
    public class TextBox : TextBoxBase, IAddChild, ITextBoxViewHost
    {
        public static readonly DependencyProperty TextWrappingProperty = TextBlock.TextWrappingProperty.AddOwner(typeof (TextBox), (PropertyM
        public static readonly DependencyProperty MinLinesProperty = DependencyProperty.Register("MinLines", typeof (int), typeof (TextBox),
        public static readonly DependencyProperty MaxLinesProperty = DependencyProperty.Register("MaxLines", typeof (int), typeof (TextBox),
        public static readonly DependencyProperty TextProperty = DependencyProperty.Register("Text", typeof (string), typeof (TextBox), (Prop
        public static readonly DependencyProperty CharacterCasingProperty = DependencyProperty.Register("CharacterCasing", typeof (CharacterC
        public static readonly DependencyProperty MaxLengthProperty = DependencyProperty.Register("MaxLength", typeof (int), typeof (TextBox)
        public static readonly DependencyProperty TextAlignmentProperty = Block.TextAlignmentProperty.AddOwner(typeof (TextBox));
        public static readonly DependencyProperty TextDecorationsProperty = Inline.TextDecorationsProperty.AddOwner(typeof (TextBox), (Proper
        private object _newTextValue = DependencyProperty.UnsetValue;
        private static DependencyObjectType _dType;
        private bool _minmaxChanged;
        private bool _isInsideTextContentChange;
        private bool _isTypographySet;
```

Figure 8-16. *TextBox dependency properties*

It is important to understand this concept for two reasons. The first reason is to understand which properties can leverage data binding. Also, when you create your own WPF user controls that expose custom properties and you want to set those property values using data binding in your WPF views, you will need to know how to define them as dependency properties in your control. This can be accomplished by ensuring that you do the following:

1. Register the properties in your custom control as a DependencyProperty.

2. Use GetValue within your property's getter to retrieve the value from the DependencyProperty.

3. Use SetValue within your property's setter to set your DependencyProperty value.

When registering a property as a DependencyProperty, you must follow a specific naming convention, ensuring that the suffix Property is appended to the property name and is declared as a static read-only property, as follows:

```
public static readonly DependencyProperty MyCustomTextProperty = DependencyProperty.
Register("MyCustomText", typeof(string), typeof(MyCustomControl));
```

In the DependencyProperty.Register method, you must pass in the actual name of the property, the property's type, and the owner's type.

Next you will need to define the property's getter and setter using the following format:

```
public string MyCustomText
{
    get { return (string)GetValue(MyCustomTextProperty); }
    set { SetValue(MyCustomTextProperty, value); }
}
```

Finally, you will need to define the DataContext for your user control. The DataContext tells your view who is the data provider. Within your user control, you can set the DataContext to itself. However, setting the DataContext on the user control itself does not work. You will need to set the DataContext on the content of the user control, as follows:

```
(this.Content as FrameworkElement).DataContext = this;
```

Listing 8-32 shows the complete example of a basic string property backed by a DependencyProperty in a user control.

Listing 8-32. Defining a DependencyProperty in a User Control

```
public partial class MyCustomControl : UserControl
    {
        public MyCustomControl()
        {
            InitializeComponent();
            (this.Content as FrameworkElement).DataContext = this;
        }

        public static readonly DependencyProperty MyCustomTextProperty =
                DependencyProperty.Register("MyCustomText", typeof(string),
                                            typeof(MyCustomControl));

        public string MyCustomText
        {
            get { return (string)GetValue(MyCustomTextProperty); }
            set { SetValue(MyCustomTextProperty, value); }
        }
    }
```

To use this custom control in your WPF View, you will need to define the user control's namespace in XAML and then add the control, as shown in Listing 8-33.

Listing 8-33. Replacing the TextBlock with a Custom User Control

```
<Window x:Class="WpfDemo.MainWindow"
        xmlns="http://schemas.microsoft.com/winfx/2006/xaml/presentation"
        xmlns:x="http://schemas.microsoft.com/winfx/2006/xaml"
        xmlns:vm="clr-namespace:WpfDemo.ViewModels"
        xmlns:local="clr-namespace:WpfDemo"
        Title="MainWindow">
    <Window.Resources>
        <vm:MainViewModel x:Key="MainViewModel" />
    </Window.Resources>
    <StackPanel DataContext="{StaticResource MainViewModel}">
        <CheckBox x:Name="DetailsCheckBox" Content="Enter details?"></CheckBox>
        <TextBox IsEnabled="{Binding ElementName=DetailsCheckBox, Path=IsChecked}"
                 Text="{Binding StatusMessage, Mode=TwoWay}" />
        <local:MyCustomControl MyCustomText="{Binding StatusMessage, Mode=OneWay}"/>
    </StackPanel>
</Window>
```

Instead of binding to a Text property, as you did with TextBlock in the previous example, notice that now you are binding to the MyCustomText property of the user control.

Summary

This chapter provided an overview of using XAML in your Windows Presentation Foundation applications, covering only the fundamental concepts. You learned the basic structure of a WPF application, understanding that XAML enables you to keep your UI components separate from your application's logic. You also learned the various ways to lay out controls within a view, as well as how to style controls. Finally, you learned how to implement the MVVM pattern and data-binding techniques to manage data flow within the application.

We have only scratched the surface of the capabilities that the Extensible Application Markup Language provides when you are designing XAML-based applications. For a deep dive on using XAML within your WPF applications, we highly recommend reading *Pro WPF 4.5 in C#: Windows Presentation Foundation in .NET 4.5* by Matthew MacDonald (Apress, 2012).

In the next chapter, we will show you how your XAML knowledge can transcend desktop to mobile applications, enabling you to develop engaging Windows Phone 8.1 applications. We will cover the basic structure of a Windows Phone app and how you can design your application for various screen sizes and page orientations.

CHAPTER 9

■ ■ ■

The Windows Phone User Interface

Applications that run on Windows Phone devices are referred to as *Windows Phone apps*. Microsoft released the Windows Phone 7 mobile operating system, which was the successor to Windows Mobile, in October 2010. Windows Phone 7 became popular among .NET developers because it enabled them easily to build and publish apps to a public app store. Windows Phone 7 app development leveraged the .NET Framework, which simplified the transition for .NET developers from desktop and web development to the mobile app development space. Developers could use either Silverlight or XNA with C# to build mobile apps, and they could release their apps to the Windows Phone Marketplace.

In October 2012, Microsoft released Windows Phone 8, which was based on the Windows NT kernel. Windows Phone 8 included a small subset of APIs in common with the Windows 8 operating system, thus enabling about 30 percent code reuse between the two platforms. It also introduced new app models to enable developers from various programming backgrounds to develop Windows Phone apps using their language of choice. Windows Phone 8 apps could be created using C++ and DirectX, HTML5 and JavaScript, or Silverlight and C#. Code reuse between Windows Store and Windows Phone apps was accomplished through the use of portable class libraries, which included a set of APIs that were common between the two platforms. Portable class libraries are external DLLs, which are compiled independently and added as a reference to each platform-specific project. The Windows Phone Marketplace was renamed to the Windows Phone Store around this time as well.

In 2014, Windows Phone 8.1 was released, which included a converged Windows Runtime API, enabling up to 90 percent code reuse, including a shared XAML framework between Windows Store and Windows Phone apps. Windows Phone 8.1 provided many more options for developers. They were now able to select from a new the *Windows Runtime app model* to create Windows Phone apps. The Windows Runtime app model lends itself to the concept of universal apps for Windows, which enables the two platforms to share UI code, assets, and files through *Shared Projects*. A Shared Project serves as a file linker, which simply copies the shared files into each platform-specific project at compile time. The result is that the shared files are compiled within each platform's executable code. Windows Phone applications developed using the Windows Runtime app model are referred to as *Windows Phone Store apps*.

Since this book's primary focus is on XAML, this chapter will focus on designing the user interface for Windows Phone Store apps. We will show you how to tailor your application to support various screen sizes, as well as how to style your user interface through the use of themes, templates, and resources. Finally, we will discuss the various ways that you can present data collections to provide an interactive, engaging user experience.

■ **Note**   In April 2015, Microsoft announced that its new operating system, Windows 10, will enable developers to create applications that can run on any Windows 10–enabled device, including tablets, phones, wearables, Xbox, and HoloLens. When Windows 10 is released, .NET developers will be able to develop XAML/C# applications that run cross-platform. The XAML fundamentals we cover in this book will help to prepare you for this next wave of application development.

The Basics

Many of the core concepts surrounding XAML UI design, which were discussed in Chapter 8, are relevant in this chapter, and they serve as the foundation for the next two chapters. If you skipped Chapter 8, now is the time to go back and read it before moving forward.

Windows Phone 8.1 SDK

Before you can develop apps for Windows Phone 8.1, you must install the Windows Phone SDK, which is available with Visual Studio 2013 Update 2 or newer. The Windows Phone 8.1 SDK includes the Windows Phone and Windows Runtime APIs, emulators, and universal app templates. If you do not have access to a licensed edition of Visual Studio, we recommend installing Visual Studio Community 2013 with Update 4, which is available free of charge from the Visual Studio Downloads page at https://www.visualstudio.com/en-us/downloads.

Note that you must select the Windows Phone SDK check box when installing Visual Studio 2013, because it is not selected by default. During the installation process, in the "Optional features to install" step, select the Windows Phone 8.0 SDK, as shown in Figure 9-1. Although the label indicates that you will be installing the Windows Phone 8.0 SDK, you can rest assured that the Windows Phone 8.1 SDK will be installed.

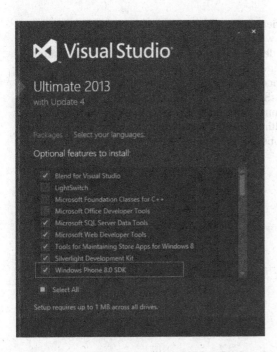

Figure 9-1. *Installing the Windows Phone SDK with Visual Studio 2013*

Multiresolution Support

The range of Windows Phone devices on the market today is extensive. Nokia Lumia devices are the most popular in the marketplace. A wide range of handheld devices is offered, from high-end tablets to modest low-end devices. As a Windows Phone developer, you will need to design your app to support different screen sizes and resolutions to ensure that it renders properly across multiple devices. Your app must support a minimum screen width of 384px, when displayed in portrait mode, and 640px, when displayed in landscape mode. We will discuss how to configure your app to support portrait and landscape mode in the "Page Orientation" section, later in this chapter.

Table 9-1 lists the screen resolutions of the emulator images that are available in the Windows Phone 8.1 SDK.

Table 9-1. *Windows Phone 8.1 Emulator Resolutions and Aspect Ratio*

Resolution	Pixel Resolution	Raw Pixels Per View Pixel	Display Resolution	Aspect Ratio
WVGA	400×667	1.2	480×800	15:9
WXGA	384×640	2.0	768×1280	15:9
720p	400×711	1.8	720×1280	16:9
1080p	450×800	2.4	1080×1920	16:9
	491×873	2.2	1080×1920	16:9

To determine the device's resolution and current orientation, you can use the DisplayInformation class, from the Windows.Graphics.Display namespace, which exposes events to allow you to monitor changes in the display. It also includes read-only properties, which provide information such as the number of pixels per logical inch, raw dots per inch along the x- and y-axes of the display screen, the number of physical pixels for each layout pixel, and the current device orientation. You can use this information to gather pertinent information about the device on which the application is running. Listing 9-1 provides a code sample that calculates the device's display resolution using the RawPixelsPerViewPixel as a multiplier against the current application window's height and width measurements. Listing 9-2 illustrates the XAML markup needed to display the resulting measurements onscreen.

Listing 9-1. Calculate the Device's Display Resolution

```
using System;
...
using Windows.UI.Xaml;
using Windows.UI.Xaml.Controls;
using Windows.UI.Xaml.Navigation;
using Windows.Graphics.Display;

namespace ResolutionDemo
{
    ...

        protected override void OnNavigatedTo(NavigationEventArgs e)
        {
            DisplayInformation info = DisplayInformation.GetForCurrentView();
            double scaleFactor = info.RawPixelsPerViewPixel;

        //calculate the display resolution
            double displayResolutionWidth = Window.Current.Bounds.Width * scaleFactor;
            double displayResolutionHeight = Window.Current.Bounds.Height * scaleFactor;

            pixelResolution.Text = string.Format("Pixel resolution: {0}x{1}",
                Window.Current.Bounds.Width, Window.Current.Bounds.Height);

            displayResolution.Text = string.Format("Display resolution: {0}x{1}",
                displayResolutionWidth, displayResolutionHeight);
        }
    }
}
```

Listing 9-2. Sample XAML Markup to Show Resolution Comparison

```
<Page
    x:Class="ResolutionDemo.MainPage"
    xmlns="http://schemas.microsoft.com/winfx/2006/xaml/presentation"
    xmlns:x="http://schemas.microsoft.com/winfx/2006/xaml"
    Background="{ThemeResource ApplicationPageBackgroundThemeBrush}">
    <Page.Resources>
        <Style TargetType="TextBlock">
            <Setter Property="TextWrapping" Value="Wrap" />
            <Setter Property="FontSize" Value="24" />
```

```
                <Setter Property="Margin" Value="10" />
        </Style>
    </Page.Resources>
    <Grid x:Name="mainGrid">
        <Grid.RowDefinitions>
            <RowDefinition Height="Auto" />
            <RowDefinition Height="Auto" />
            <RowDefinition Height="Auto" />
        </Grid.RowDefinitions>
        <TextBlock x:Name="pixelResolution" />
        <TextBlock x:Name="displayResolution" Grid.Row="1" />
        <StackPanel Orientation="Horizontal"
                    Grid.Row="2">
            <TextBlock Text="Grid Actual Width: " />
            <TextBlock x:Name="gridWidthDetails"
                        Text="{Binding Path=ActualWidth, ElementName=mainGrid}" />
        </StackPanel>
    </Grid>
</Page>
```

Deploying this code to the WXGA 4.5-inch emulator results in the display shown in Figure 9-2.

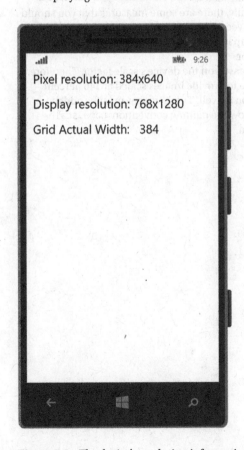

Figure 9-2. *The device's resolution information is displayed in the WVGA 4.5-inch emulator*

Notice that the actual width of the controls on the page are based on pixel resolution. You shouldn't concern yourself too much with each device's pixel measurements since you should not be using fixed measurements when designing your pages.

Scaling

If you rely on fixed measurements, you will notice that controls in your app may render just fine in one resolution but may appear too small or too large in another resolution. By using dynamic layouts and allowing the Windows Runtime system to handle the way in which elements are organized within the page, it ensures that your app will look consistent across devices regardless of the screen's pixel density.

Within Windows Phone applications, the system will automatically scale UI elements based on the following scale factors:

1.0: 100 percent, no scaling

1.4: 140 percent scaling

2.4: 240 percent scaling

The system determines which scale factor to use based on the device's physical screen size, screen resolution, screen DPI, and form factor. Notice that in Listing 9-1, we used the RawPixelsPerViewPixel property on the DisplayInformation class to determine the scale factor.

Although the Windows system handles scaling automatically, there are some measures that you should take when including images within your application. First, use vector-based graphics as much as possible since they scale up or down quite well. If you need to use bitmap images, add them as resources within your application and provide a separate image for each scaling factor.

The application will automatically load the proper image based on the device's scale factor. Therefore, for each original image that you include in your project, be sure to provide images scaled at 140 percent and 240 percent of the original image size within the application as well. These images must be added to the same folder within your application, and you should follow the naming convention: name.scale-scalefactor.ext. Figure 9-3 illustrates this naming convention.

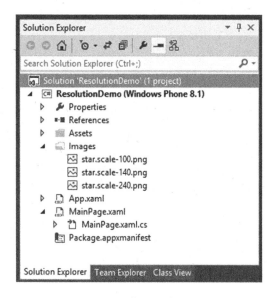

Figure 9-3. *Including images to support multiple scale factors*

Within your XAML, you can simply reference the image as follows: `<Image Source="Images/star.png" />`

Windows Phone will retrieve the appropriate image based on its determination of the scale factor to use based on the current device.

Run the app in each of the emulators. You should notice a result similar to that depicted in Figure 9-4.

■ **Tip** Notice in Figure 9-4 that the original image, `star.scale-100.png`, is not displayed. The Windows Phone 8.1 emulators only provide images with a scale factor greater than 1.0, so you will not see the original image when testing in the emulator.

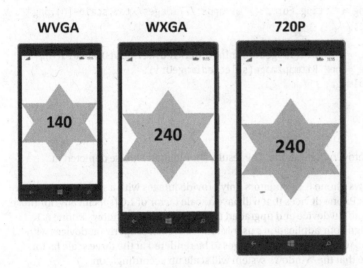

Figure 9-4. *Star image automatically loaded by Windows based on the scale factor*

As mentioned earlier, the Windows system determines which scale factor to use based on various properties of the current device, and it loads the image that is based on the calculated scaling factor threshold. When referencing the image from XAML using the base name of the file, without the scale factor included, Windows will locate the required file as long as you follow the file naming convention discussed earlier in this section.

Although XAML handles file loading without any effort on your part, you may encounter a situation where you will need to load bitmap images manually from the code-behind file. In this case, use the `RawPixelsPerViewPixel` property to determine which bitmap image to load based on the scale factor calculation: `RawPixelsPerViewPixel * 100`. On Windows Phone, there are only three scale factors for which you must account, so determining which image to load will take only a few lines of code, as shown in Listing 9-3.

Listing 9-3. Load a Bitmap Based on the Device's Scale Factor

```
using System;
...
using Windows.UI.Xaml;
using Windows.UI.Xaml.Controls;
using Windows.UI.Xaml.Navigation;
using Windows.Graphics.Display;
```

```
namespace ResolutionDemo
{
    ...
        protected override void OnNavigatedTo(NavigationEventArgs e)
        {
            DisplayInformation info = DisplayInformation.GetForCurrentView();
            double scaleFactor = info.RawPixelsPerViewPixel * 100;

            string selectedScaleFactor = (scaleFactor <= 100) ? "100" :
                                         (scaleFactor <= 140) ? "140" :
                                         "240";

            string imageUriString = string.Format(@"ms-appx:///Images/star.scale-{0}.png",
            selectedScaleFactor);

            Uri selectedImageUri = new Uri(imageUriString, UriKind.RelativeOrAbsolute);
            BitmapImage bmpImage = new BitmapImage(selectedImageUri);
            MyImage.Source = bmpImage;
        }
    }
}
```

Run the app in the various emulator configurations. The results should match those depicted in Figure 9-4.

As mentioned earlier, the Windows Phone 8.1 emulators only provide images with a scale factor greater than 1.0. However, there are Windows Phone devices that will have a scale factor of 1.0 (specifically, for those users who purchased a Windows Phone 8.0 device and upgraded the device's OS to Windows Phone 8.1 when it became available). If you design your application's user interface to look properly on devices with a minimum screen resolution of 384×640 and you provide images to be rendered at the three scale factors discussed earlier, then you will ensure that the Windows system will scale up accordingly on higher-resolution devices, and your UI will look and behave in a consistent manner across devices.

Themes, Resources, and Styles

Windows Phone systems use themes to control the visual representation of the system applications and third-party applications. A *theme* consists of a set of resources that define how visual elements are displayed on the device, and it is comprised of predefined settings for pages and UI controls, such as background colors, accent colors, font styles, and font sizes, for example.

Background and Accent Colors

The Windows Phone SDK provides two background color themes: Dark mode and Light mode. Dark theme mode displays with a black background, while Light theme mode displays with a white background.

Twenty accent colors are available in both Dark and Light theme modes, as shown in Figure 9-5.

Figure 9-5. Accent colors available in Windows Phone 8.1

To configure your theme on a Windows Phone, launch the Settings app, and select the start + theme item from the list. Figure 9-6 depicts the start + theme screen, which contains the selection lists for the background and accent color settings.

Figure 9-6. *Windows Phone devices run in Dark or Light theme modes, along with a configured accent color*

The reason that theming on Windows Phone is important to you is because any Windows Phone app that you may develop will automatically inherit the device's selected theme by default, unless you override the default theme with your own theme. However, it is still important to understand how themes work and to ensure that your application is visibly appealing when run on a device that is set either to Dark or Light theme mode.

Avoid explicitly configuring font text color to use White or Black; otherwise, you run the risk of the font disappearing against the same color background when the device theme is changed. Instead, make use of the predefined resources for Windows Phone to configure styles for visual elements in your application.

Theme Resources

The Windows Phone SDK provides multiple collections of predefined theme resources that you can leverage when styling your application. When configuring elements to use theme resources, you can be sure that the styles applied will correlate to the current theme that the device is currently configured to run.

Brush resources are available that define the standard color themes that are utilized within Windows Phone applications. It is best to use a brush resource, rather than a specific color, to ensure that your application adapts to any theme changes that are applied by the user. For example, using a predefined theme resource to set font color ensures that the color is not washed out against the current background theme. In Dark theme mode, the font color will be set to White, while in Light theme mode, the color will be set to Black. Table 9-2 lists the SolidColorBrush resources available on Windows Phone.

Table 9-2. *SolidColorBrush Resources*

Name	Description
PhoneAccentBrush	SolidColorBrush of the foreground color
PhoneForegroundBrush	SolidColorBrush of the foreground and border color
PhoneBackgroundBrush	SolidColorBrush of the default background color for pages and controls
PhoneContrastBackgroundBrush	SolidColorBrush used for the background color of contrasting elements
PhoneContrastForegroundBrush	SolidColorBrush used for the foreground color of contrasting elements
PhoneDisabledBrush	SolidColorBrush used for the disabled foreground and border color
PhoneSubtleBrush	Subtle foreground and border color brush
TransparentBrush	Provides transparent background on elements that apply this brush
PhoneSemitransparentBrush	Provides a partially transparent background brush
PhoneChromeBrush	SolidColorBrush used to match the Application Bar background in the current theme

If you require a resource type that returns Color rather than a SolidColorBrush type, Color resources are available that are in line with the available Brush resources, such as PhoneBackgroundColor, PhoneForegroundColor, PhoneDisabledColor, and so forth.

To reference a theme resource within your XAML markup, set the value of the property to a named ThemeResource as follows:

```
<object Property="{ThemeResource NamedResource}" />
```

For example, to set the Foreground color on a TextBlock to the device's accent color, add this markup to your page:

```
<TextBlock Foreground="{ThemeResource PhoneAccentBrush}" />
```

Font resources are available that define the font style and sizes you can leverage in your application, as listed in Table 9-3.

Table 9-3. *Font Size Resources*

Name	Value
TextStyleSmallFontSize	10.659
TextStyleMediumFontSize	16
TextStyleLargeFontSize	18.139
TextStyleExtraLargeFontSize	25.5
TextStyleExtraLargePlusFontSize	29.86
TextStyleExtraExtraLargeFontSize	34.139

Similar to Brush resources, configure the FontSize of your TextBlock elements to use the named ThemeResource:

```
<TextBlock FontSize="{ThemeResource TextStyleMediumFontSize}" />
```

Predefined Styles

Similar to predefined resources, the Windows Phone SDK provides predefined styles that you can use to maintain a consistent look and feel across TextBlock controls within your application. When adding a page to a Windows Phone 8.1 application, the Page background is configured to use the ApplicationBackground themed resource by default:

```
<Page Background="{ThemeResource ApplicationPageBackgroundThemeBrush}">
```

You can find the complete list of XAML theme resources that are available for your Windows Phone 8.1 applications on the MSDN site: http://bitly.com/XAMLThemeResources.

Application Architecture

When designing a Windows Phone Store application, it is important to understand the application architecture. Similar to WPF applications, the starting point for a Windows Phone application is the Application class, which determines the page that will be loaded on startup, contains shared resources and properties, and allows you to override, or register, application life-cycle events enabling custom behavior to be handled when the application is launched, activated, suspended, or resumed from a suspended state. Table 9-4 describes these key events.

Table 9-4. *The Main Application Life-Cycle Events on Windows Phone*

Life-Cycle Event	Override Event	Description
Launched	The override event is OnLaunched.	Windows Phone generates boilerplate code to handle this event. It is imperative that you leave that code intact; however, you may include additional code logic within this event. The LaunchActivatedEventArgs parameter is passed into this event, which provides useful information such as how the app was launched, the TileId that the user tapped to launch the app (if applicable), and the application's previous execution state.
Activated	The override event is OnActivated.	Override this event if you want to perform custom actions, such as updating and displaying any notifications that the user might have missed while the application was deactivated.
Suspending	No override. You must register an event handler. Here's an example: this.Suspending += this.OnSuspending;	Register an event handler for the Suspending event if you need to store the application's state, such as user data, to persistent storage. Your app may be automatically terminated by the operating system if it is running low on resources or shut down before the user is able to resume the app, so it is imperative to store application data at that point in time in order to ensure that the user does not experience data loss when returning to your app.
Resuming	No override. You must register an event handler. Here's an example: this.Resuming += this.OnResuming;	Register an event handler for the Resuming event if you need to restore the application's state from the data that was cached when it was suspended.

Page Orientation

Windows Phone enables you to design your pages such that they can be viewed in portrait and/or landscape mode. As long as you ensure that your layouts are dynamic, when the orientation is changed, your UI will adapt according to the changed height and width measurements based on the new orientation.

Within Windows Phone Store apps, you can set the supported orientations within the Application tab in the app's package manifest, named Package.appxmanifest. Double-click the package manifest in the Visual Studio Solution Explorer. You should see a view similar to what is depicted in Figure 9-7.

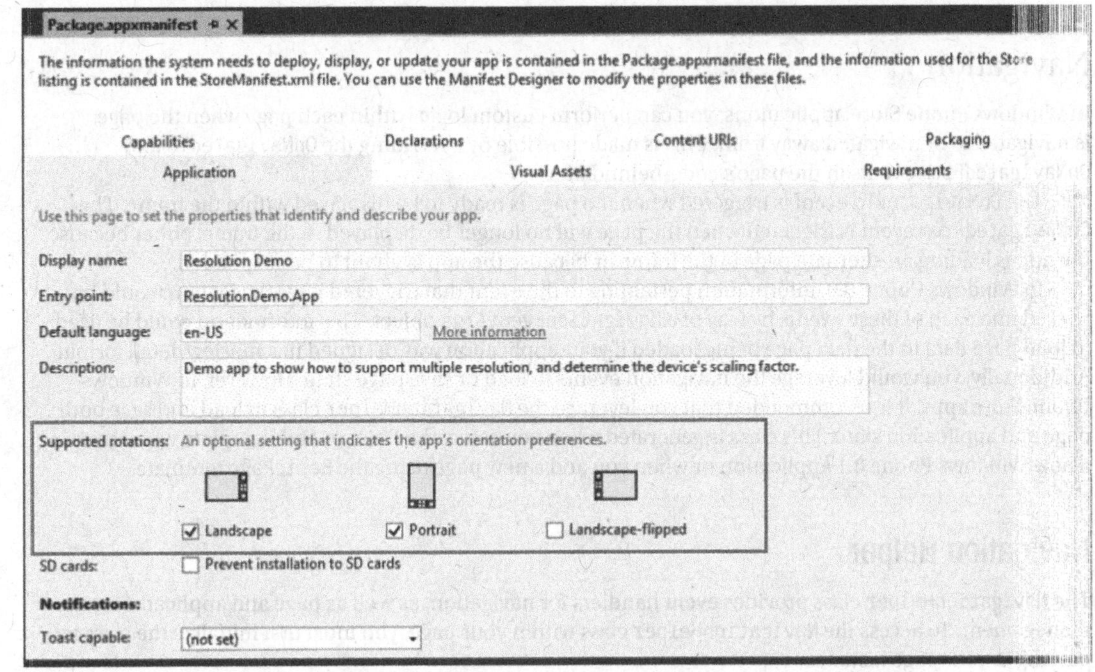

Figure 9-7. *Selecting the app's supported screen orientations in the package manifest*

The package manifest contains metadata about your application, including your application's entry point, which is the Application class by default. It also includes the tile images and application logo, device features or capabilities that your application will leverage, hardware that the device must support for your app to work as expected, and packaging details that will be displayed in the Windows Phone Store when the app is published.

You may also select which orientations your application will support by ensuring that each supported orientation is checked, as shown in Figure 9-7. Configuring your application's orientation setting in the package manifest will ensure that all of the pages within your app will support the selected orientations.

Alternatively, you may prefer to set the supported orientations from each page's code-behind individually. The advantage to this approach is that you can set the supported orientation to a different value on a page-by-page basis by setting the value of the AutoRotationPreferences property on the DisplayInformation class.

For example, let's say you are developing a game in which the main game play screen must run in landscape mode only, while the app's settings page will be displayed in portrait mode only. In the OnNavigatedTo event within your MainPage, include the following line of code to support landscape and landscape flipped orientations: DisplayInformation.AutoRotationPreferences = DisplayOrientations. LandscapeFlipped | DisplayOrientations.Landscape;

In the OnNavigatedTo event within your SettingsPage, simply set the AutoRotationPreferences property as follows:

```
DisplayInformation.AutoRotationPreferences = DisplayOrientations.Portrait;
```

Navigation

In Windows Phone Store applications, you can perform custom logic within each page when the page is navigated to or navigated away from. This is made possible by overriding the OnNavigatedTo and OnNavigatedFrom events in the page's code-behind file.

The OnNavigatedTo event is triggered when the page is ready to be displayed within the frame. The OnNavigatedFrom event is triggered when the page will no longer be displayed in the frame, either because the app is loading an alternate page in the frame or because the app is about to be suspended.

In Windows Phone 8.0, information pertaining to the event that triggered page navigation would be passed into each of these events by way of a NavigationEventArgs object. This information could be used to load page data in the next page being loaded if your application was designed in a master/detail format. Additionally, you would leverage the navigation events to load or save page state. However, in Windows Phone Store apps, it is recommended that you leverage the NavigationHelper class to load and save both page and application state. This class is generated when you select the Pivot or Hub template when creating a new Windows Phone 8.1 application or when you add a new page using the BasicPage template.

Navigation Helper

The NavigationHelper class provides event handlers for navigation, as well as page and application state management. To access the NavigationHelper class within your page, you must first initialize the class by passing in your page instance.

If you want to manage page or application state, you can then wire up the LoadState and SaveState events within the code-behind of your pages. When you create a page using the BasicPage template, this code is generated for you, as shown in Listing 9-4.

Listing 9-4. NavigationHelper Code That Is Generated When Creating a Page from the BasicPage Template

```
public sealed partial class DetailsPage : Page
{
    private NavigationHelper navigationHelper;
    private ObservableDictionary defaultViewModel = new ObservableDictionary();

    public DetailsPage()
    {
        this.InitializeComponent();

        this.navigationHelper = new NavigationHelper(this);
        this.navigationHelper.LoadState += this.NavigationHelper_LoadState;
        this.navigationHelper.SaveState += this.NavigationHelper_SaveState;
    }
```

```
    public NavigationHelper NavigationHelper
    {
        get { return this.navigationHelper; }
    }

    private void NavigationHelper_LoadState(object sender, LoadStateEventArgs e)
    {
    }

    private void NavigationHelper_SaveState(object sender, SaveStateEventArgs e)
    {
    }

    #region NavigationHelper registration

    protected override void OnNavigatedTo(NavigationEventArgs e)
    {
        this.navigationHelper.OnNavigatedTo(e);
    }

    protected override void OnNavigatedFrom(NavigationEventArgs e)
    {
        this.navigationHelper.OnNavigatedFrom(e);
    }

    #endregion
}
```

When the page is loading, leverage the NavigationHelper_LoadState event to retrieve application state from your chosen data store location, whether it is local storage, a local database, or in the cloud.

When the app is suspending or when the user is navigating to an alternate page, make use of the NavigationHelper_SaveState to store any transient UI data so that it can be retrieved and loaded into the page when the user navigates back to the page or resumes the application.

Page Navigation

Even the simplest of applications may require page navigation to at least one additional page, if only to load a basic Settings or Support page for the user. When developing a Windows Phone Store application from one of the available built-in templates, the application's navigation code to launch the main page is generated for you in the OnLaunched event in the App.xaml.cs file, as shown in Listing 9-5. This is an example of the way that navigation is handled in Windows Phone Store applications, and it serves as the approach that you will take in managing navigation for any other pages.

Listing 9-5. First Page Navigation in the Application's OnLaunched Event

```
Frame rootFrame = Window.Current.Content as Frame;
...
// When the navigation stack isn't restored navigate to the first page,
// configuring the new page by passing required information as a navigation
// parameter
```

```
if (!rootFrame.Navigate(typeof(MainPage), e.Arguments))
{
    throw new Exception("Failed to create initial page");
}
```

What did you notice about how navigation is handled? It appears that a frame, rather than the main window, controls navigation.

Windows Phone Store applications run within a single window. When the application launches, a frame is created and is set as the window's content, which can be accessed through the `Window.Current.Content` property. The frame serves as the host container for pages, not the window. In this way, it is the frame that triggers and tracks navigation between pages. To utilize the frame to navigate to a specific page, simply cast the `Window.Current.Content` property as a frame and then call the `Navigate` method, passing in the type of page that you want to load, as was demonstrated in Listing 9-5.

What happens when you need to pass information to the next page? For example, if your main page displays a list of items, what happens when a user taps an item? Will it navigate to a detailed page containing more information about the item selected? In this case, you may choose to pass a unique item ID so that the Details page knows which item information to load into the page. You can simply pass in this additional information to the target page as the second parameter in the `Navigate` method as follows:

```
Frame.Navigate(typeof(DetailsPage), itemId);
```

The second parameter expects an object type, so you are not limited by the data that you want to send to the next page. Now that you've passed the necessary information to the Details page, how is it received and processed before the next page loads? If you take another look at the code in Listing 9-5, you will see that the frame is passing the argument to the `DetailsPage`, which in turn receives the information in its `NavigationEventArgs` parameter. It then passes it on to the `OnNavigatedTo` event in the `NavigationHelperClass`, which triggers the `LoadState` event to be raised in the target page. Your original parameter will be passed into the `LoadStateEventArgs` object, which you can retrieve from its `NavigationParameter` property, as shown in Listing 9-6.

Listing 9-6. Retrieving the NavigationParameter Passed into the DetailsPage

```
private void NavigationHelper_LoadState(object sender, LoadStateEventArgs e)
{
    if (e.NavigationParameter != null)
    {
        int itemId = -1;
        int.TryParse(e.NavigationParameter.ToString(), out itemId);
        if (itemId > 0)
        {
            //then load your item's details
        }
    }
}
```

Backward Navigation

Backward page navigation occurs when users travel back through the history of pages that they have loaded within the application, similar to hitting the Back button in a browser window. The behavior to which Windows Phone users have grown accustomed involves traveling through the page history, referred to as the *backstack*, using the device's back key. This is related to Windows Phone original design principles.

In Windows Phone Silverlight apps, the device's back key would navigate through the backstack. Once at the main page, if there were no further pages within the backstack, hitting the back key would then close the application and return the user either to another previously launched app or to the Start screen.

In Windows Phone Store apps, this has changed. The device's back key closes the app by default, even when there are pages in the backstack. Therefore, you will first need to override this behavior to check for a backstack history and then navigate through the backstack, instead of closing the application.

As mentioned earlier, the frame is responsible for tracking page navigation. The frame stores the history of navigation within its BackStack property, which returns a list of PageStackEntry objects. The PageStackEntry list is comprised of the pages that were loaded by the application in the order they were loaded. To navigate back to the previous page within your app, you should check to determine whether there are pages on the backstack using the Boolean property Frame.CanGoBack. If it returns true, there are page entries within the frame's BackStack, and you may then initiate the backward navigation by calling the GoBack() method on the frame.

The next step is to include this code when the device's hardware back key is pressed. You can achieve this by wiring up the HardwareButtons.BackPressed event, which is contained within the Windows.Phone. UI.Input namespace. You can register this event within each page, as shown in Listing 9-7.

Listing 9-7. Overriding the Keypress Event of the Device's Back Button

```
public DetailsPage ()
{
    this.InitializeComponent();
    Windows.Phone.UI.Input.HardwareButtons.BackPressed += OnHardButtonsBackPressed;
}

private void OnHardButtonsBackPressed(object sender, Windows.Phone.UI.Input.
BackPressedEventArgs e)
{
    if (this.Frame.CanGoBack)
    {
        e.Handled = true;
        this.Frame.GoBack();
    }
}
```

Once you manually handle backward navigation, you must cancel the default backward navigation behavior by setting e.Handled = true. This will ensure that your application is not closed accidentally.

Additionally, if a page within your application displays a pop-up dialog, you will want to account for this in your BackPressed event as well. The first check to include will determine whether the pop-up dialog is open. If it is, the first tap of the hardware back key should close the pop-up. The next tap of the hardware back key should then check whether there is a page in the BackStack to allow backward navigation. If so, it should then navigate to the previous page. Finally, if there is no pop-up dialog open or any pages in the BackStack, the tap of the back button should then close the application. This action requires no code, since it is the default behavior when the button is tapped. Be sure to cancel navigation only when you are performing an action as a result of the button tap. Canceling backward navigation if neither of the earlier conditions is met will cause your user to be stuck within your application with nowhere to go. This will ensure that your application will fail certification when submitted to the Windows Phone Store.

■ **Tip** When creating a Windows Phone Store application using either the Pivot or Hub template, you will not need to handle the BackPressed event of the device's back button manually, because this code is already wired up within a NavigationHelper class. It includes commands that handle backward navigation, and it provides a common override for the hardware's BackPressed event. This is a cleaner implementation, which saves you from writing the same code within each page to manage the BackPressed event manually.

Caching Pages

Windows Phone Store apps now include the option to cache pages upon navigation. This is configured using the NavigationCacheMode property on each page, which accepts one of the following enumeration values:

>   NavigationCacheMode.Disabled: Always load a new instance of the page when navigating to the page.

>   NavigationCacheMode.Enabled: The page is cached, but this may be destroyed if the cache limit is exceeded.

>   NavigationCacheMode.Required: The page is cached, and the cache instance is loaded when the user navigates to the page.

In this way, you can configure whether a new instance of the page will always be created each time user navigates to the page or whether a loaded instance of the page will be saved in the cache and then loaded from cache on subsequent visits to that page. Caching pages will result in improved application performance. By default, the NavigationCacheMode is set to Disabled. If you want to make use of page caching, you will need to configure the NavigationCacheMode explicitly within each page's constructor.

Templates

A *template* is used in XAML to configure the presentation of data within a view. A common scenario in which templates are utilized includes designing the display for a collection of items. Since the items may be objects of any type, you need to tell the host container what information to display from that object and how to present it.

DataTemplate

A DataTemplate represents the visual display of an object, and it supports data binding to user controls that are included in the template, if the controls expose dependency properties to which to bind. There are various ways to define a DataTemplate. To define a DataTemplate in XAML, you simply need to wrap the desired content within a DataTemplate element, as follows:

```
<DataTemplate>
    <StackPanel Orientation="Horizontal">
        <Image Source="{Binding CompanyLogo}" />
        <TextBox Text="{Binding CompanyName}" />
    </StackPanel>
</DataTemplate>
```

A DataTemplate is similar to a Page in that it expects a single object to be set as its content. Therefore, to support multiple items within a DataTemplate, you must use a container control, such as a StackPanel or Grid. The content of a DataTemplate is contained within a property called VisualTree.

You can define a DataTemplate within the application resources dictionary in the App.xaml file or within a specific page's resources dictionary; however, you must then assign it a unique key value.

```
<DataTemplate x:Key="MyDataTemplate">
```

Now that you have the DataTemplate defined as a resource, which makes use of data binding, you are likely asking yourself the following questions:

- How do I make use of a DataTemplate within a view?
- Where do I set the DataContext so that the DataTemplate knows from where to retrieve the data-bound properties?
- Does the DataTemplate always have to be defined as an application or page resource?

Well, to answer the first question, collection-based controls, such as the ComboBox, ListView, and GridView are able to leverage a DataTemplate as long as it is assigned to the control's ItemTemplate property.

We will discuss the answers to the second and third questions in the next section, as we cover the ItemTemplate property in detail.

ItemTemplate

Controls that display an items list, such as the ComboBox, ListView, and GridView controls, expose a property named ItemTemplate, which is used to set and retrieve a single DataTemplate object. The template assigned to the ItemTemplate property will be applied to each item displayed within the control.

Another option for configuring a DataTemplate, aside from defining it as a page or application resource, is to define it as the content for the control's ItemTemplate property in XAML. For example, to configure the ItemTemplate for a ListView, you would include the following markup:

```
<ListView ItemsSource="{Binding Companies}" >
    <ListView.ItemTemplate>
        <DataTemplate>
            <StackPanel Orientation="Horizontal">
                <Image Source="{Binding CompanyLogo}" />
                <TextBox Text="{Binding CompanyName}" />
            </StackPanel>
        </DataTemplate>
    </ListView.ItemTemplate>
</ListView>
```

The markup for GridView or ComboBox will be similar, just replacing ListView in the element tag with the name of the desired control. When configuring a DataTemplate in this way, you will not need to set a key on the template, because the template is applicable only to this control, and it cannot be referenced by any other control.

When the DataTemplate is defined within the application or page resource dictionary, you must set the ItemTemplate property to refer to this resource using the template's assigned key as follows:

```
<ListView ItemTemplate="{StaticResource MyDataTemplate}">
```

As mentioned in the previous section, data templates support data binding, but how does the template know where the data is coming from? The list item's object serves as the `DataContext` for the binding. Therefore, when binding properties within the `DataTemplate`, they must map to properties that exist within the list item; otherwise, a binding error will occur silently at runtime, and data will not be displayed within the list.

Displaying Collections

The most common types of mobile applications involve displaying and managing lists in some way, shape, or form. How many apps do you use that deal with data collections? Popular apps that come to mind include Twitter, Facebook, Vine, and SnapChat. Then there are the standard utility apps, such as e-mail, address book, and device settings. All of these applications allow you to view and manage data.

In Windows Phone Store applications, you can use the `ListView` or `GridView` control to display a collection of items. To populate either of these controls, set the `ItemsSource` property either within XAML or in the code-behind. Within XAML, you can use data binding to set the control's `ItemsSource` to a static collection defined as a resource in the page. Here's an example:

```
<ListView ItemsSource="{StaticResource Companies}">
```

However, in most cases, the collection will change while the user has the application open. Items can be added, removed, or modified through user interaction, application updates can be received from a web service, or both. In this case, your good MVVM practices will come in handy to make short work of this task. Simply add an `ObservableCollection` within the view model that you created for your view, and bind the collection to the `ItemsSource` property, as follows:

```
<ListView ItemsSource="{Binding Companies}">
```

As mentioned within the "Templates" section earlier in this chapter, each item displayed within the `ListView` or `GridView` will use the `ItemsSource` collection as the `DataContext` by default. As long as the controls defined within your control's `DataTemplate` is configured to bind to properties exposed by the collection item's type, then data will flow through to the UI, populating the collection-based control as expected.

ListView

A `ListView` is used to display items in a vertical, scrolling list. Oftentimes, the lists are configured such that when a user taps an item, the application navigates to a Details page to display more information about the selected item. Figure 9-8 depicts an example of using the `ListView` control within the main page of the application to display a list of companies.

Figure 9-8. *Items within the ListView control are displayed as a vertical, scrolling list*

Notice that the ListView items consist of a combination of controls, using an ItemTemplate, as discussed in the previous section. This enables you to design items that are visually appealing by displaying data in a unique way, incorporating images, text, and any other controls to display item information.

The ListView control's selection behavior may be configured using the SelectionMode property, which may be set to one the following enumeration values:

> Single: A single item is selected when the user taps the item. SelectionMode is set to Single by default.

> Multiple: Displays a check box next to each item in the list, enabling multiple item selections. The user must place a check mark next to each item of interest.

> None: Item selection is not enabled.

When an item is tapped in the list, the ListView's SelectionChanged event is triggered, as long as its SelectionMode is set to Single or Multiple. It is possible to wire up a handler to this event to provide custom logic based on list item selections, such as navigating to another page. This may be accomplished in XAML by setting the SelectionChanged attribute to the name of your event handler. Here's an example:

```
<ListView x:Name="CompanyListView" SelectionChanged="OnListViewSelectionChanged">.
```

Or, you may register the event in the page's code-behind as follows:

```
CompanyListView.SelectionChanged += OnListViewSelectionChanged;
```

The SelectionChanged event expects two parameters: an object that represents the sender and the event argument type, SelectionChangedEventArgs. Since you named the event handler OnListViewSelectionChanged, you need to add the following handler within the code-behind.

```
private void OnListViewSelectionChanged(object sender, SelectionChangedEventArgs e)
{
}
```

The SelectionChangedEventArgs exposes two properties of interest: AddedItems and RemovedItems. The AddedItems collection contains the item (or items) that the user selected in the ListView. The RemovedItems collection contains the item (or items) that were deselected.

Alternatively, you can determine which item was selected by checking the ListView's SelectedItem property when running in single selection mode or by checking the SelectedItems collection when running in multiple selection mode. Let's take a look at how this all comes together.

Listing 9-8 illustrates an example of wiring up the SelectionChanged event on the ListView control within the XAML markup. Notice that you don't specify a SelectionMode. In this case, the ListView will enable single item selection by default.

Listing 9-8. Configuring the SelectionChanged Event in the ListView to Capture When an Item Selection Occurs

```
<ListView x:Name="CompanyListView"
        ItemsSource="{Binding Companies}"
          SelectionChanged="OnListViewSelectionChanged">
    <ListView.ItemTemplate>
        <DataTemplate>
            <StackPanel Orientation="Horizontal">
                <Image Source="{Binding LogoImagePath}" />
                <TextBlock Text="{Binding CompanyName}"
                        VerticalAlignment="Center"
                        Margin="10,0,0,0"
                        FontSize="{StaticResource TextStyleLargeFontSize}" />

            </StackPanel>
        </DataTemplate>
    </ListView.ItemTemplate>
</ListView>
```

Following along with the example shown in the XAML markup, set the ListView control's ItemsSource to an ObservableCollection, where each item in the list represents a Company model. Design the ItemTemplate to display the company's logo and name. The Company model is defined as follows:

```
public class Company
{
    public string CompanyName { get; set; }
    public string LogoImagePath { get; set; }
    public string Headquarters { get; set; }
    public int YearFounded { get; set; }
}
```

Next you will need to add some logic to the custom event handler that was added to the code-behind. In this example, you simply want to navigate to a Details page when an item is tapped in the list. To accomplish this, add a page to the project that will be used to display additional information about the selected item. As mentioned in the "Page Navigation" section earlier in this chapter, use the BasicPage template when adding a new page to the project so that the navigation helper methods are generated as well. Within this new page, named DetailsPage, include XAML markup to display the company name, logo, and additional details about the company. Listing 9-9 depicts sample XAML markup to accomplish this, along with some basic styling and spacing to provide a clean, polished look.

Listing 9-9. Details Page Containing Markup to Display Additional Company Information

```
<Page
    x:Class="ListViewDemo.DetailsPage"
    xmlns="http://schemas.microsoft.com/winfx/2006/xaml/presentation"
    xmlns:x="http://schemas.microsoft.com/winfx/2006/xaml"
    xmlns:d="http://schemas.microsoft.com/expression/blend/2008"
    xmlns:mc="http://schemas.openxmlformats.org/markup-compatibility/2006"
    mc:Ignorable="d"
    Background="{ThemeResource ApplicationPageBackgroundThemeBrush}">
    <Page.Resources>
        <Style TargetType="TextBlock">
            <Setter Property="FontSize"
                    Value="{StaticResource TextStyleMediumFontSize}" />
            <Setter Property="Margin"
                    Value="10" />
        </Style>
    </Page.Resources>
    <Grid x:Name="LayoutRoot"
        DataContext="{Binding SelectedCompany}">
        <Grid.ChildrenTransitions>
            <TransitionCollection>
                <EntranceThemeTransition/>
            </TransitionCollection>
        </Grid.ChildrenTransitions>

        <Grid.RowDefinitions>
            <RowDefinition Height="Auto"/>
            <RowDefinition Height="*"/>
        </Grid.RowDefinitions>

        <StackPanel Grid.Row="0" Margin="19,0,0,0" Orientation="Horizontal">
            <Image Source="{Binding LogoImagePath}"
                   VerticalAlignment="Center"/>
            <TextBlock Text="{Binding CompanyName}"
                       VerticalAlignment="Center"
                       Margin="10,0"
                       Style="{ThemeResource HeaderTextBlockStyle}"
                       CharacterSpacing="{ThemeResource PivotHeaderItemCharacterSpacing}"/>
        </StackPanel>

        <Grid Grid.Row="1"
              x:Name="ContentRoot"
```

```
                    Margin="19,30,19,0">
                <Grid.RowDefinitions>
                    <RowDefinition Height="Auto"/>
                    <RowDefinition Height="Auto" />
                </Grid.RowDefinitions>
                <Grid.ColumnDefinitions>
                    <ColumnDefinition Width="Auto"/>
                    <ColumnDefinition/>
                </Grid.ColumnDefinitions>
                <TextBlock Text="Founded:" />
                <TextBlock Text="{Binding YearFounded}"
                        Grid.Column="1" />
                <TextBlock Text="Headquarters:"
                        Grid.Row="1" />
                <TextBlock Text="{Binding Headquarters}"
                        TextWrapping="Wrap"
                        Grid.Row="1"
                        Grid.Column="1" />

        </Grid>
    </Grid>
</Page>
```

Note that the LayoutRoot Grid has its DataContext set to a SelectedCompany property. Ideally, you will create a ViewModel for the DetailsPage, which exposes this property. Momentarily, you will need to set the ViewModel's SelectedCompany property to the company that the user tapped on the MainPage. To achieve this, you need to make sure you are passing the selected company to the DetailsPage.

Within the MainPage code-behind, in the OnListViewSelectionChanged event handler, add the code to check the SelectedItem property on the ListView control, and navigate to the DetailsPage passing the selected Company as a parameter to the secondary page, as shown in Listing 9-10.

Listing 9-10. Modifying the SelectionChanged Event Handler to Navigate to the DetailsPage When a ListView Item Is Tapped

```
private void OnListViewSelectionChanged(object sender, SelectionChangedEventArgs e)
{
    if (CompanyView.SelectedItem != null)
    {
        this.Frame.Navigate(typeof (DetailsPage), CompanyView.SelectedItem);
    }
}
```

Last but not least, within the NavigationHelper_LoadState in the DetailsPage, retrieve the selected Company object from the LoadStateEventArgs.NavigationParameter property and set it to the ViewModel's SelectedCompany property, as shown in Listing 9-11.

Listing 9-11. Set the DataContext of the DetailsPage to the Selected Company

```
private DetailsViewModel viewModel = new DetailsViewModel();

private void NavigationHelper_LoadState(object sender, LoadStateEventArgs e)
{
    Company selectedCompany = e.NavigationParameter as Company;
```

```
    if (selectedCompany != null)
    {
        viewModel.SelectedCompany = selectedCompany;
    }

    this.DataContext = viewModel;
}
```

Run the application, and tap an item in the list to view additional details about the company, as shown in Figure 9-9.

Figure 9-9. *Navigating to a details page containing more information about the company that was tapped in the ListView*

GridView

The GridView is similar to the ListView, except that it renders items in a grid rather than as a list. Items within the collection are displayed horizontally and wrap around to the next row. Its behavior is similar to the WrapPanel control discussed in Chapter 8, in the section "Container Controls." The GridView is suited for displaying an image gallery or for creating a cardview-style layout.

The GridView shares many of the same properties and events as the ListView control because both items derive from the same type: ListViewBase. In the ListView demo, we referenced properties and events that are also available in the GridView. We can change the element markup on the MainPage to reference GridView instead of ListView and run it without errors. The display may not be as appealing, as shown in Figure 9-10, but it works nonetheless.

Figure 9-10. *Modified MainPage to render the collection in a GridView control*

The layout defined in the ItemTemplate for the ListView control does not look as appealing when used within a GridView. Let's change it so that only the company logos are displayed. Remove the TextBlock from the GridView's ItemTemplate markup, and add a Margin to the StackPanel to provide proper spacing between each company logo, as follows:

```
<GridView.ItemTemplate>
    <DataTemplate>
        <StackPanel Margin="5,10,0,0">
            <Image Source="{Binding LogoImagePath}"
                    Stretch="None"/>
        </StackPanel>
    </DataTemplate>
</GridView.ItemTemplate>
```

Run the application. The changes to MainPage should appear, as shown in Figure 9-11.

Figure 9-11. *Modifying the ItemTemplate within the GridView to display company logos only*

With the MainPage displayed, tap an item in the GridView to navigate to the DetailsPage. It just worked without requiring any additional code changes. The implementation details of handling the SelectionChanged event is no different from what we demonstrated for the ListView control.

Presentation Controls

In Chapter 8, we discussed the various container controls that you can utilize to manage the layout of user controls within a view. In Windows Phone 8.1, many of those container controls are available, including the StackPanel, Grid, and Canvas to name a few. All of the knowledge that you acquired about these controls in Chapter 8 is transferable to Windows Phone because the markup and behavior is the same. In this chapter, we will focus on the various content presentation controls that are available in Windows Phone 8.1.

Presentation controls are another form of container controls. The difference from standard container controls is that the approach used to arrange UI controls within a single page is transparent to the user. Your users don't care if you used a StackPanel over a Grid, and why would they? As long as they can do whatever it is they need to do in your app, then that is all that matters, and five-star reviews will follow, right? Well, not quite.

You really have to impress your user and provide them with a great experience within your application. Presentation controls will help you to do just that. They are a set of advanced controls that set the tone for the manner in which a user will interact with your application. However, they should be used only when it makes sense to do so, such as for applications that will provide multiple sections or lists of data and when you want to present it in an appealing, easy-to-navigate layout. For applications, such as games or simple utility apps, these controls will not be necessary.

Hub

The *Hub control* is used to display a series of sections containing data or controls. The user can view the various sections by panning from side to side. In Windows Phone 8.0, this was known as the *Panorama control*. The visual elements defined within the Hub control extend beyond the bounds of the screen's width so that as a user swipes left or right, it feels as though they haven't left the main page. They are just shifting their view to see the items that are off-screen.

The layered effects of a background image, data overlay, and built-in animations within the Hub control provide an appealing visual user experience when panning across the sections, giving the user the feeling of scrolling across the page of a magazine.

Since the main purpose of the Hub control is to allow users to move through the view from side to side, this control is supported in Portrait mode only.

The Hub control is comprised of the following main elements:

- ***Background image***: Setting a background image on a Hub control is optional. However, this is a major aspect that adds to the visual appeal of this control.

- ***Hub header***: This consists of plain text and/or an image representing the application. For example, use an image that matches the one displayed on the application's tile. Ideally, the header will enable users to identify easily which application they are using.

- ***Hub section***: This contains controls or additional data in a logical grouping. For example, a Hub section may contain a gallery of images, while another section is comprised of status updates from a social media feed. A Hub control may be made up of one or more Hub sections; however, for performance reasons and for an optimal user experience, do not exceed five sections.

- ***Hub section header***: Including a section header is not required. If a header is specified, make sure that it describes the intent of the section with a single word or short phrase.

- ***Thumbnails***: These may be used as a navigation source to display additional data or media on a secondary page.

Let's take a look at a Hub control in action. Launch Visual Studio to create a new project, and select the Hub App (Windows Phone) template, as shown in Figure 9-12.

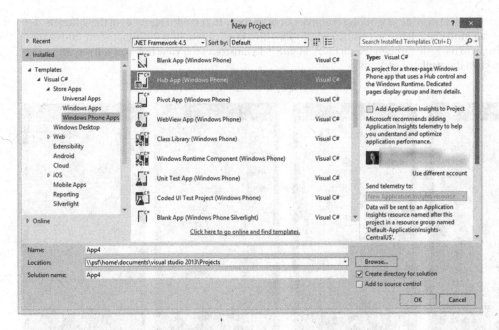

Figure 9-12. *Creating a new Hub app using the Visual Studio template*

Once the project is loaded into Visual Studio, take a moment to inspect the XAML that was generated in the HubPage.xaml file, as shown in Listing 9-12.

Listing 9-12. Markup Generated for the Windows Phone Hub Page

```
<Hub x:Name="Hub"
    x:Uid="Hub"
    Header="application name"
    Background="{ThemeResource HubBackgroundImageBrush}">
        <HubSection x:Uid="HubSection1"
                    Header="SECTION 1"
                    DataContext="{Binding Groups}"
                    HeaderTemplate="{ThemeResource HubSectionHeaderTemplate}">
            <DataTemplate>
                ...
            </DataTemplate>
        </HubSection>
    <HubSection x:Uid="HubSection2"
                    Header="SECTION 2"
                    DataContext="{Binding Groups}"
                    HeaderTemplate="{ThemeResource HubSectionHeaderTemplate}">
            <DataTemplate>
                ...
            </DataTemplate>
        </HubSection>
    ...
</Hub>
```

The Hub template provides a working example out of the box. To provide examples of the different layouts, you can implement it in each section within your own application. Run the application, and swipe from left to right to navigate through the sections. Figure 9-13 illustrates the view that you will see when looking at each of the available sections.

Figure 9-13. *The Hub control provides an appealing panning effect when swiping across to view the hub sections*

Each Hub section uses a `DataTemplate` to configure the section's appearance, layout, and UI controls. Within each section, you can lay out the UI elements as needed, making use of the `ListView` or `GridView` controls to host item collections and wiring up `SelectionChanged` events to trigger navigation to supplementary details pages, as we discussed in the previous section.

Pivot

The Windows Phone *Pivot control* enables the display of one or more data sets as a list, with each list being displayed as a Pivot Item. The user can navigate between the Pivot Items by swiping from right to left, or from left to right. The Pivot control is useful for displaying large data sets and filtering on a specific data set. You can allow users to drill down to view more details about a specific item displayed in the Pivot Item's list by tapping the item to navigate to a secondary page containing further information.

Now take a moment to create a Windows Phone Pivot app to inspect the markup and code that is automatically generated. Launch Visual Studio and select the Pivot App (Windows Phone) template. Once the project is loaded in Visual Studio, take a moment to inspect the XAML that was generated in the `PivotPage.xaml` file, as shown in Listing 9-13.

Listing 9-13. Markup for Windows Phone Pivot Page

```
<Pivot x:Uid="Pivot" Title="MY APPLICATION"
       x:Name="pivot"
       CommonNavigationTransitionInfo.IsStaggerElement="True">
    <!--Pivot item one-->
    <PivotItem
```

```xml
        x:Uid="PivotItem1"
        Margin="19,14.5,0,0"
        Header="first"
        DataContext="{Binding FirstGroup}"
        CommonNavigationTransitionInfo.IsStaggerElement="True">
        <ListView
            ItemsSource="{Binding Items}"
            IsItemClickEnabled="True"
            ItemClick="ItemView_ItemClick"
            ContinuumNavigationTransitionInfo.ExitElementContainer="True">
            <ListView.ItemTemplate>
                <DataTemplate>
                    <StackPanel Margin="0,0,0,9.5">
                        <TextBlock
                            Text="{Binding Title}"
                            TextWrapping="Wrap"
                            Pivot.SlideInAnimationGroup="1"
                            CommonNavigationTransitionInfo.IsStaggerElement="True"
                            Style="{ThemeResource ListViewItemTextBlockStyle}"
                            Margin="0,0,19,0"/>
                        <TextBlock
                            Text="{Binding Description}"
                            TextWrapping="WrapWholeWords"
                            Pivot.SlideInAnimationGroup="2"
                            CommonNavigationTransitionInfo.IsStaggerElement="True"
                            Style="{ThemeResource ListViewItemContentTextBlockStyle}"
                            Margin="0,0,19,0"/>
                    </StackPanel>
                </DataTemplate>
            </ListView.ItemTemplate>
        </ListView>
</PivotItem>

<!--Pivot item two-->
<PivotItem
        x:Uid="PivotItem2"
        Margin="19,14.5,0,0"
        Header="second"
        DataContext="{Binding SecondGroup}">
        <!--Double line list no text wrapping-->
        <ListView
            ItemsSource="{Binding Items}"
            IsItemClickEnabled="True"
            ItemClick="ItemView_ItemClick"
            Loaded="SecondPivot_Loaded"
            ContinuumNavigationTransitionInfo.ExitElementContainer="True">
            <ListView.ItemTemplate>
                <DataTemplate>
                    <StackPanel Margin="0,0,0,9.5">
                        <TextBlock
                            Text="{Binding Title}"
```

```
                            Pivot.SlideInAnimationGroup="1"
                            CommonNavigationTransitionInfo.IsStaggerElement="True"
                            Style="{StaticResource ListViewItemTextBlockStyle}"/>
                        <TextBlock
                            Text="{Binding Description}"
                            Pivot.SlideInAnimationGroup="2"
                            CommonNavigationTransitionInfo.IsStaggerElement="True"
                            Style="{StaticResource ListViewItemContentTextBlockStyle}"/>
                    </StackPanel>
                </DataTemplate>
            </ListView.ItemTemplate>
        </ListView>
    </PivotItem>
</Pivot>
```

Similar to the Hub template, the Pivot App template provides a working example out of the box. Figure 9-14 depicts a Pivot control with two Pivot Items.

Figure 9-14. *The Pivot control displays content within Pivot Items, which can be viewed by swiping from side to side*

Each item is comprised of a ListView to display the same data collection styled in various ways. In a real-world application, the lists would be distinct and separate, providing different collections of pertinent data. For example, a Recipes app may provide sections to separate breakfast, lunch, dinner, and dessert recipes.

Application Bar

In the previous sections, we demonstrated how to display items within collections-based controls, triggering navigation to an alternate page when items in the list are tapped. However, what happens when you want to perform an action on the selected item aside from page navigation? How would you provide menu actions to enable users to add or delete items from the list?

The Windows Phone SDK includes an *Application Bar*, which should be used for this purpose, as shown in Figure 9-15.

Figure 9-15. An Application Bar provides quick access to actions that can be performed on the current page

Note that we are leveraging the Companies application, which was developed as part of the "*Displaying Collections*" section earlier in this chapter. Simply modify the CompanyListView control to enable multiple item selection by setting its SelectionMode property to Multiple, and remove the event registration for the OnSelectionChanged event, since we will take action on selected items only when an Application Bar button is tapped.

Now, let's add the Application Bar to the page, as depicted in Figure 9-15. The Application Bar within a Windows Phone application must reside at the bottom of the page, according to Windows Phone Design Principles. The Application Bar is able to display up to four action buttons. These buttons should be used for quick actions that affect the data on the current page.

The Application Bar also provides an area for secondary commands, or menu items, which the user can access by tapping the ellipsis button, as shown in Figure 9-16.

Figure 9-16. *Tap the ellipsis button to reveal AppBar button labels and additional menu items*

Secondary commands can be used to initiate actions that may not necessarily be relevant to the current page. For example, providing an action to rate the application or a link to navigate to a settings page are good candidates for secondary command actions.

To add an Application Bar within a Windows Phone page, add the following markup within the Page element:

```
<Page.BottomAppBar>
    <CommandBar>
        <AppBarButton Label="add"
                      Icon="Add"
                      Click="AddAppBarButton_Click" />
        <CommandBar.SecondaryCommands>
            <AppBarButton Label="settings"
                      Click="SettingsButton_OnClick" />
        </CommandBar.SecondaryCommands>
    </CommandBar>
</Page.BottomAppBar>
```

As you can see, the Application Bar is represented with the CommandBar element. To position the Application Bar at the bottom of the page, add the CommandBar markup to the Page.BottomAppBar element. You may display only one Application Bar on a page at a time, and it must reside at the bottom of the page.

The CommandBar contains two collections for storing commands: PrimaryCommands and SecondaryCommands. In Windows Phone 8.1 applications, the PrimaryCommands collection represents the image buttons that are displayed on the Application Bar. The PrimaryCommands collection is the default property on the CommandBar in a Windows Phone 8.1 application. Therefore, by adding the AppBarButton elements directly inside the CommandBar element, they will be added to the PrimaryCommands collection.

Primary command buttons must include an image to represent its corresponding action so that the user is easily able to identify and understand its intended purpose. Set the button's Icon property to a glyph from the Segoe UI Symbol font by referencing its enumerated member name. To obtain a list of the symbols available for the AppBarButton.Icon property, refer to the Symbol enumeration documentation on the Windows Dev Center site, located at http://bitly.com/AppBarSymbol. Next, set the button's Label property to include a short description of the button's action.

Finally, register the button's Click event to wire up an event handler in the page's code-behind, which will enable you to add the necessary logic that will be executed when the button is tapped. Listing 9-14 depicts an example of managing the deletion of selected ListView items from the main page of the application.

Listing 9-14. Deleting Selected Items from the ListView

```
private void OnDeleteButtonClicked(object sender, RoutedEventArgs e)
{
    var selectedCompanies = CompanyListView.SelectedItems.ToArray();
    foreach (Company item in selectedCompanies)
    {
        viewModel.DeleteCompany(item);
    }
}
```

The SecondaryCommands collection contains AppBarButton elements that represent additional menu items, which are displayed when the Application Bar's ellipsis button is tapped. The AppBarButton elements are configured in the same manner as those within the PrimaryCommands collection, except that there is no need to define an Icon property, since this property is ignored when the AppBarButton is defined as a secondary command.

Summary

This chapter provided an overview of designing compelling user experiences in your Windows Phone Store applications using XAML and C#. You learned the basic structure of a Windows Phone Store application and how you can design your application for various screen sizes and page orientations. We also discussed the various presentation controls available and how you can use them to display application content while maximizing screen real estate. Finally, you learned how to incorporate Windows Phone 8.1 features within your application, including adding page navigation, leveraging themes and resources, displaying collections within ListView and GridView controls, and configuring the Application Bar.

In the next chapter, we will explore the XAML used to design the user interface for Windows Store applications, as well as how to share data with other applications using Share contracts.

CHAPTER 10

■ ■ ■

The Windows User Interface

With the inception of Windows 8, Microsoft made it possible for developers to create and publish applications, known as Windows Store apps, which could be installed on desktops, laptops, or tablets running Windows 8. Similar to Windows Phone apps, developers could easily publish their applications to make them available across a wide global audience. However, only a small subset of APIs were reusable across the Windows Store and Windows Phone applications, which quickly became a major sticking point among developers who were attempting to target Windows systems and Windows Phone devices.

The announcement of Windows 8.1 at the Microsoft Build conference in April 2014 provided quite a bit of excitement among .NET developers because it introduced a converged API between Windows Store and Windows Phone Store applications. The reality of being able to share a larger portion of code logic, including XAML and UI assets, brought developers another step closer to the potential of targeting multiple platforms with a single codebase. Well, almost. Multiple platforms simply meant being able to target tablets, PCs, and devices running Windows. Baby steps, right?

As we touched on in Chapter 9, Microsoft has announced that the dream of developing one application to target multiple Windows platforms will be a reality with the release of Windows 10 in late July 2015. The concepts that we discussed throughout this book surrounding the XAML user interface design will still apply when you make the move to Windows 10 development.

That being said, much of the content we covered in Chapter 8 and Chapter 9 also apply to designing the Windows Store user interface, so we won't rehash what we've already discussed. If you skipped over those chapters in haste, take a step back and read them before moving on in this chapter to ensure that you have a solid foundation for the advanced topics that we will be covering here.

The Basics

Before digging into Windows Store development, we will need to cover the pertinent information regarding the Windows SDK, developer licensing, and the basic design principles surrounding the Windows Store user interface.

Windows Software Development Kit

To develop Windows Store applications, the Windows SDK for Windows 8.1 must be installed on the development machine. It contains all of the necessary APIs and tools, including the Windows App Certification Kit, which is used to test apps for certification in the Windows Store. The good news here is that there is nothing additional that you will need to do to obtain the SDK since it is automatically installed with Visual Studio 2013 Update 2 or newer.

Developer License

Before you can create a Windows Store app in Visual Studio, you must install a developer license on your development machine. The license enables you to test your Windows Store applications prior to certification and publication in the store. When you attempt to create a new Windows Store app or open an existing Windows Store app using Visual Studio 2013, you will be prompted to obtain a developer license, as shown in Figure 10-1.

Figure 10-1. *Prompt to install developer license for Windows 8.1*

Review the terms of the license. If you want to proceed, then click the I Agree button. You will then be prompted with the User Account Control dialog, as shown in Figure 10-2.

Figure 10-2. *Click Yes in User Account Control dialog to install the license*

Click the Yes button to continue with the installation. Once the license is installed on your machine, it is valid for a period of one year. When the license has reached its expiration date, you will be prompted to install a new license at that time.

Basic Design Principles

Windows Store apps follow a clean, modern design practice, incorporating some of the distinctive features available in the Windows 8.1 operating system. To design Windows Store applications effectively, it is important to understand the key elements that make store applications so unique.

When launched, Windows Store applications run full-screen, as illustrated in Figure 10-3.

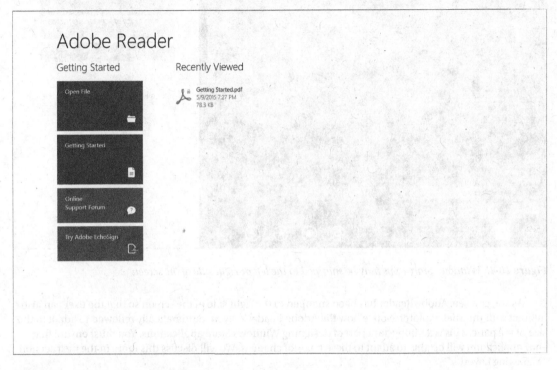

Figure 10-3. Adobe Reader Windows Store app

Users can drag a running Windows Store application to the left or right of the screen to force the app to snap to the respective side within a pane. This allows the user to interact with multiple Windows Store applications at the same time, as shown in Figure 10-4.

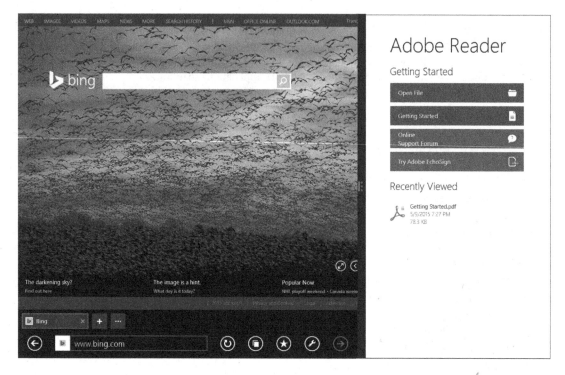

Figure 10-4. *Windows Store apps may be snapped to the left or right side of the screen*

As you can see, Adobe Reader has been snapped to the right side of the screen so that the user can also interact with Internet Explorer. Notice how the Adobe Reader's layout automatically reflowed to adapt to the size of the pane. This is an important part of designing Windows Store applications. You must ensure that your application will be able to adapt to these types of changes. We will discuss this more in the next section, "Managing Layouts."

Another important design element to consider is the Application Bar. As we mentioned in Chapter 9, the markup to include an Application Bar within Windows Phone applications is the same markup that you will use for Windows Store applications. While Windows Phone applications could display only a single Application Bar at the bottom of the page, Windows Store applications have the option to display up to two Application Bars on a single page—one at the top of the page and the other at the bottom. An Application Bar will be displayed at the top of the page if placed within the `Page.TopAppBar` element. Alternatively, an Application Bar will be displayed at the bottom of the page if placed within the `Page.BottomAppBar` element. The Application Bars will appear when the user swipes from the bottom edge of the screen downward or when the user right-clicks. Figure 10-5 illustrates an example of making use of both the top and bottom Application Bars in a Windows Store app.

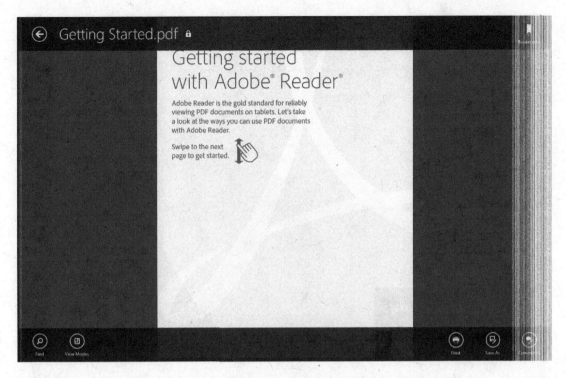

Figure 10-5. *The primary and secondary Application Bars available within a Windows Store app*

Since we have already discussed the details and implementation of the Application Bar in Chapter 9, we won't cover it here since the same information applies to using it within your Windows Store applications.

Windows 8.1 provides a set of Charms that enable applications to integrate with core features within the operating system, such as Search, Settings, and Share. The Charms bar can be brought into view when swiping from the right edge inward, hovering the mouse pointer in the top or bottom right corner, or pressing the Windows+C shortcut key combination. Figure 10-6 shows the Charms bar.

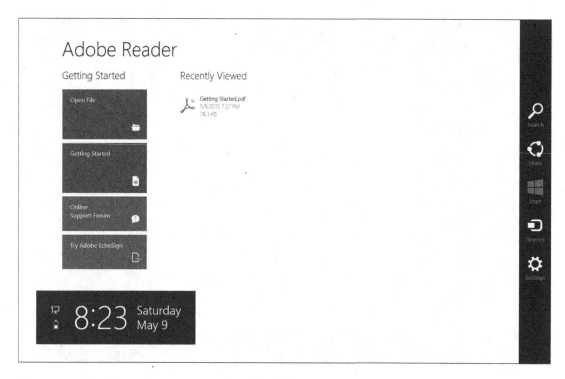

Figure 10-6. *The Charms bar appears on the right side of the screen*

In addition, Windows Store apps may make use of flyouts to collect information from the user, show more details about an item, or ask the user to confirm an action. Figure 10-7 depicts a couple of examples for using flyouts in your application. We will discuss this feature in detail in the "Flyouts" section later in this chapter.

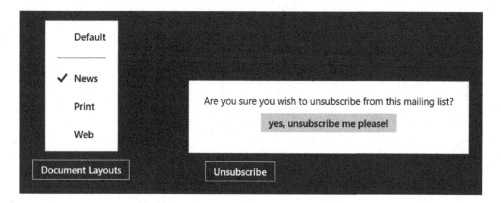

Figure 10-7. *Flyouts can be used to provide pop-up menu options or display a message prompt*

Gestures

Windows Store apps should all be designed for touch. This is easy to do so since all UI controls will respond to the following, which are common gestures recognized by the operating system.

- *Tap*: Tapping invokes the primary action on the element that receives the tap (for example, tapping a button).

- *Press and hold*: Pressing and holding displays detailed information about the selected element (for instance, displaying a tooltip).

- *Slide to pan*: Swiping left or right will pan across the page (for example, Hub control behavior).

- *Cross slide to select*: Sliding a short distance, perpendicular to the panning direction, will select an item (for instance, selecting an item in the list).

- *Cross slide to move*: You can drag and drop a control across the page.

- *Pinch and stretch to zoom*: You can drag fingers close together to pinch or drag fingers apart to stretch. These gestures are used to resize an element or to switch between the views in the SemanticZoom control.

- *Rotate*: You can select an item and turn to rotate the selected item.

- *Swipe from edge*: Depending on the location from which the swipe starts and the direction that the swipe takes, a specific action is performed.

  - Swiping from the right edge displays the Charms bar.
  - Swiping from the bottom edge displays the Application Bar.
  - Swiping from the left edge displays running apps.
  - Swiping from the top edge to the right/left splits the window.
  - Swiping from the top edge down to the bottom edge closes the app.

Managing Layouts

Windows Store apps may be run on devices of varying sizes—from 10" tablets to desktop systems leveraging full-size monitors, as well device orientation. Tablets may be run in portrait or landscape mode, so it's natural to consider which orientation your application will support.

In addition to screen size and orientation, applications must also consider the available screen real estate. As mentioned earlier in this chapter, Windows Store applications may run full-screen or be snapped in a pane that can be resized to various widths. The minimum width for which you must design depends on the supported minimum width set within the application's manifest file, Package.appxmanifest, as shown in Figure 10-8.

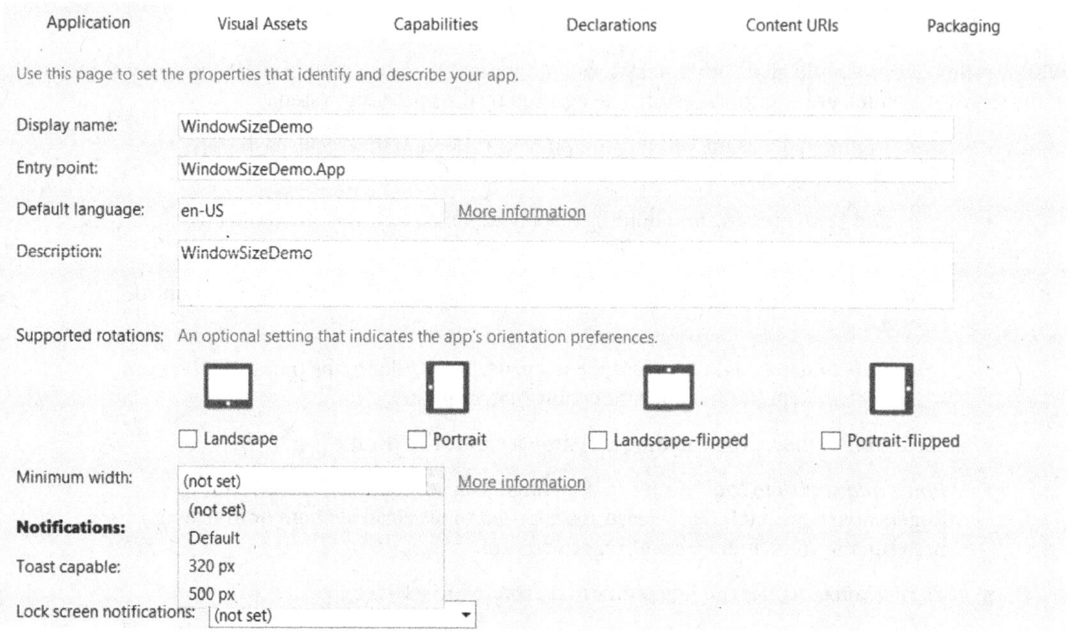

Application	Visual Assets	Capabilities	Declarations	Content URIs	Packaging

Use this page to set the properties that identify and describe your app.

Display name: WindowSizeDemo

Entry point: WindowSizeDemo.App

Default language: en-US   More information

Description: WindowSizeDemo

Supported rotations: An optional setting that indicates the app's orientation preferences.

☐ Landscape   ☐ Portrait   ☐ Landscape-flipped   ☐ Portrait-flipped

Minimum width: (not set)   More information

Notifications:
(not set)
Default
Toast capable: 320 px
500 px
Lock screen notifications: (not set) ▼

Figure 10-8. Configuring the minimum width supported by the application in the application manifest

By default, the minimum supported width will be 500px. If you want to support a width of 320px, simply select that option within the "Minimum width" field in the manifest.

The application's height will always occupy the full height of the screen. Only the application width real estate will vary since multiple apps can be run side-by-side and the user will have the ability to resize panes dynamically. Your application must continue to render properly despite the screen size that it is afforded by the user.

When designing your Windows Store application, you must determine how your application will look as its available width expands or contracts. As we mentioned in Chapter 8 and Chapter 9, avoid using fixed sizes in your XAML views. Allow the XAML subsystem to adjust automatically to the screen size that your application is afforded by the user.

Visual States

There will be cases when you will want to ensure that your page renders in a different format when the application window is snapped or resized. You can accomplish this by defining the visual states that your page will support using the `VisualState` class from the `Windows.UI.Xaml` namespace. The `VisualState` class enables you to configure the appearance of a control when it is in a specific state. However, to manage a collection of visual states as well as the logic for transitions between controls, you must make use of the `VisualStateManager`. Within XAML, you will define one or more visual states using the `VisualStateManager.VisualStateGroups` collection, as shown in Listing 10-1.

Listing 10-1. Configuring Visual States in XAML

```xaml
<VisualStateManager.VisualStateGroups>
    <VisualStateGroup x:Name="MyVisualStateGroup">
        <VisualState x:Name="Snapped">
        </VisualState>
        <VisualState x:Name="Narrow">
        </VisualState>
        <VisualState x:Name="Default" />
    </VisualStateGroup>
</VisualStateManager.VisualStateGroups>
```

In the example in Listing 10-1, we have defined three visual states: Snapped, Narrow, and Default. Don't get too hung up on the names since you can name the visual states using whatever convention makes sense to you. The names you provide here will be referenced in the code-behind, which we will get to shortly.

Storyboards and Animations

Once you have decided the various widths that you want to support, you must determine how your page will appear in each of those views. For example, if a StackPanel is rendering controls horizontally while the application window is in full view, you may want to change it to render controls vertically when the application is snapped to the left or right edge of the screen. Changing the way the control is rendered can be thought of as a visual transition. Visual transitions can be used to change any Windows Runtime dependency property on a control.

In XAML, you will be able to define the visual transitions that you want to be applied to a control as it moves from one visual state to another. This is accomplished through the use of storyboards and animations. Animations add movement within your application, providing appealing transitions as property values on a control are changed. Storyboards control the animations that are run using a timeline.

You can create animations for Color, Double, Point, and Object properties using the animations listed in Table 10-1.

Table 10-1. Windows Runtime Animations

Animation	Animates the Value of...
ColorAnimation	A Color property between two target values over a specified Duration
ColorAnimationUsingKeyFrames	A Color property along a set of keyframes
DoubleAnimation	A Double property between two target values over a specified Duration
DoubleAnimationUsingKeyFrames	A Double property along a set of keyframes
ObjectAnimationUsingKeyFrames	An Object property along a set of keyframes over a specified Duration
PointAnimation	A Point property between two target values over a specified Duration
PointAnimationUsingKeyFrames	A Point property along a set of keyframes

Using the example mentioned earlier, Listing 10-2 demonstrates how to change the StackPanel orientation when the window is snapped.

Listing 10-2. Configure the StackPanel to Change Orientation When the Page Is Snapped

```
<VisualStateManager.VisualStateGroups>
    <VisualStateGroup x:Name="MyVisualStateGroup">
        <VisualState x:Name="Snapped">
            <Storyboard>
                <ObjectAnimationUsingKeyFrames
                        Storyboard.TargetName="MyStackPanel"
                        Storyboard.TargetProperty="Orientation">
                    <DiscreteObjectKeyFrame KeyTime="0">
                        <DiscreteObjectKeyFrame.Value>
                            <Orientation>Vertical</Orientation>
                        </DiscreteObjectKeyFrame.Value>
                    </DiscreteObjectKeyFrame>
                </ObjectAnimationUsingKeyFrames>
            </Storyboard>
        </VisualState>
    ...
    </VisualStateGroup>
</VisualStateManager.VisualStateGroups>
```

Listing 10-2 demonstrates the use of the ObjectAnimationUsingKeyFrames class to transition the StackPanel from horizontal to vertical orientation by defining the StackPanel's new orientation property within the DiscreteObjectKeyFrame.Value element.

```
<DiscreteObjectKeyFrame KeyTime="0">
    <DiscreteObjectKeyFrame.Value>
        <Orientation>Vertical</Orientation>
</DiscreteObjectKeyFrame>
```

The number of animations that you want to include within a single storyboard is not limited. You can change as many property values as you need there. For example, if you also wanted reduce the text size of the Title text block when the window is snapped, you could include an additional animation in the storyboard definition for the Snapped visual state as follows:

```
<DoubleAnimation Duration="0"
                To="21"
                Storyboard.TargetProperty="FontSize"
                Storyboard.TargetName="TitleTextBlock" />
```

Note that, in this case, the FontSize is changed through the To property on the DoubleAnimation element.

When configuring an animation for a specific control, you must specify the target control's name and the property to which the animation must be applied. You can accomplish this by setting the attached properties TargetName and TargetProperty on the animation: <ObjectAnimationUsingKeyFrames Storyboard.TargetName="MyStackPanel" Storyboard.TargetProperty="Orientation">.

Notice that when the TargetName has been configured, the TargetProperty will automatically populate its selection list with only those properties that are applicable to the target UI element, enabling you to have complete control over the appearance of any object within the page.

You must also specify a Duration or KeyTime to indicate how long the animation will take to complete. When defining a duration for a visual state transition, use zero-duration animations to ensure that the application remains responsive. Setting a longer duration may negatively affect performance on the UI thread and lock up the application until the animation completes.

OnSizeChanged

Now that you know how you can define a view for each of the visual states that your application will support, how does the VisualStateManager know how to render the page?

To ensure the appropriate visual state is rendered when the application window's width is resized, you must register for the Page's OnSizeChanged event. The OnSizeChanged event receives the SizeChangedEventArgs parameter, which exposes two Size properties: NewSize and PreviousSize. You can use these properties to retrieve the Height and Width of the application window before and after it was resized.

Within the OnSizeChanged event, you will need to call the VisualStateManager.GoToState method, passing in the desired visual state to render. In this case, you will use the e.NewSize.Width property to determine which visual state to render. You must decide the maximum width that each visual state will support. Will a width of 500px or less trigger your Snapped view, or will it be 320px? What will the next maximum supported width be after that? These are design considerations that you must define based on your application. Listing 10-3 demonstrates an example of how to trigger the appropriate visual state based on the window's new width size.

Listing 10-3. The OnSizeChanged Event Will Be Used to Trigger the Appropriate VisualState Through the VisualStateManager

```
//custom enumeration to represent each of
//the custom visual states configured in XAML
public enum MyVisualStates
{
    Snapped,
    Narrow,
    Default
}

public sealed partial class MainPage : Page
{

    public MainPage()
    {
        this.InitializeComponent();
        this.SizeChanged += MainPage_SizeChanged;
    }

    void MainPage_SizeChanged(object sender, SizeChangedEventArgs e)
    {
        VisualStateManager.GoToState(this, GetCustomVisualState(e.NewSize.Width), true);
    }

    private string GetCustomVisualState(double width)
    {
        if (width <= 500)
        {
            return MyVisualStates.Snapped.ToString();
        }
```

```
    if (width <= 800)
    {
        return MyVisualStates.Narrow.ToString();
    }

    return MyVisualStates.Default.ToString();
    }

}
```

Taking the time to configure visual states within your application will ensure that your users have a seamless experience regardless of the screen real estate that is available to your app at runtime. Although it does require some legwork up front, the end result will be a polished, high-quality application that will be appealing to your users.

Searching Data

One of the fundamental features that all data-driven applications should provide is a mechanism to allow users to search and filter through data to find a particular item or group of items.

The Windows 8.1 SDK includes a SearchBox control to enable you to include advanced search capabilities within your application. Although the SearchBox itself is a simple control with no real functionality driving it, the control includes integration points, which you can leverage to incorporate search using your own custom logic. It includes additional features that make it easy to display a polished search interface, such as displaying suggestions based on the user's current entry, as shown in Figure 10-9.

Figure 10-9. *SearchBox with a list of suggestions displayed based on the user's search criteria*

You may subscribe to one or more of the following events to add functionality to the SearchBox:

- SuggestionRequested: Handle this event to provide new suggestions in the search pane based on the user's search text.

- QueryChanged: Handle this event to take action as the user types in the SearchBox. This may affect performance, so use with caution.

- QuerySubmitted: Handle this event to control the action that is triggered when the user submits a search query.

- ResultSuggestionChosen: Handle this event to control the action that is triggered when the user selects a suggested search result.

To include a SearchBox within a Windows Store page, simply include the element's markup, <SearchBox /> along with any properties or events that you want to set. Here's an example:

```
<SearchBox x:Name="CompanySearchBox"
        MinWidth="200"
        HorizontalAlignment="Right"
        QuerySubmitted="SearchBoxOnQuerySubmitted"
        SuggestionsRequested="SearchBoxOnSuggestionsRequested" />
```

As mentioned earlier, the SearchBox will display a list of suggestions, or a search history list, when the page is rendered. To turn off the list display, simply set its Boolean property, SearchHistoryEnabled, to False.

When the SearchHistoryEnabled property is set to True, the list will display up to 20 items in total. The first five items will be displayed in the pop-up, while the remaining items in the list may be scrolled into view.

To set the search history list to populate forcibly or to clear it, you can instantiate a SearchSuggestionManager object. This object provides an AddHistory method to allow you to add strings to the search history list. In turn, it also provides a ClearHistory method to enable you to clear the search history list.

If you want to display a Search Results page when the user submits the query entry by hitting Enter, you can easily incorporate this into your application by adding the Search Results Page template, as shown in Figure 10-10.

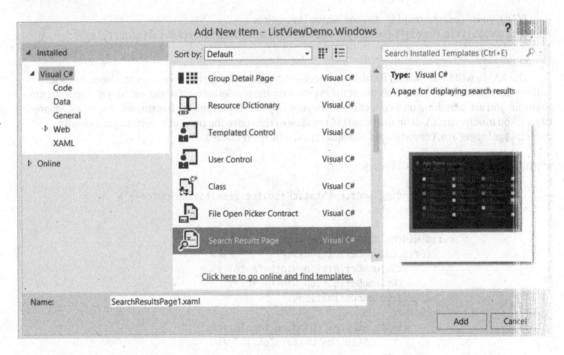

Figure 10-10. *Adding a search results page to the application*

The Search Results Page template provides the UI layout and most of the code needed to render a polished results list. With a few minor tweaks, you will have a fully functional results page with little effort. You can create your own custom results page, if you so choose. This just provides a quick and easy alternative.

In the Search Results page code-behind, within the navigationHelper_LoadState event, add an entry to the DefaultViewModel dictionary for the Results collection. You will need to code your own custom search logic within your ViewModel to retrieve the results based on the query text entered. For example, in the case where you are searching only on company names, your ViewModel may expose a simple method to retrieve all companies that contain the query text entered as follows:

```
public ObservableCollection<Company> GetSearchResults(string queryText)
{
    return new ObservableCollection<Company>(Companies
            .Where(c => c.CompanyName.Contains(queryText))
            .ToList<Company>());
}
```

Within the search results code-behind file, you would simply add a line of code to include the results of this call to the DefaultViewModel["Results"] entry, as shown here:

```
private void navigationHelper_LoadState(object sender, LoadStateEventArgs e)
{
    var queryText = e.NavigationParameter as String;

    ...

    //Add your custom results to the DefaultViewModel
    this.DefaultViewModel["Results"] = App.MainViewModel.GetSearchResults(queryText);
}
```

The XAML within the search results page needs to be modified slightly to ensure the bound properties within the resultsGridView match the items exposed on the model on which you will be searching. In this example, you are searching on a collection of Company objects. Therefore, each result will depict a Company object. You modify the XAML in the resultsGridView to reference the properties within your Company object: LogoImagePath, CompanyName, Headquarters, and YearFounded.

```
<GridView x:Name="resultsGridView"
        ...
        ItemsSource="{Binding Source={StaticResource resultsViewSource}}">
        <GridView.ItemTemplate>
            <DataTemplate>
                <Grid Width="294" Margin="6">
                    <Grid.ColumnDefinitions>
                        <ColumnDefinition Width="Auto" />
                        <ColumnDefinition Width="*" />
                    </Grid.ColumnDefinitions>
                    <Border ...>
                        <Image Source="{Binding LogoImagePath}"
                                Stretch="UniformToFill" />
                    </Border>
                    <StackPanel Grid.Column="1"
                                Margin="10,-10,0,0">
                        <TextBlock Text="{Binding CompanyName}"
                                    TextWrapping="NoWrap"
                                    Style="{StaticResource BodyTextBlockStyle}" />
```

```
                    <TextBlock Text="{Binding Headquarters}"
                               TextWrapping="NoWrap"
                               Style="{StaticResource BodyTextBlockStyle}" />
                    <TextBlock Text="{Binding YearFounded}"
                               TextWrapping="NoWrap"
                               Style="{StaticResource BodyTextBlockStyle}" />
                </StackPanel>
            </Grid>
        </DataTemplate>
    </GridView.ItemTemplate>
    ...
</GridView>
```

Finally, you need to modify the MainPage code-behind to add functionality to the SearchBox. In this example, you ensure that the following actions are handled with respect to the SearchBox:

- Display the search history list only when the control has focus.

- Add suggestions to the search history list when the onsuggestionsrequested event is raised.

- Clear the search history list each time the page is loaded or when the list will be populated with a new list of suggestions.

- Navigate to the search results page when the querysubmitted event is raised.

Note that this is a simple example of how to include SearchBox functionality. You have the flexibility to add logic that makes sense within the context of your application. Listing 10-4 shows the resulting code from the example.

Listing 10-4. Code-Behind Needed to Manage SearchBox

```
private readonly SearchSuggestionManager searchManager;

public MainPage()
{
    this.InitializeComponent();

    this.NavigationCacheMode = NavigationCacheMode.Required;
    this.DataContext = App.MainViewModel;

    //only show the search history list when the search box has focus
    CompanySearchBox.GotFocus += delegate(object sender, RoutedEventArgs args)
    {
        CompanySearchBox.SearchHistoryEnabled = true;
    };
    CompanySearchBox.LostFocus += delegate(object sender, RoutedEventArgs args)
    {
        CompanySearchBox.SearchHistoryEnabled = false;
    };

    //clear previous search history each time the application is launched
    searchManager = new SearchSuggestionManager();
    searchManager.ClearHistory();
}
```

```
private void SearchBoxOnQuerySubmitted(SearchBox sender, SearchBoxQuerySubmittedEventArgs args)
{
    Frame.Navigate(typeof (CompanySearchResults), args.QueryText);
}

private void SearchBoxOnSuggestionsRequested(SearchBox sender,
SearchBoxSuggestionsRequestedEventArgs args)
{
    //clear search history, and add new suggestions to the search history list
    searchManager.ClearHistory();
    IEnumerable<Company> results = App.MainViewModel.GetSearchResults(args.QueryText);

    foreach (Company company in results)
    {
        searchManager.AddToHistory(company.CompanyName);
    }
}
```

If configured properly, upon typing text into the SearchBox and hitting the Enter key on the MainPage, the search results page should appear with a similar layout as the one that is depicted in Figure 10-11.

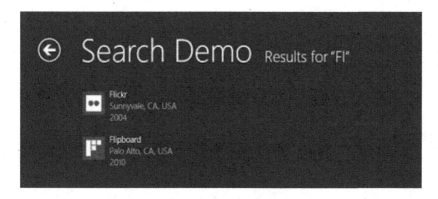

Figure 10-11. *Search results page displaying list of matching items*

As you can see, the Search Results Page template provides you with a great starting point. However, we highly recommend that you leverage the knowledge you have gained so far to customize the theme and style of this page to match your application's look and feel.

Flyouts

The Windows 8.1 SDK provides a Flyout control that can be used to gather user information, display a message, prompt for confirmation, or provide menu options.

The Basics

The Flyout control enables users to dismiss the control simply by touching anywhere on the screen outside of the Flyout. You may customize the content of the Flyout control by displaying any elements that you see fit within a container control. You are not constricted to displaying static text alone. You can incorporate input fields, images, buttons, or any other rich content you so desire. You also may apply your application's theme or custom styles to provide visual appeal to the control.

In the event that you want to display a list of menu options, the content of the Flyout control may be set to the MenuFlyout element. The MenuFlyout element enables you to define the list of options that will be presented to the user and to wire up events to handle the user's selection. Menu items within a MenuFlyout may consist only of regular menu items, toggle menu items, and/or separator bars. We will demonstrate the use of the MenuFlyout element later in this section.

To perform custom actions when the Flyout control is loading, displayed, or dismissed, you may subscribe to the Flyout control's Opening, Opened, or Closed events, respectively.

Usage and Syntax

Flyouts can be implemented within a page through a button, Application Bar button, or programmatically. To display a flyout when a button is tapped, simply include the desired Flyout markup within the Button element, as follows:

```
<Button>
   <Button.Flyout>
      <Flyout>
      <!-- include your desired content here -->
      </Flyout>
   </Button.Flyout>
</Button>
```

When the Flyout is associated with a button in this way, no additional code is needed to display the flyout. Tapping the button will automatically trigger the flyout to open.

If you want to control where the Flyout is rendered when the button is tapped, you may set the Flyout's Placement property to one of the following enumerated values: Top, Bottom, Left, Right, Full. Setting the control's Placement to one of the first four properties will ensure that it displays at the specified location in relation to its parent button. Setting Placement to Full will cause the Flyout to expand and display in the center of the screen, as illustrated in Figure 10-12.

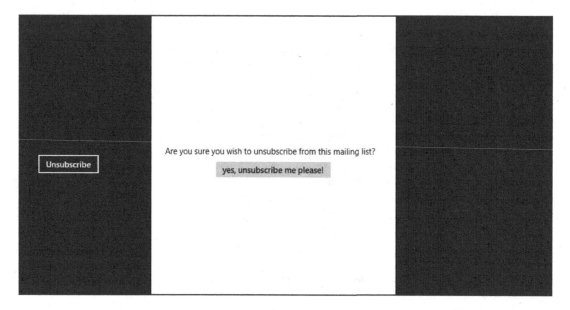

Figure 10-12. *When the Flyout's Placement property is set to Full, it will display center screen*

You can also integrate a `Flyout` control within an `AppBarButton` using similar markup as follows:

```
<AppBarButton>
    <AppBarButton.Flyout>
        <!-- place desired content here -->
    </AppBarButton.Flyout>
</AppBarButton>
```

Just as with the button, incorporating a `Flyout` within an `AppBarButton` will cause the `Flyout` to display when the `AppBarButton` is tapped.

As mentioned earlier, you may be able to create a `MenuFlyout` to present the user with contextual options to take action on the current page, as shown in Listing 10-5. A `MenuFlyout` can contain only the following child elements:

- `MenuFlyoutItem`: Displays a simple menu item. Use this menu item when an action must be taken immediately upon selection. Subscribe to the `Click` event to handle user selection.

- `ToggleMenuFlyoutItem`: Displays a menu item that will appear with a check mark next to it when tapped. Use this menu item to provide the user with a choice of options. Monitor the value of the `IsChecked` property on the `ToggleMenuFlyoutItem` to determine whether the item has been selected.

- `MenuFlyoutSeparator`: Displays a horizontal gray bar. It is not a functional menu item, and it is simply used to separate menu items into groups.

Listing 10-5. An Example of Using the MenuFlyout to Provide Multiple Options to the User

```
<AppBarButton Label="send to" Icon="Send">
    <AppBarButton.Flyout>
        <MenuFlyout>
            <MenuFlyoutItem Text="All Click="SendToAllOnClick" />
            <MenuFlyoutSeparator />
            <ToggleMenuFlyoutItem Text="Email"
                                  IsChecked="{Binding IsEmailSelected, Mode=TwoWay}" />
            <ToggleMenuFlyoutItem Text="Facebook"
                                  IsChecked="{Binding IsFacebookSelected, Mode=TwoWay}" />
        </MenuFlyout>
    </AppBarButton.Flyout>
</AppBarButton>
```

Programmatic Display

If you want to attach a Flyout to a FrameworkElement other than a button, you must declare the Flyout as a Resource, associate the Flyout control to the FrameworkElement using the FlyoutBase.FlyoutAttached property, and programmatically trigger the Flyout to display by calling the FlyoutBase.ShowAttachedFlyout method from the code-behind when the FrameworkElement is tapped.

For example, let's say you wanted to create a card game where an Image control is used to display a card. When a special card is tapped, you want to provide the user with a list of options to enable them to decide how that card will be used in the game.

To associate a Flyout with an Image control, define your Flyout as a page resource and then associate the Flyout to the Image control, as shown in Listing 10-6.

Listing 10-6. Define Flyout as a Resource and Associate It to the Image

```
<Page ...>
<Page.Resources>
    <MenuFlyout x:Key="SpecialActionMenuFlyout">
        <MenuFlyoutItem Text="Power Up"
                        Tag="PowerUp"
                        Click="SpecialActionOnClick"/>
        <MenuFlyoutItem Text="Damage Enemy"
                        Tag="Damage"
                        Click=" SpecialActionOnClick"/>
        <MenuFlyoutItem Text="Restore Health"
                        Tag="Restore"
                        Click=" SpecialActionOnClick"/>
    </MenuFlyout>
</Page.Resources>

...

    <Image Source="{Binding SpecialCard}"
           Tapped="OnSpecialCardTapped"
           FlyoutBase.AttachedFlyout="{StaticResource SpecialActionMenuFlyout}" />
...
</Page>
```

In the Page's code-behind file, call the FlyoutBase.ShowAttachedFlyout method, simply passing in the Image control.

```
private void OnSpecialCardTapped (object sender, TappedRoutedEventArgs e)
{
    FlyoutBase.ShowAttachedFlyout((FrameworkElement)sender);
}
```

And that's all there is to it! With a few extra steps, you can easily associate Flyout controls to any FrameworkElement in your application.

Flyout Styles

Now that you know how to incorporate flyouts into your application, let's take a closer look to see how the Flyout control can be customized to conform to the application's theme.

FlyoutPresenter

The content within a Flyout control can be styled in the same way that you would style standard FrameworkElements within XAML. However, the Flyout control itself may not be styled directly. Instead, it must be styled by configuring its FlyoutPresenterStyle. The FlyoutPresenterStyle defines the overall appearance of the Flyout control. You will be able to customize the style of the control's dependency properties, such as FontSize, Background, Foreground, and Padding to name just a few. When defining the FlyoutPresenterStyle, you must set its TargetType="FlyoutPresenter" and include setters for the dependency properties that you want to customize, as follows:

```
<Flyout>
    <Flyout.FlyoutPresenterStyle>
        <Style TargetType="FlyoutPresenter">
            <Setter Property="BorderBrush" Value="White" />
            <Setter Property="Background" Value="CornflowerBlue" />
            <Setter Property="Foreground" Value="White" />
                ...
        </Style>
    </Flyout.FlyoutPresenterStyle>
    <!-- Flyout content -->
</Flyout>
```

MenuFlyoutPresenter

Similar to the Flyout control, you may configure the style on the MenuFlyout using the MenuFlyoutPresenterStyle property, ensuring that the TargetType is set to MenuFlyoutPresenter.

```
<MenuFlyout>
    <MenuFlyout.MenuFlyoutPresenterStyle>
        <Style TargetType="MenuFlyoutPresenter">
            ...
        </Style>
    </MenuFlyout.MenuFlyoutPresenterStyle>
    <!-- Menu Flyout content -->
</Flyout>
```

Contracts

The Windows 8.1 SDK provides contracts that you can leverage within your application to interact with the native system features and functionality, such as sharing content between applications and integrating with the Settings menu.

Share Contract

The share contract enables applications to share data with and/or receive data from other applications in the form of plain text, links, and files. You can designate your application to participate as the share source, which will serve data to an application of the user's choosing. Only those applications that are configured to serve as a share target will be available as an option with which to share data. You can also configure your application to serve as the target source. In this way, when a user selects to share data from an external application, such as Facebook or Instagram, your application will appear in the list as a target application that is available to receive the content.

To ensure that your application is configured to share data with other applications, you must add the Windows.ApplicationModel.DataTransfer namespace to your application page. Within your application page's constructor, you must retrieve an instance of the DataTransferManager object and subscribe to its DataRequested event. The DataRequested event is triggered whenever the user invokes a share action through the Charms bar. Therefore, you will make use of this event to include any data that you want to share with any external applications.

Finally, the data you want to share must be passed through a DataRequest object. Note that the Title of the DataRequest object is a mandatory field and must be set. Listing 10-7 shows a basic example of configuring the main page of the application to participate in the share contract so that it can share data with external applications.

Listing 10-7. Configure the Page to Participate in the Share Contract

```
private void OnDataRequested(DataTransferManager sender, DataRequestedEventArgs e)
{
    DataRequest request = e.Request;
    request.Data.Properties.Title = "Share Demo";
    request.Data.Properties.Description = "Demonstrating the use of the Share Contract";

    request.Data.SetText("Sharing text with another application.");
}
```

Listing 10-7 illustrates how easy it is to share text with external applications. However, what if you wanted to share an image? This does require a few extra lines of code; however, it is very straightforward.

To share an image, you must convert it into a RandomAccessStreamReference, which will then be passed to the DataRequest object through a call to the SetBitmap method, as shown in Listing 10-8.

Listing 10-8. Sharing an Image with an External Application

```
private async void OnDataRequested(DataTransferManager sender, DataRequestedEventArgs e)
{
    var deferral = e.Request.GetDeferral();

    DataRequest request = e.Request;
    request.Data.Properties.Title = "Share Demo";
```

```
request.Data.Properties.Description = string.Format("Demonstrating the use of the
Share Contract");

StorageFile imageFile = await Windows.ApplicationModel.Package.Current.
InstalledLocation.GetFileAsync("MontegoBay.png");

var stream = RandomAccessStreamReference.CreateFromFile(imageFile);
request.Data.SetBitmap(stream);
request.Data.Properties.Thumbnail = stream;

deferral.Complete();
}
```

In Listing 10-8, we are loading the image from a file that we packaged with the application by calling the GetFileAsync method. Notice that we are using the async/await operators. In this case, we need to request a deferral, since we are invoking an asynchronous process. To accomplish this, we call the GetDeferral method on the DataRequest object so that the application is able to load the image and generate the DataPackage asynchronously. We wrap up the request by calling the Complete method on the deferral object. Now when we run the application, we can invoke the Charms bar and click the Share button to share our image with an external application, as shown in Figure 10-13.

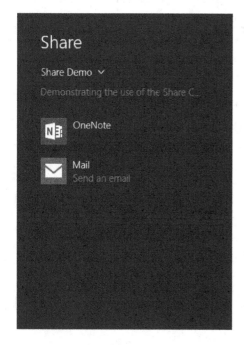

Figure 10-13. *The application's custom share title and description is displayed in the Share Flyout along with applications that are share targets*

Selecting an application from the list of available share targets will cause the application to load in a snapped page with the share data displayed in view, as shown in Figure 10-14.

Figure 10-14. *The share target application is loaded in a snapped pane with the shared data in view*

Settings Contract

The settings contract enables you to integrate your application's settings within the Settings flyout accessible from the Charms bar. By default, all Windows Store applications are designed with a default Settings pane and are configured to participate in the settings contract. You may include up to seven commands within the Settings pane. If you do not include a custom Settings flyout within your application, the default Settings pane will contain the name of the application, your publisher name, a command that will display a Settings flyout containing application permissions information, and a command that will enable users to rate your app. The "Rate and review" command is available only once the application is published to the Windows Store.

Summary

This chapter provided an overview of the design principles and features that should be considered when designing your Windows Store applications. You learned about how to design your application to adapt to different layouts and how to incorporate Windows 8.1 contracts within your application to provide an engaging user experience. We also discussed the use of flyouts to provide contextual menu options.

In the next chapter, we will discuss how to package your Windows applications for publication in the Windows Store.

CHAPTER 11

■ ■ ■

Deploying and Maintaining Your Application

Now that you are equipped with all the skills needed to develop high-quality XAML applications, the next step is to explore your options for using a version control system to protect your codebase. In addition, we will discuss the need for setting up a build server with continuous integration so that you can continue to enhance your application, all while providing iterative releases and ensuring that the code you check in remains clean and functional. Finally, we will cover how you can deploy your Windows 8.1 and Windows Phone 8.1 applications to the Windows Store.

Version Control

An important aspect of application development is the use of version control to provide a safe repository for your application's source code, allow development teams to merge changes to a central location, and track the history of changes that the application has undergone.

The Basics

Let's start with a brief discussion of the main components and features that you need to understand as they relate to current version control systems.

> *Repository*: The central location into which all code changes eventually make their way. A version control system should have a dedicated server, which is the central repository consisting of the files that need to be tracked. The central repository will also maintain a history of the changes made to each file, along with any comments related to those changes.

> *Master/trunk*: The originating branch that serves as the baseline for a project on which development progresses.

> *Branch*: A copy of the master branch or another child branch to a separate location so that any changes made to the files do not affect its parent. A developer or development team will utilize a branch to implement a new feature or perform bug fixes, without working directly off the master. You can call these features *branches* since they should be short-lived in nature and exist only when working on a single task. Feature branches should be disposed of once the changes have been merged back into the parent branch.

Merge: The action taken to integrate changes made within one branch to another. Best practices recommend using branching to make code changes and then merging to the master once the feature is complete and has gone through the proper checks and balances to ensure that it is stable for release.

Merge conflict: Occurs when changes to a file contradict the version of that file stored on the server. This often occurs as a result of multiple developers modifying the same file and attempting to check in changes subsequently. Usually, the first developer to check in wins. The lucky developer who gets to deal with the merge conflict decides which changes are applied and which changes should be discarded. Or, in the case where all the code changes must be applied, that person decides the order in which those conflicting code blocks appear in the file.

Resolve: Occurs when the developer who addressed the merge conflict has completed the merge. In this case, the developer will mark the file as resolved so that the version control system knows it's in good condition to be checked in. The developer resolving any merge conflicts must ensure that the changes checked in prior to this check-in aren't negatively impacted or completely overwritten.

Check in: The action that pushes changes made on a local machine to the version control system's central repository. In Team Foundation Version Control, you will often hear check-ins being referred to as *commits*. However, in Git, this would be known as a *push*. We will discuss the additional terminology for this system in the "Git" section later in this chapter.

Check out: The action of creating a local working copy from the repository. A user may specify a specific revision to check out or obtain the latest revision from the repository. In older version control systems, a file checkout prevented multiple developers from modifying the file at the same time. In current version control systems, this has been vastly improved so that multiple developers can work on the same set of files in parallel, and they can check in their changes separately, ensuring that any conflicts that arise are resolved prior to completing the check-in process.

Revert/roll back: There are two scenarios at play here. You can revert, or roll back, any pending changes to your working copy that have not yet been checked in to the central repository. In this case, the changes are lost forever, and there is no record of this change on the server. If you want to undo, or roll back a change on the server, you can do so only if you have the necessary privileges to make those changes to the central repository. Make sure that you, or the version control system administrator, performs the rollback using the appropriate commands to ensure that the history of the changeset is not lost as a result of the rollback.

Changeset: The file, or set of files, bundled within a single check-in.

Get latest: The action of copying the latest code from the version control system. You can get the latest code from the master, a selected branch, a selected directory within master or branch, or a specific file.

In an ideal environment, your version control process should look a little something like this when working on a new task or bug fix:

1. Create a feature branch off the master.

2. Pull down the latest code from the server to your local machine.

3. Make the necessary code changes, including writing the required unit tests.

4. Be a good citizen. That is, test your changes, and ensure that your unit tests pass and the code builds successfully.

5. Check in your changes to the server.

6. Request a code review. Wait for approval, and ensure that all unit tests and integration tests on the server pass.

7. When given the green light, merge your changes to the master. Resolve any merge conflicts that arise.

8. Delete your feature branch.

9. Lather, rinse, repeat.

As simple as that sounds, things can go wrong even with the best of intentions.

Choosing a Version Control System

Many version control systems are available, such as Team Foundation Version Control, Git, Subversion, and CVS, to name a few. The type of version control system that you will use may be already in place and dictated by the organization or the team. If you're tasked with choosing which system to use, it is important that you take the time to research a few systems in order to understand which one will serve the team's needs. Let's take a look at a couple of the popular version control systems available today.

Team Foundation Version Control

Team Foundation Version Control (TFVC) is a centralized version control system that can be set up on premises or in the cloud through Visual Studio Online. The complete history of the source code changes is maintained on a single server. When users check out files, a snapshot of the files is copied to the local machine. Users make their changes and check in any to the server, which then stores the updated file and logs the change along with the developer's comments in the version control history.

Team Foundation Version Control enables you to define workspaces, supports branching and merging, and allows you to define permissions all the way down to the file level. TFVC is suitable for projects of all sizes, and it can easily scale up to support millions of files per branch.

TFVC works with Team Foundation Server, a collaboration platform, which includes project process templates such as Agile, Scrum, and CMMI templates. It also provides tools that enable development teams and stakeholders to track and monitor a project's progress and audit code changes. In addition, TFVC allows you to create custom build scripts and manage your deployment options. To use TFVC, you must set up Team Foundation Server in-house (or in the cloud with Visual Studio Online) to serve as the central location to store source code.

To learn more about how to use TFVC, refer to the online MSDN article "Use Team Foundation Version Control" at http://bitly.com/TFVCSetup.

Git

Git is an open source, distributed version control system that is designed to handle projects of all sizes. When users check out files, they also receive a history of the source code changes. In this way, users can easily work disconnected, being able to view changesets and commit changes locally until they are back online.

A Git server will serve as the central repository into which all code changes and related metadata, such as changesets and developer comments, will eventually make their way. You can set up a Git server in-house, use Team Foundation Server using Git to TFS, or use a service such as GitHub.

Git has some custom terminology with which you will need to become familiar if you are using this version control system within your organization. Table 11-1 defines the more common terms that you will need to learn.

Table 11-1. *Common Git Terminology*

Term	Description
Clone	The act of downloading a local copy of a repository on your local machine.
Fork	A copy of another repository. You can fork off the master or another branch and make changes to it without affecting the original branch. Forks remain attached to the original branch, which enables developers to submit requests to have changes merged into the original branch, with the approval of the original branch's collaborators.
Commit	The act of checking in a file or set of files to the local repository. Every time a commit is performed, it creates a unique ID that identifies the changeset details for the commit. Details of the commit are stored including the date/time of the commit, the developer who made the changes, and any developer comments.
Push	Sending committed changes to the remote repository. The files that were committed, along with the details of the commits, are uploaded to the remote repository.
Pull	Getting the latest code from the repository and merging them into your local repository.
Fetch	Getting the latest code from the repository without merging them into your local repository.
Pull request	Creates a request to have your changes merged to the master or another branch. The designated collaborators may approve or reject the request.

In a nutshell, Git enables you to work on a branch and commit changes to that branch. The changes, however, are committed to the repository on your local machine. Nothing has gone up to the central repository on the server just yet. When you are ready to move your changes to the server, you must perform a Git push.

Once your changes are on the server, you can then create a pull request to have your changes reviewed. Once the pull request is approved, you can then merge your changes to the master.

This is just the layman's version of a basic check-in process using Git. Really understanding Git and getting up to speed on all of the available commands requires an entire book. We recommend reading *Pro Git* by Scott Chacon and Ben Straub (Apress, 2014).

Visual Studio 2013 Integration

Team Foundation Version Control and Git to TFS are integrated within Visual Studio 2013.

To start using TFVC or Git to TFS to manage your application's code, you must connect to the Team Foundation Server that contains your source code repositories. Select Team ➤ Connect to Team Foundation Server, as shown in Figure 11-1.

Figure 11-1. *Connecting to Team Foundation Server from Visual Studio 2013*

In the Team Explorer pane, click the Select Team Projects link, as shown in Figure 11-2.

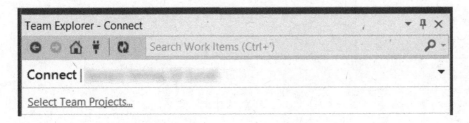

Figure 11-2. *Select Team Projects link in the Team Explorer pane*

You will then be prompted to connect to a Team Foundation Server (TFS), as shown in Figure 11-3. If you have previously configured Team Foundation Server connections, they will be available for selection in the Select A Team Foundation Server drop-down list. However, if this is your first time connecting to TFS, then click the Servers button to configure the connection to an existing Team Foundation Server.

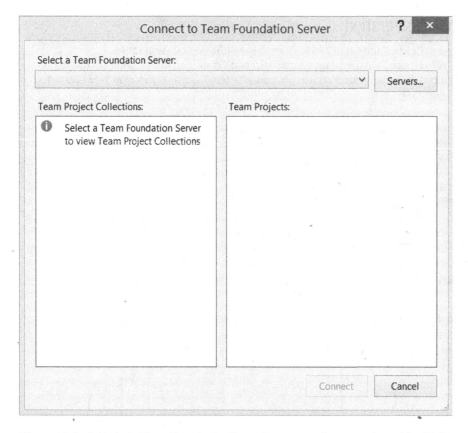

Figure 11-3. *Selecting a Team Foundation Server instance and team project with which to work*

Once you have connected to a Team Foundation Server instance and selected the team project with which you want to work, click Connect.

Team Foundation Version Control

Within the Team Explorer pane, click the "Configure your workspace" link, as shown in Figure 11-4. A workspace mapping represents the directory location on your local machine, which will contain your working copy of the project.

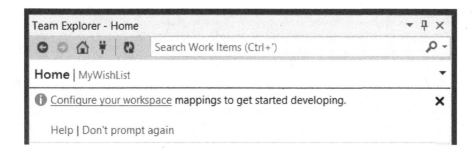

Figure 11-4. *Configuring workspace mappings*

Within the Team Explorer pane, click the Map & Get button, illustrated in Figure 11-5, to configure the workspace mapping and retrieve any files that are contained within the workspace path on the server.

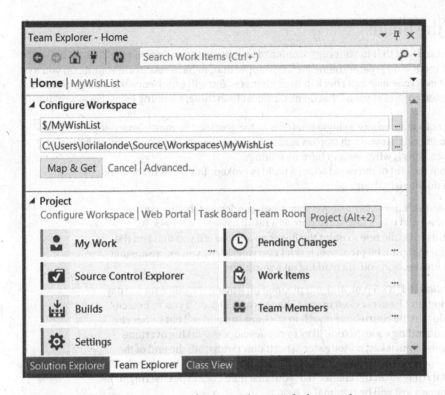

Figure 11-5. *Configuring your workspace and getting the latest code*

At this point, your environment is properly configured. You can make changes to your project's files on your local machine and check in files to Team Foundation Server as needed. Any changes that you make locally, which are not checked in to the server, will be lost in the event that your machine, or files, become corrupted between check-ins. In this case, we recommend that you check in early and often to avoid losing a day's or week's worth of work.

Continuous Integration

Now that you have selected a version control system, the next step requires configuring a build server for continuous integration. At a high level, continuous integration includes one or more of the following checks based on the configuration on the build server:

1. Compile the application code whenever a check-in is performed.

2. If the build fails, send out a notification if configured to do so.

3. If the build is successful, run automated unit and integration tests.

4. If the tests fail, send out a notification, if configured.

Continuous integration (CI) enables you to safeguard your application's code by catching problems at the time that the check-in occurs. The earlier the issue is caught, the easier it will be to resolve.

"Johnny Broke the Build!"

How many times have you heard that in your organization? How many times were you the culprit? We've all been guilty of it, and there is no greater shame for a developer than to have your team waiting on you to fix your misdeed so that everyone else can check in their changes. You will experience this in organizations that are using older version control systems that do not support branching, meaning everyone is working off the master.

Or, you may be part of a team where a single branch is being accessed by multiple developers. In this scenario, there is the likelihood that you will step on each other's toes, conflicts will arise more frequently, and builds will get broken. This is why we can't have nice things.

In all honesty, it's not the end of the world when a build is broken. But if you're the developer who caused the failure, then do the right thing.

1. *Notify the team.* It's never fair to leave your team wondering whether you are aware that the build is in a sad, sorry state as a result of your last check-in. Nobody wants to be the one to point the finger at you and tell you that you did this shameful thing. So, be proactive. Just let everyone know you are aware that the build is broken, and you are working on a resolution.

2. *Fix it immediately.* If it's 5 p.m. and you planned on leaving the office for the day, then you shouldn't have checked in your changes at 4:59 p.m. If you're brazen enough to do that, be courteous enough to stick around and roll back your check-in or fix the offending code. No one likes to see developers working overtime on these kinds of mistakes; so, long story short: don't wait until the end of the day to check in your changes. A good practice would be to check in regularly throughout the day so on the chance that your machine goes kaput overnight, the scope of changes lost will be minimal at best.

3. *Notify the team.* Let everyone know when the build is stable again.

Configure a CI Build

Team Foundation Server makes it easy to configure continuous integration builds. You must belong to the Build Administrators group within Team Foundation Server to create build definitions.

Within the Team Explorer pane in Visual Studio 2013, click the Builds button. Within the Builds section, click the New Build Definition link, as shown in Figure 11-6.

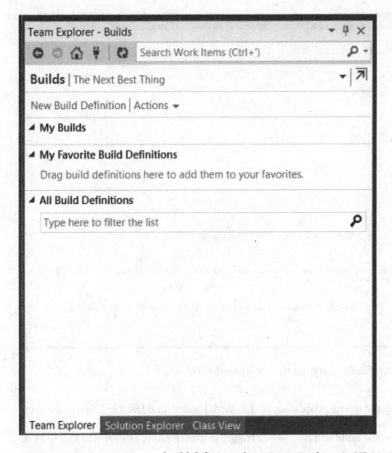

Figure 11-6. Creating a new build definition from Team Explorer in VS 2013

A New Build Definition pane will load in the Visual Studio IDE, as shown in Figure 11-7. Provide a name that makes it easy to identify the type of build it is; it must be unique, and it may not contain the special character $.

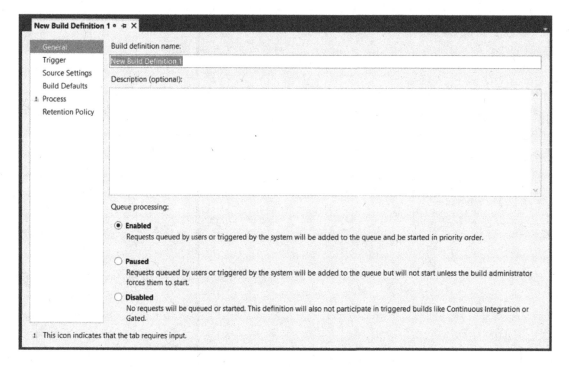

Figure 11-7. Configuring a new build definition from the Visual Studio IDE

Note that the options for the build queue processing are Enabled, Paused, and Disabled. Since you want the builds to be triggered by the system, leave the selection at Enabled for now.

Next, you need to define when the build will run. Select Trigger in the left pane, as shown in Figure 11-8.

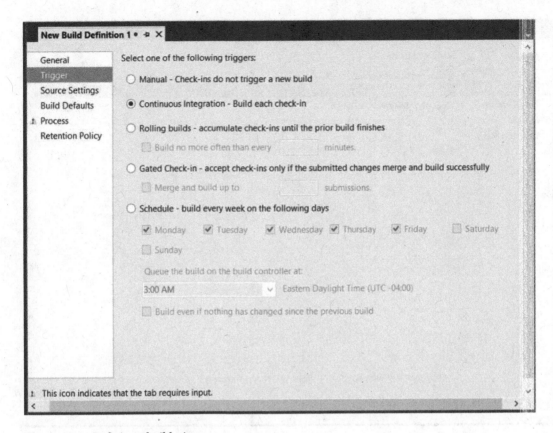

Figure 11-8. *Defining a build trigger*

A build in TFS can be triggered in one of the following ways:

- *Manual*: The developer must explicitly run the build.

- *Continuous Integration*: The build is triggered each time a check-in occurs.

- *Rolling builds*: Limit the number of builds that occur over a time period, in minutes. The valid range for the minutes text box is 0 to 2147483647.

- *Gated Check-in*: The build will attempt to merge and build the changes. If a failure occurs, the check-in will be rejected. If it succeeds, the check-in will be completed. In this way, no one will be able to check in code that will break the build. This feature is not available when configuring a build definition for a Git repository.

- *Schedule*: The build runs on a custom schedule. You may specify the days the build will run and the time of day the build will occur. You can additionally opt in to build even if no changes were made since the last build.

Since you want to configure a CI build, select the Continuous Integration option.

The next thing to do is to configure the location of the source code by specifying the Source Control Folder setting, as shown in Figure 11-9.

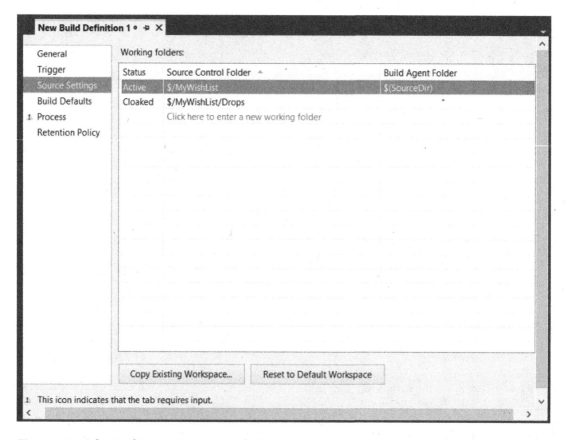

Figure 11-9. Selecting the repository against which the build will execute

The Build Agent Folder column indicates the directory on the build server that will be used to check out the source code from TFS to compile and build. The value of $(SourceDir) points to the working directory on the build machine. Its value is defined within the Working Directory settings for the build agent on the server.

Next, you will need to specify which build controller to use. A build controller is used to determine the name of the build, create the label in version control, log notes, and report the build status. It also is used to distribute the bulk of the work of the build process to its pool of build agents. If you have more than one configured build controller, select the one that you want to use for the current team project's build definition in the Build Defaults section, as shown in Figure 11-10.

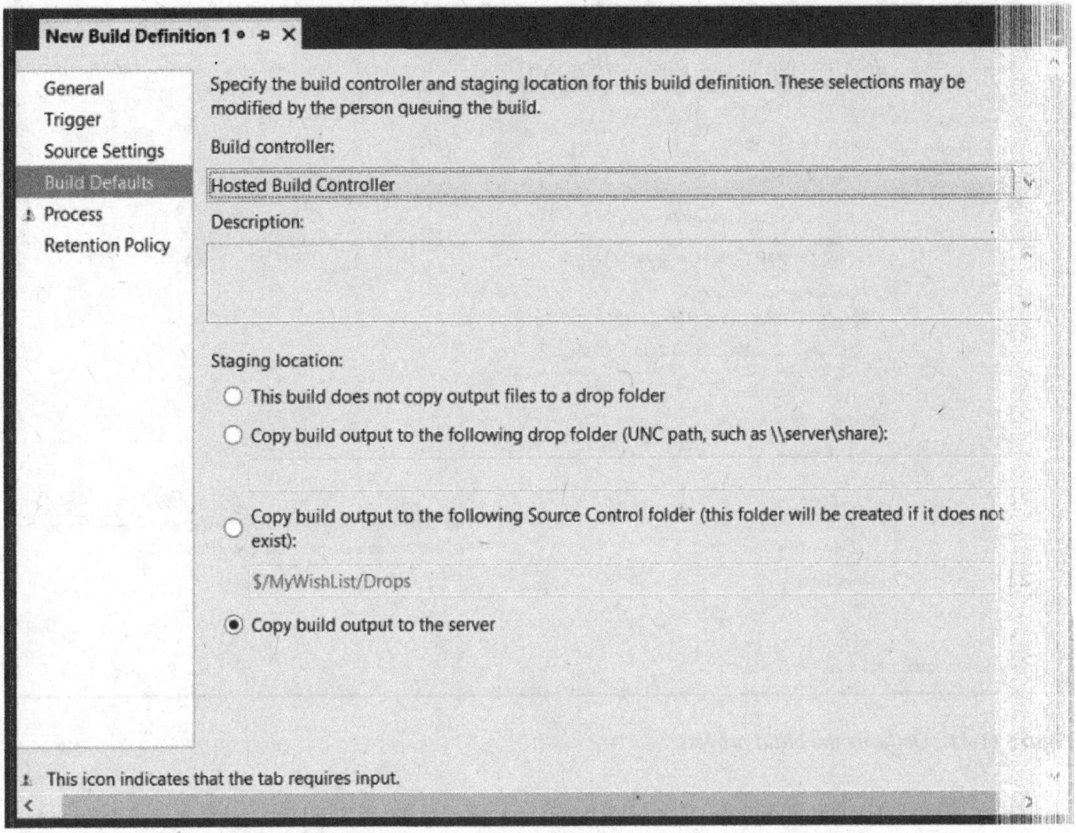

Figure 11-10. *Specifying the build controller and staging location for the build output*

You will also be able to specify whether the build output files are copied to a staging location. If so, then you can set the staging location to a file share, to a source control folder, or to Team Foundation Server.

Let's move on to configuring the build process. Click Build Process in the left pane, as shown in Figure 11-11.

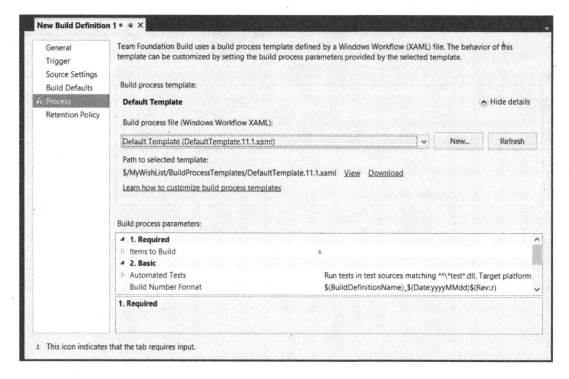

Figure 11-11. *Defining the build process*

There is a list of default templates from which you may choose. Each build process template defines a set of parameters that control how your build is run. You may select one of the default templates provided as a starting point and customize the build process parameters manually, if needed. You may upload your own build process template if you have a defined process in place that you want to apply to the team project's build definition.

At a minimum, you must define the project or solution files to build in the first build process parameter provided in the list, Items To Build. Set the focus to the value cell for this parameter, and click the ellipses button that appears to load the Items to Build dialog, as shown in Figure 11-12.

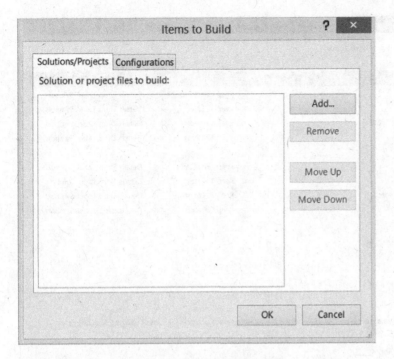

Figure 11-12. *Selecting the items to build for this build process*

Click the Add button and then select the solution or project files to build. Click OK to apply the changes, close the dialogs, and return to the build definition.

Finally, you have the option to configure how long any generated build outputs are kept in the configured staging location, grouped by build type and build state, as shown in Figure 11-13.

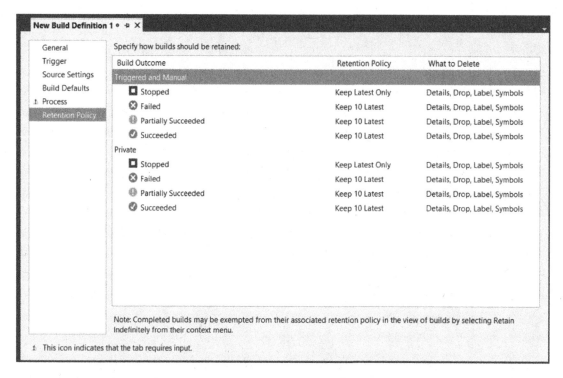

Figure 11-13. Configuring the retention policy for build outputs that were generated

For each build state within a grouping, you may select the number of builds to keep from a predefined list or select a custom value. In addition, you must indicate what will be deleted, which could be any one or more of the following:

- *Drop*: Files and folders output by the build and copied to the drop location

- *Test Results*: Results of automated tests executed during the build process or results of tests published against the build

- *Label*: Version control marker associated with specific file versions by the build process

- *Symbols*: Debugging symbols published to a symbol server during the build

Note that Details, which refers to build information, is always deleted and cannot be unchecked here. Once you are satisfied with the build definition configuration, click Save. Now you will see the build listed within the My Build Definitions group in your Team Explorer pane.

Queue a Build

Now that you have your build configured, you can start checking in your changes, knowing that the CI build will kick off automatically.

To manage your build definition or to view the status of build executions, right-click the build definition name in the Team Explorer pane to bring up its context menu, as shown in Figure 11-14.

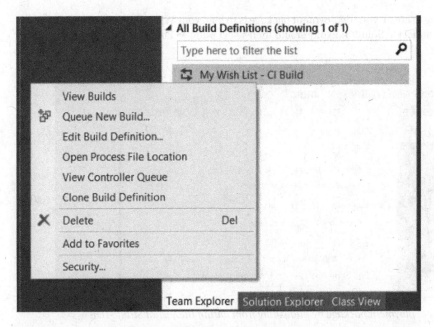

Figure 11-14. Managing your builds through the right-click context menu in the Team Explorer pane

To verify that your CI build is configured properly, make a small change to your application code and check it in. Go to the Builds tab. Do you see a build in the queue? Figure 11-15 illustrates an example of this.

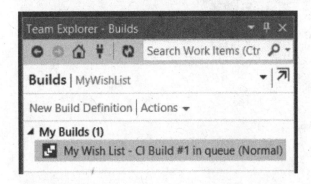

Figure 11-15. CI build added to the queue as a result of a check-in

---

■ **Note**   If you want to trigger a build without checking in code, you can do so by selecting the Queue New Build menu item from the context menu.

Deploying WPF Applications Using ClickOnce

It is easy to deploy a WPF application using ClickOnce, a deployment technology that enables you to create self-updating Windows-based applications that can be installed and run with minimal user interaction.

A quick and easy way to create your deployment package is to load your WPF application in Visual Studio 2013. Select your project in Solution Explorer and then select Build ➤ Publish <applicationName>, as shown in Figure 11-16.

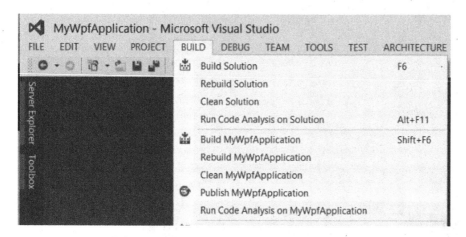

Figure 11-16. Creating a deployment package by publishing from within the Visual Studio IDE

Next, you will specify the desired location to publish the application to. This can be a local directory or network share, as shown in Figure 11-17.

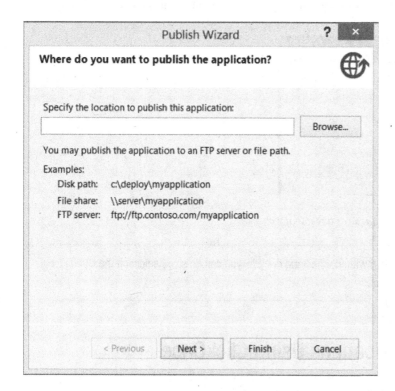

Figure 11-17. Specifying the location to publish the application

Now you must determine how the application will be accessible to users, as shown in Figure 11-18. You can choose to make it available from a web site or file share or package it to media such as a DVD. However, nowadays the more common options are a file share or web site URL.

Figure 11-18. *Selecting the manner in which the installation will be available*

Finally, you must configure whether the application will check for updates (Figure 11-19). Enabling this ensures that whenever the application is run, it will check the installation location for a newer version. If one is available, it will automatically install the new version before launching the application.

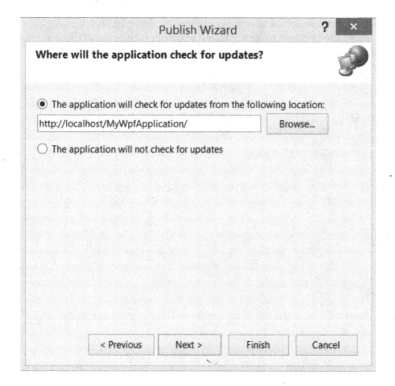

Figure 11-19. *Configuring whether the installation will automatically check for updates*

Publishing Apps to the Windows Store

When you are ready to make your Windows 8.1 and Windows Phone 8.1 applications available for public consumption, you will need to publish them to the Windows Store, which requires a Windows Dev Center account.

Windows Dev Center

Windows Dev Center enables you to publish your apps to the store; view reports on application stats, such as the number of downloads and crashes; and view and respond to user reviews. It also lets you configure push notifications to enable users to receive real-time notifications for your applications. If you want to monetize your applications through paid apps, in-app advertisements, or in-app purchases, the Windows Dev Center is the place to do that as well.

Registration

A Windows Developer account requires a one-time fee of $19 USD for individuals or $99 USD for businesses. You must register using a Microsoft Live ID. If you do not have one, then you must obtain one first. To register for a Microsoft Live account, go to http://outlook.com and click "Sign up now." Follow the steps to create your own Microsoft Live account.

Next, you will need to register for a Windows Developer account. Go to http://dev.windows.com and click the "Get a dev account" link, as shown in Figure 11-20, which will navigate to the "Register as an app developer" page.

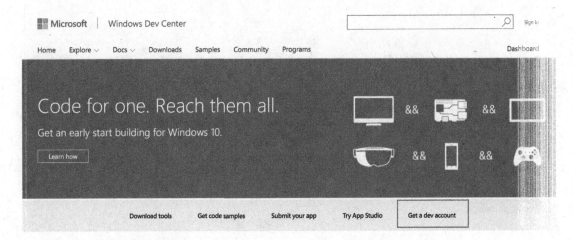

Figure 11-20. *Registering for a Windows Developer account at Windows Dev Center*

The "Register as an app developer" page provides an overview on what you may do with your developer account and the type of services available with that account, as shown in Figure 11-21. Click the "Sign up" button to continue.

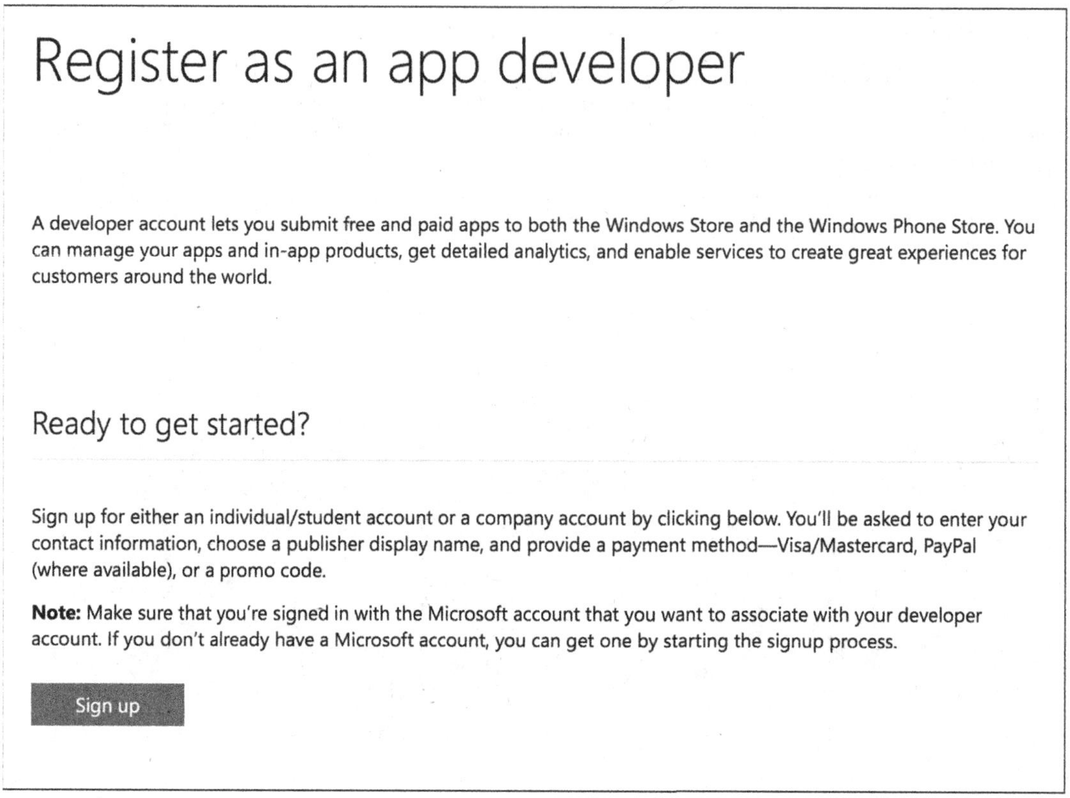

Register as an app developer

A developer account lets you submit free and paid apps to both the Windows Store and the Windows Phone Store. You can manage your apps and in-app products, get detailed analytics, and enable services to create great experiences for customers around the world.

Ready to get started?

Sign up for either an individual/student account or a company account by clicking below. You'll be asked to enter your contact information, choose a publisher display name, and provide a payment method—Visa/Mastercard, PayPal (where available), or a promo code.

Note: Make sure that you're signed in with the Microsoft account that you want to associate with your developer account. If you don't already have a Microsoft account, you can get one by starting the signup process.

> Sign up

Figure 11-21. *Signing up for an individual or company account using a Microsoft Live ID*

At this point, you will be prompted to sign in with your Microsoft Live credentials. Once you have signed in with your Microsoft Live account, you will see an information page (yes, once again) with the details on what a developer account means and the type of services that are available with a developer account, as shown in Figure 11-22. Click the Join Now button to proceed.

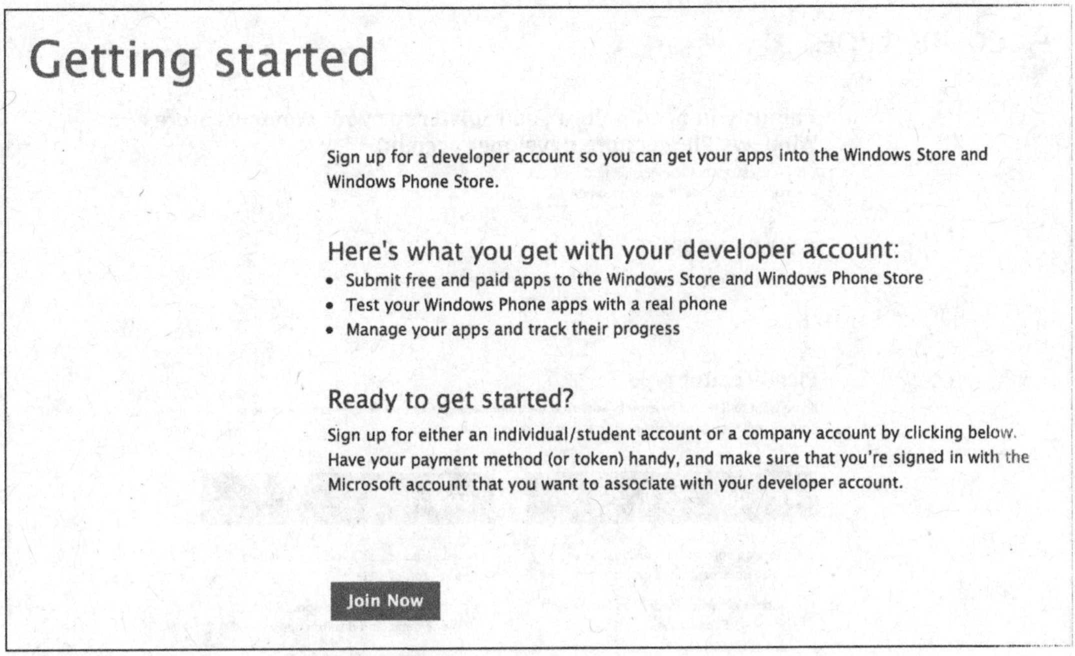

Getting started

Sign up for a developer account so you can get your apps into the Windows Store and Windows Phone Store.

Here's what you get with your developer account:
- Submit free and paid apps to the Windows Store and Windows Phone Store
- Test your Windows Phone apps with a real phone
- Manage your apps and track their progress

Ready to get started?
Sign up for either an individual/student account or a company account by clicking below. Have your payment method (or token) handy, and make sure that you're signed in with the Microsoft account that you want to associate with your developer account.

Join Now

Figure 11-22. *Upon signing in with your Microsoft Live ID credentials, click Join Now to register*

Select the country or region in which you live or will be conducting your business. Once you have made your selection, the pricing for each account type will be displayed in the selected location's currency, as shown in Figure 11-23.

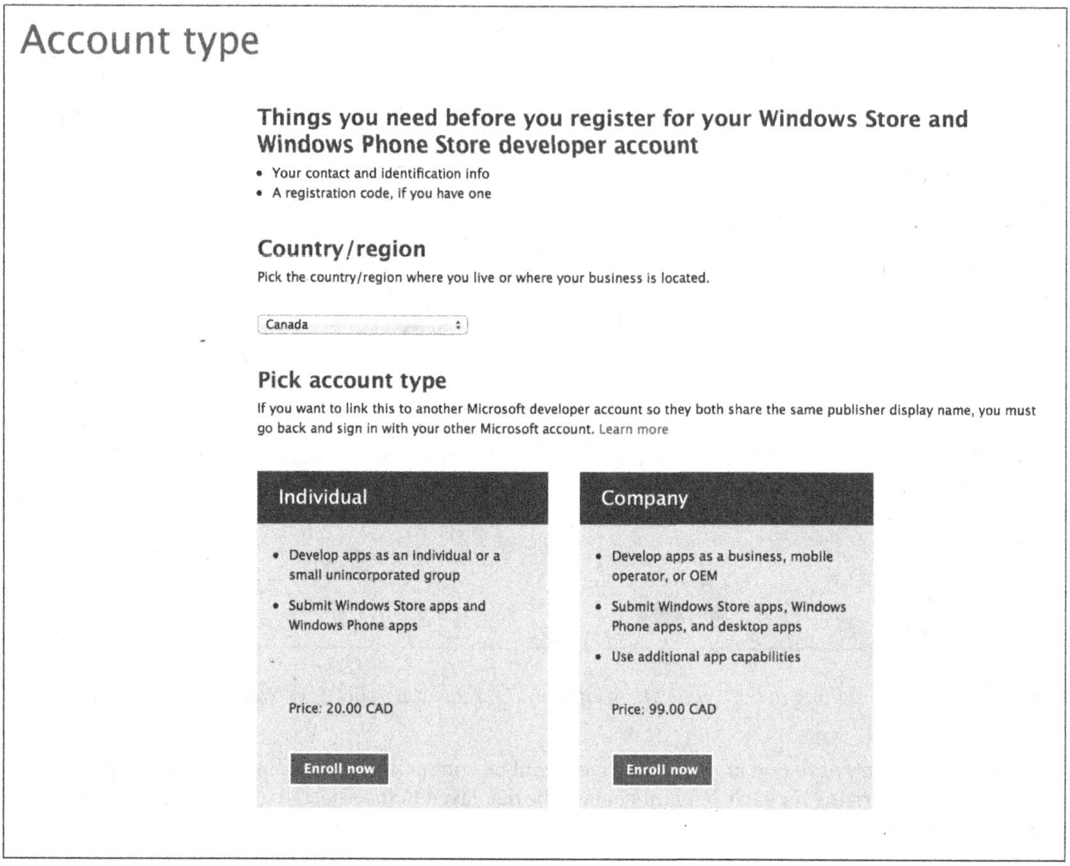

Account type

Things you need before you register for your Windows Store and Windows Phone Store developer account
- Your contact and identification info
- A registration code, if you have one

Country/region
Pick the country/region where you live or where your business is located.

Canada ▾

Pick account type
If you want to link this to another Microsoft developer account so they both share the same publisher display name, you must go back and sign in with your other Microsoft account. Learn more

Individual	Company
• Develop apps as an individual or a small unincorporated group	• Develop apps as a business, mobile operator, or OEM
• Submit Windows Store apps and Windows Phone apps	• Submit Windows Store apps, Windows Phone apps, and desktop apps
	• Use additional app capabilities
Price: 20.00 CAD	Price: 99.00 CAD
Enroll now	Enroll now

Figure 11-23. *Account pricing is displayed in the selected country's currency*

Select the account type you want to set up by clicking its respective "Enroll now" button.

Next, you must enter your account information including name, address, contact number, and so on. In addition to that, you must select a publisher name, which will be displayed in the Windows Store and associated with your apps, as shown in Figure 11-24.

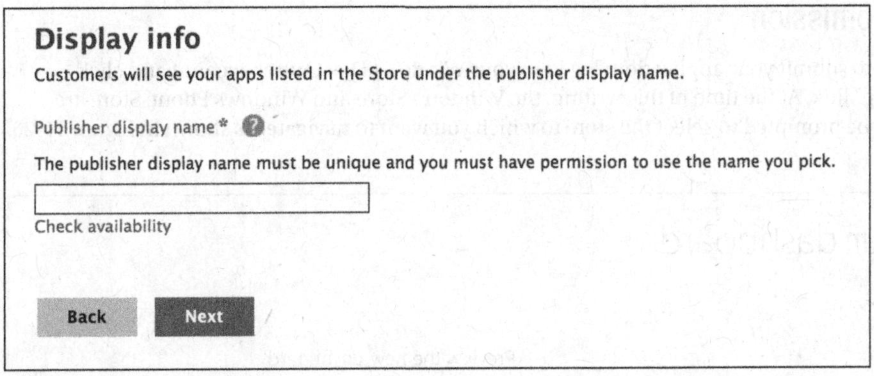

Display info

Customers will see your apps listed in the Store under the publisher display name.

Publisher display name * ❓

The publisher display name must be unique and you must have permission to use the name you pick.

Check availability

Back   Next

Figure 11-24. *Selecting a publisher display name*

The publisher name entered must be unique. You can click the "Check availability" link to validate your chosen name before attempting to proceed. If the validation succeeds, select the Next button to continue.

Now it's time to pay for the account, either by credit card or by token, as shown in Figure 11-25.

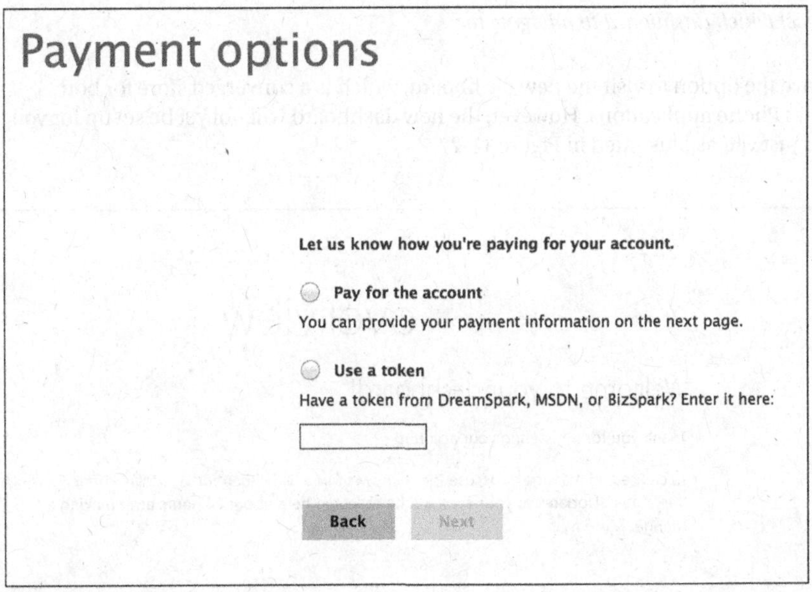

Payment options

Let us know how you're paying for your account.

⚪ **Pay for the account**
You can provide your payment information on the next page.

⚪ **Use a token**
Have a token from DreamSpark, MSDN, or BizSpark? Enter it here:

Back   Next

Figure 11-25. *Selecting a payment option*

If you have an MSDN, DreamSpark, or BizSpark account, you will be able to create a free Windows Dev Center account by entering the token that is displayed in your MSDN subscription. Select your payment option and then click the Next button to continue. Complete the payment process in order to create your developer account. Now you are ready to submit your Windows Store and Windows Phone apps to the store.

Application Submission

When you are ready to submit your application, log in to your Windows Dev Center account and click the "Submit your app" link. At the time of this writing, the Windows Store and Windows Phone Store are separate, so you will be prompted to select the store to which you want to navigate, as shown in Figure 11-26.

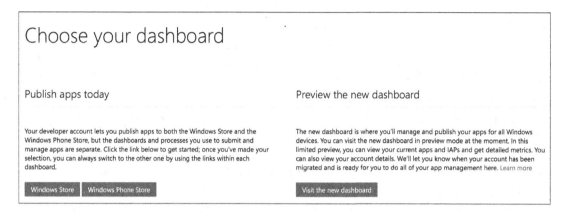

Figure 11-26. *You must select which dashboard to navigate to*

Notice that you also have the option to visit the new dashboard, which is a converged store for both Windows Store and Windows Phone applications. However, the new dashboard will not yet be set up for you to submit your applications just yet, as illustrated in Figure 11-27.

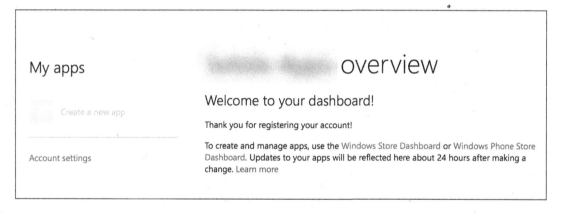

Figure 11-27. *The new dashboard does not allow app submissions at this time*

Windows Store

The Windows Store process for app submission requires some preliminary steps to package and certify that the app is ready for submission.

Packaging Your Windows Store App

Before you can submit your application to the Windows Store, you must associate your app with the store, capture at least one screenshot of the running application, and create the necessary app packages to upload to the store. This can be accomplished through the Visual Studio IDE. Load your Windows 8.1 application in Visual Studio 2013. Right-click your app's name in Solution Explorer and select the Store menu item, as shown in Figure 11-28.

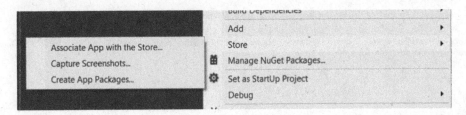

Figure 11-28. *Preparing your Windows 8.1 app for publication to the store from Visual Studio*

The first thing you will need to do is to associate your app with the Windows Store. Select the Associate App with the Store menu item, which will launch the dialog displayed in Figure 11-29.

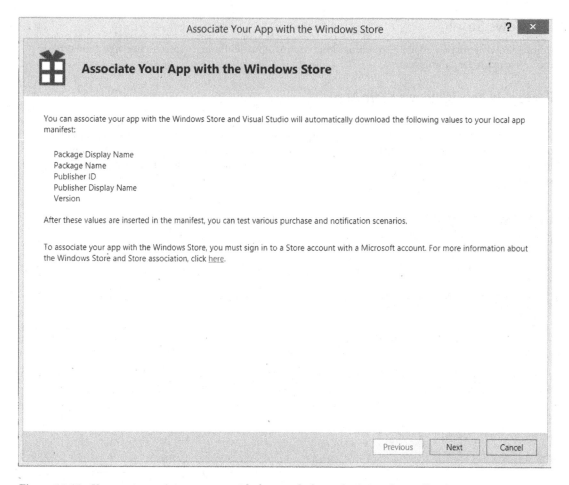

Figure 11-29. You must associate your app with the store before submitting the application

At this point, you will walk through a series of steps to reserve an app name and opt in to create the app's package to upload to the store. You will also configure the app package's output location on your machine and select the packages to create, as shown in Figure 11-30.

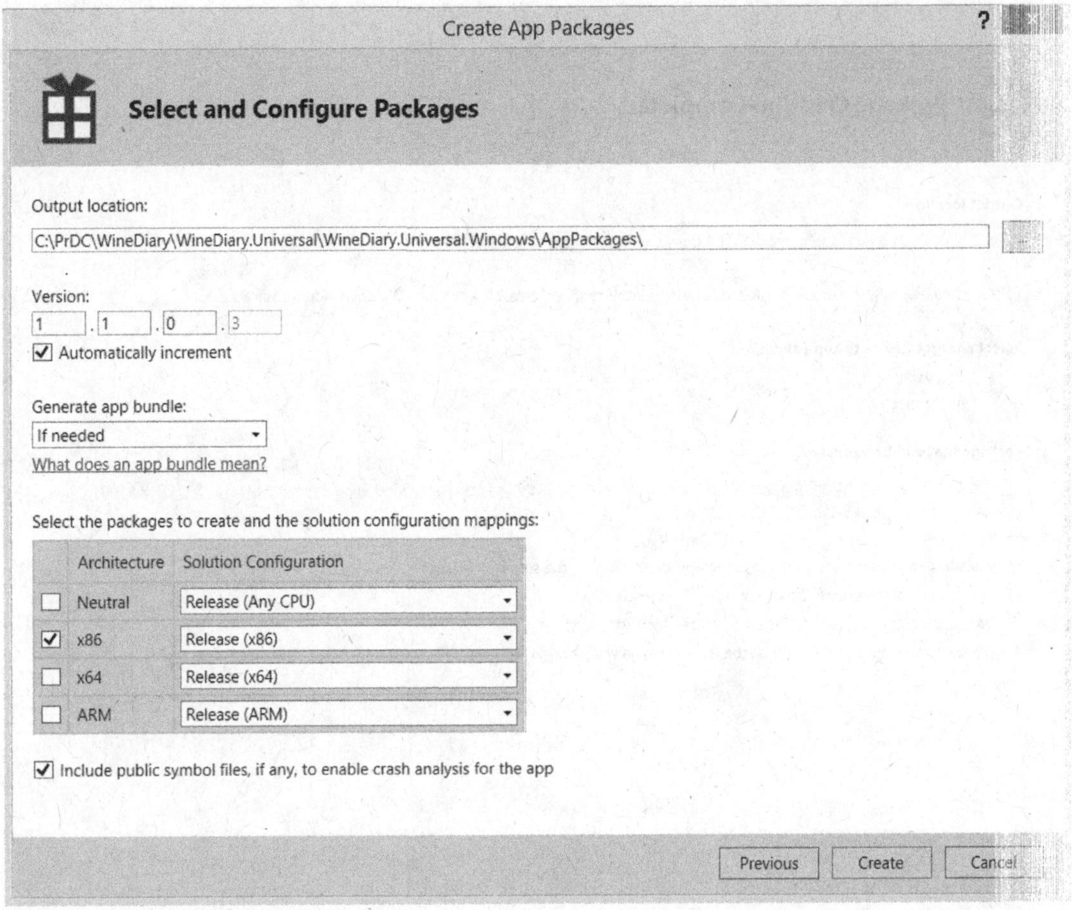

Figure 11-30. *Configuring your app packages*

Once you have configured your app packages accordingly, click Create to generate the package. Once the package has been created successfully, you will be able to review the details in the Package Creation Completed screen, as shown in Figure 11-31.

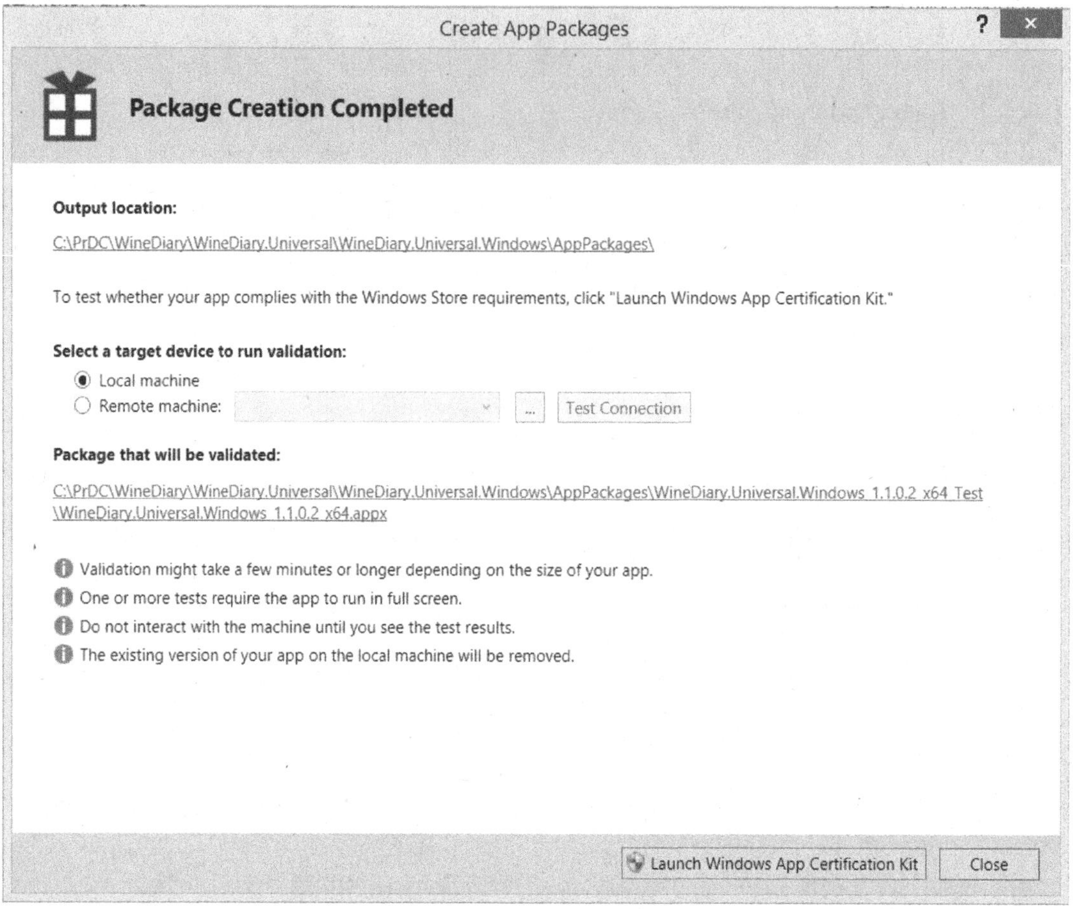

Figure 11-31. *Once the package has been created, it must be verified against Windows App Certification Kit*

You must also perform validation against the application's package to verify that it is ready for submission to the store. This will help you to discover any errors that could arise during the certification process, saving you time from going back and forth with the app submission process. In the Package Creation Completed screen, select the device on which to run the app validation, either locally or on a remote machine. Click the Launch Windows App Certification Kit button to launch the certification process.

The Windows App Certification Kit enables you to select which validation tests to perform, as shown in Figure 11-32. It is recommended that you run all tests before submitting your app to the store.

Figure 11-32. *Selecting the validation tests to run*

Click Next to execute the series of tests. Your app will load and unload a few times during this process. Do not interfere with the app interaction while the tests are being performed.

Once all the tests have executed, you will be notified if the validation process passed or failed, as shown in Figure 11-33.

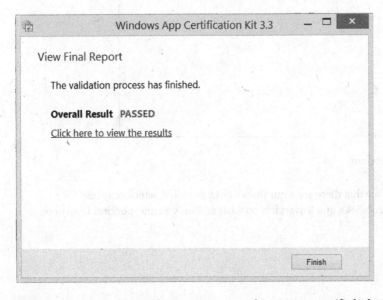

Figure 11-33. *Once the validation process completes, you are notified whether the certification passed or failed*

If the validation process failed, click the link to view the results of the tests. Scroll down through the list to find where the failure occurred and correct the issues. Build your application again and repeat the app package creation and app validation process. Once your application has passed validation, you may proceed to submit your app to the Windows Store.

Initiating App Submission

Let's take a look at what you need to do to submit a Windows Store application. From the Choose Your Dashboard page, select the Windows Store button to navigate to the Windows Store dashboard, as shown in Figure 11-34.

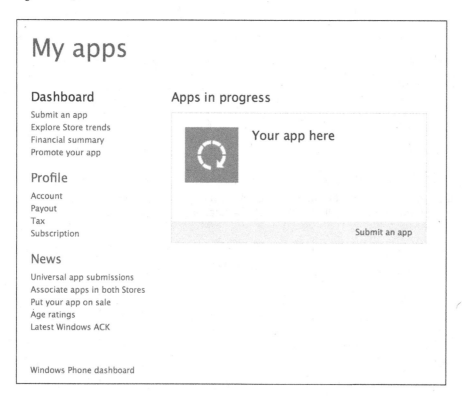

Figure 11-34. *Windows Store dashboard*

From the dashboard, you can see that there are a number of links available, which may be overwhelming at first. Table 11-2 provides a quick overview on what actions you may perform from here.

Table 11-2. *Windows Store Actions*

Link	Description
Submit an app	Initiates a wizardlike walk-through to submit your Windows Store application to the store. We will provide a high-level overview of the steps involved in application submission later in this section.
Explore Store trends	Takes you to a page with a link to the latest Windows App Builder blog post. This post provides details on recent store trends across categories and markets, as well as details on device adoption. It is important to stay on top of these trends because they may provide you with ideas on what types of apps to build, where to focus your development efforts, and which languages to support.
Financial summary	Financial reports based on any paid transactions through your application.
Promote your app	Enables you to create ad campaigns to promote your apps, by creating ads that will appear in other apps in the store. This requires that you create an account in the pubCenter portal, at `https://pubcenter.microsoft.com/Dashboard`. Within the pubCenter portal, you will be able to design your ad, configure your campaign budget, and track ad impressions and clicks.
Account	View and modify your account profile information, including your publisher name and your developer information. You can also view your unique publisher ID.
Payout	Set up your bank information to receive payments from Microsoft, as a result of paid transactions through your apps. If you plan on monetizing your applications by making them paid apps, including in-app purchases or integrating in-app advertisements, then you must set up both your payment and tax information before submitting apps to the store.
Tax	Fill out tax forms within your developer account to set up paid apps or transactions within your app that will generate revenue. You will not be able to set up your tax profile until you have set up your payment information.
Subscription	Deprecated. In the past, developer accounts needed to be renewed every year. However, Microsoft has changed this recently so that developer accounts no longer expire. This link simply takes you to an information page that says this same thing.
News links	Links to Windows blog posts and Windows Store/Windows Phone documentation for detailed information on the link topics.
Windows Phone dashboard	Quick link to the Windows Phone dashboard.

Now let's take a look at how to submit a Windows Store application. Click the "Submit an app" link to start the process, as shown in Figure 11-35.

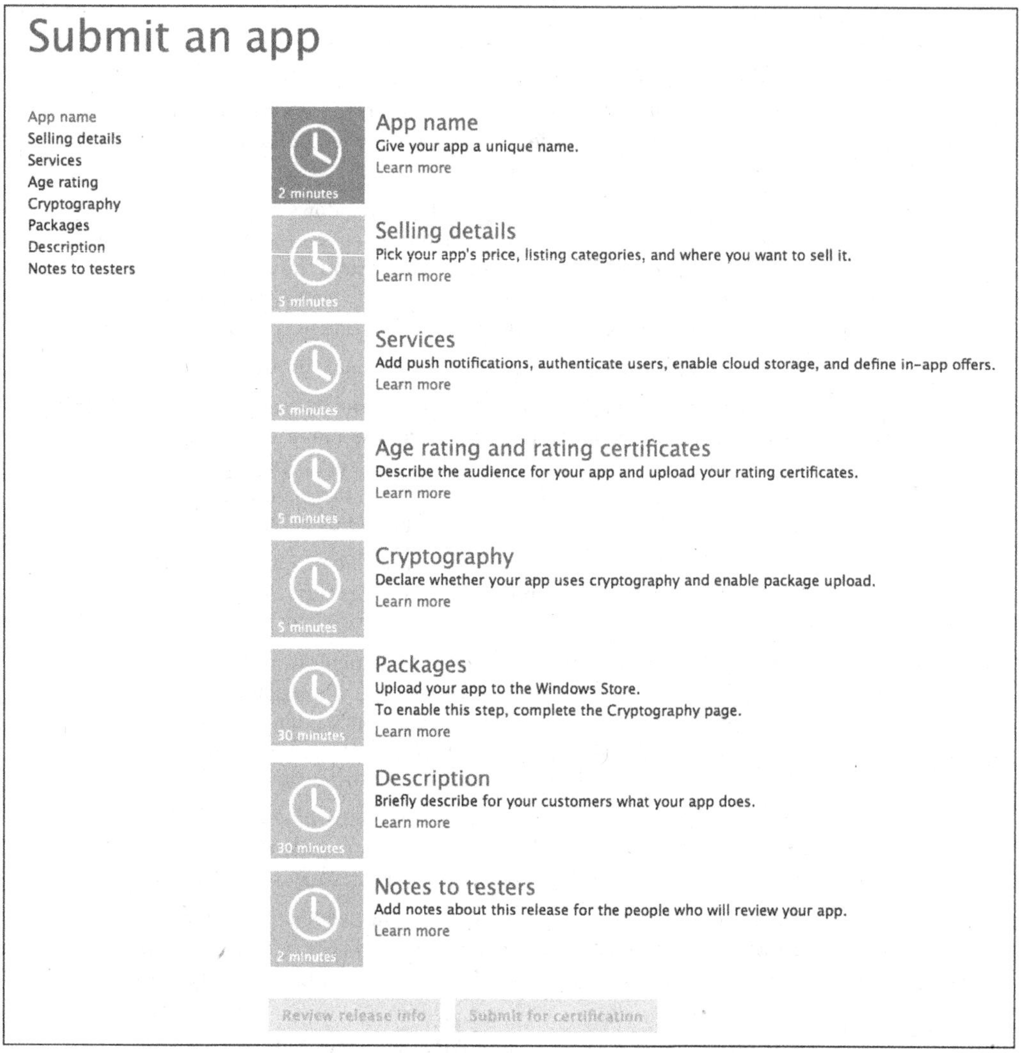

Submit an app

App name
Selling details
Services
Age rating
Cryptography
Packages
Description
Notes to testers

App name
Give your app a unique name.
Learn more

2 minutes

Selling details
Pick your app's price, listing categories, and where you want to sell it.
Learn more

5 minutes

Services
Add push notifications, authenticate users, enable cloud storage, and define in-app offers.
Learn more

5 minutes

Age rating and rating certificates
Describe the audience for your app and upload your rating certificates.
Learn more

5 minutes

Cryptography
Declare whether your app uses cryptography and enable package upload.
Learn more

5 minutes

Packages
Upload your app to the Windows Store.
To enable this step, complete the Cryptography page.
Learn more

30 minutes

Description
Briefly describe for your customers what your app does.
Learn more

30 minutes

Notes to testers
Add notes about this release for the people who will review your app.
Learn more

2 minutes

Review release info   Submit for certification

Figure 11-35. Submitting an app to the Windows Store

Notice that the app submission process provides a wizardlike interface to help walk you through the necessary steps.

App Name

The first, and most important, step is to name your application. This is referred to as *reserving* the app name, as shown in Figure 11-36. You can start the app submission process simply to reserve the name of your application before you even start developing it.

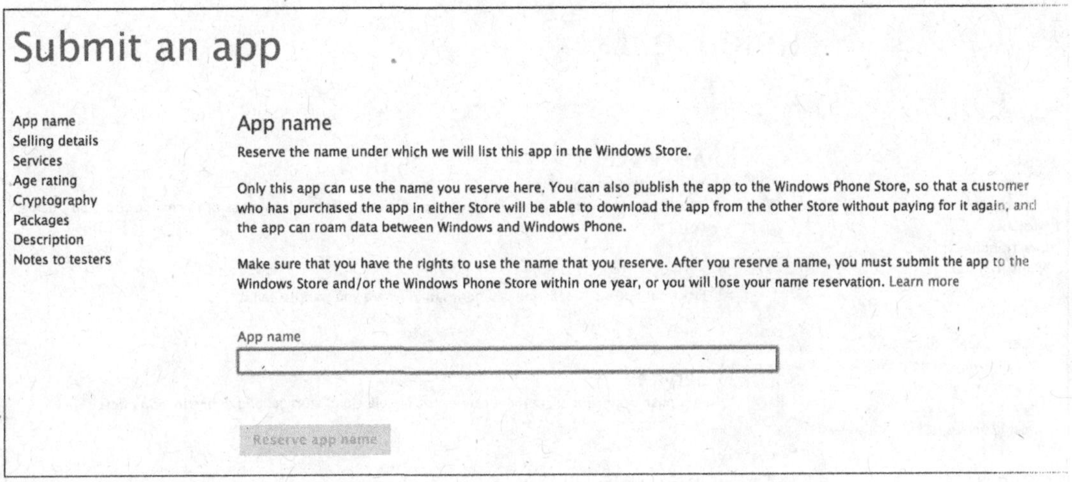

Submit an app

App name
Selling details
Services
Age rating
Cryptography
Packages
Description
Notes to testers

App name

Reserve the name under which we will list this app in the Windows Store.

Only this app can use the name you reserve here. You can also publish the app to the Windows Phone Store, so that a customer who has purchased the app in either Store will be able to download the app from the other Store without paying for it again, and the app can roam data between Windows and Windows Phone.

Make sure that you have the rights to use the name that you reserve. After you reserve a name, you must submit the app to the Windows Store and/or the Windows Phone Store within one year, or you will lose your name reservation. Learn more

App name

[   ]

[Reserve app name]

Figure 11-36. *Reserving an app name*

The name must be unique—if anyone else has already created an app with that name, you're out of luck. Pick a new one. Once you reserve an app name, no one else can use that name.

If the application is not submitted to the store under the reserved name within a year's time, the name will no longer be associated with your account. It will be released to allow someone else to use the name. The reserved name can also be associated with your Windows Phone Store dashboard. In this way, if you decide to publish a Windows Phone version of your app, your users may be able to install it on their phone. This provides two benefits to your users:

- If the app is purchased, the user needs to pay for it only one time.

- Data will roam between both the Windows Store and the Windows Phone app, providing a great user experience.

Once you have successfully reserved an app name, notice that the next four steps become enabled in your app submission page, as shown in Figure 11-37.

Figure 11-37. *Reserving an app name enables the next four steps in the app submission process*

Selling Details

The next step is to configure whether your app will be published as free or paid, as well as in which markets it will be available. If publishing a paid application, you may additionally configure it to be available as a time-based trial version, as shown in Figure 11-38.

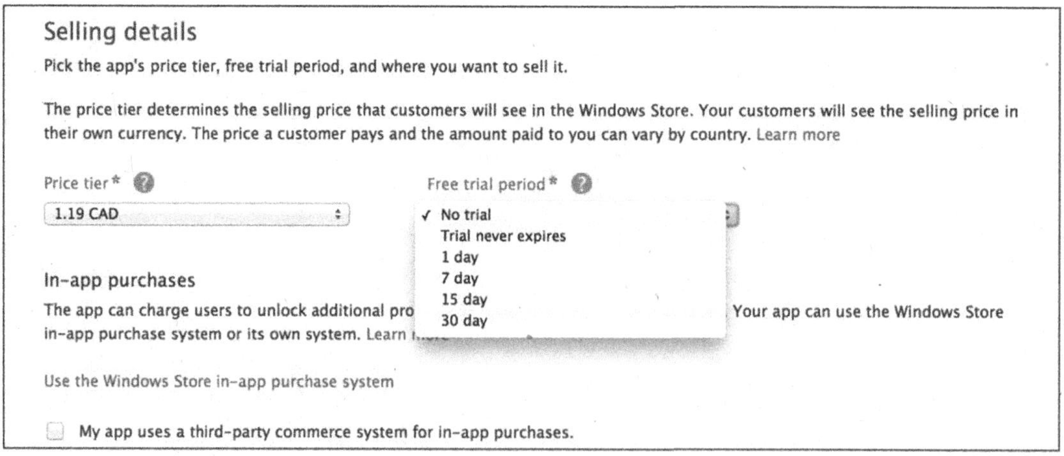

Figure 11-38. *Trial versions may be enabled for paid apps*

Optionally, you may configure in-app purchases at this time. If you are using the Windows Store in-app purchase system, click the link to navigate directly to the Services step in the app submission process. Otherwise, click the check box to indicate that you are using a third-party commerce system for in-app purchases.

Next, you must also select the markets in which the app will be available. You must select at least one country or region. There is an option to select all markets. However, you must understand that some countries have restrictions on which apps are available in those markets. Refer to the Windows documentation, "Choosing your markets," at http://bitly.com/WindowsMarketInfo for more details. Also, if your application is available for purchase, you must fill out a valid tax profile for each country in which it will be available for sale.

Next, you must select the category and subcategory under which your app will be grouped in the Windows Store and the date when it will be released. Optionally, you may indicate whether the app requires a touch-screen device or if the device must meet minimum requirements for DirectX and available RAM. Once you have the selling details configured, click the Save button at the bottom of the page to continue.

Services

The next step is to configure any additional services that your application will require, such as cloud services and in-app purchases. These services will require additional code to be included in your application to truly integrate these features. We are simply setting up the server-side infrastructure that is needed to provide the necessary association between your app and the Windows Store for these services.

To configure your app for push notifications, user authentication, or cloud storage, you will need to leverage Azure Mobile Services. Therefore, you will need to sign up for a Microsoft Azure account. A quick link is provided on the Services page to do so. Note that you must sign up using a Microsoft Live account. If you already have a Microsoft Azure account, another quick link is provided to the Azure sign-in page. Azure Mobile Services is beyond the scope of this book. To learn more about how to use Azure Mobile Services to provide advanced cloud services within your app, read the online documentation at http://bitly.com/LearnAzureMobileServices.

If you plan on including in-app purchases within your application, you can configure one or more offers on the Services page, as shown in Figure 11-39.

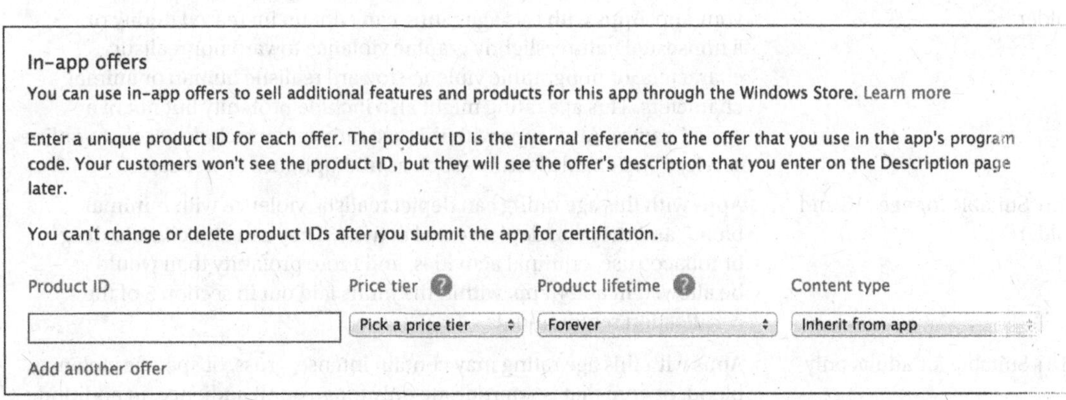

In-app offers

You can use in-app offers to sell additional features and products for this app through the Windows Store. Learn more

Enter a unique product ID for each offer. The product ID is the internal reference to the offer that you use in the app's program code. Your customers won't see the product ID, but they will see the offer's description that you enter on the Description page later.

You can't change or delete product IDs after you submit the app for certification.

Product ID	Price tier ❓	Product lifetime ❓	Content type
	Pick a price tier ⇕	Forever ⇕	Inherit from app ⇕

Add another offer

Figure 11-39. Windows Store makes it easy to include in-app offers within your application

Simply enter a product ID, which represents the offer that your app will recognize, select the price of the offer, when (or if) the offer will expire, and the type of content that will be available through this offer. To include multiple offers, click the "Add another offer" link to configure each offer you want to provide. Once you have configured your services or if you are not providing any of these services within your app, click the Save button to move onto the next step.

Age Rating and Rating Certificates

When submitting Windows Store applications, you must select an age rating since the Store uses age ratings to help your customers find apps that meet their needs. Table 11-3 includes the available age rating groups and associated descriptions, as listed in the Windows Store.

Table 11-3. Windows Store Age Ratings*

Age Rating	Description
3+ Suitable for young children	These applications are considered appropriate for young children. There may be minimal comic violence in nonrealistic, cartoon form. Characters should not resemble or be associated with real-life characters. There should be no content that could be frightening, and there should be no nudity or references to sexual or criminal activity. Apps with this age rating also cannot enable features that could access content or functionality unsuitable for young children. This includes, but is not limited to, access to online services, collection of personal information, or activating hardware such as microphones or webcams.
7+ Suitable for ages 7 and older	Apps with this age rating have the same criteria as the 3+ applications, except these apps can include content that might frighten a younger audience and can contain partial nudity, as long as the nudity does not refer to sexual activity.
12+ Suitable for ages 12 and older	Choose this rating if you are not sure which age rating to select for your app. Apps with this age rating can contain increased nudity of a nonsexual nature, slightly graphic violence toward nonrealistic characters, or nongraphic violence toward realistic human or animal characters. This age rating might also include profanity but not of a sexual nature. Also, apps with this age rating may include access to online services and enable features such as microphones or webcams.
16+ Suitable for ages 16 and older	Apps with this age rating can depict realistic violence with minimal blood, and they can depict sexual activity. They can also contain drug or tobacco use, criminal activities, and more profanity than would be allowed in a 12+ app, within the limits laid out in section 5 of the certification requirements.
18+ Suitable for adults only	Apps with this age rating may contain intense, gross, or specific violence, blood, or gore that is appropriate only for an adult audience, in addition to content that is appropriate for a 16+ app.

*Windows Store Documentation, age ratings and rating boards:
`http://bitly.com/WindowsStoreAgeRatings`

If your app makes use of third-party services, you must choose the strictest age rating to ensure that you comply with those service policies as well. For example, if your app integrates with Facebook, you must select the 16+ age rating since Facebook does not allow users who are younger than 13.

Also, it is important to note that the Windows Store will not publish adult-only apps, unless the app is a game and has been rated by a third-party ratings board. If your app is a game, you will need to provide additional rating information and upload a rating file or a rating certificate, depending on the market in which the game is made available.

Once you have configured the age rating or uploaded any required rating certificates, click Save to continue.

Cryptography

This step simply requires you to indicate whether your app uses cryptography or encryption such as data encryption, uses antivirus protection, or uses a secure communication channel, to name a few. At this point, your only option is to click either Yes or No.

If you clicked Yes, then you will have additional selections to make to gather more details on the type of encryption or cryptography being used. If you clicked No, then you will be prompted to confirm that your app is available for distribution without any restrictions. Click Save to continue.

At this point, the Packages step should be enabled in the app submission process.

Packages

Now it's time to upload your app package! In this step, you will upload the app package that was created during the packaging process, which we detailed earlier in this chapter. The package can be found in the directory of your Windows 8.1 application, under the AppPackages folder. Drag your .appxupload file from the AppPackages directory to the drop target on the Packages page in the store, as shown in Figure 11-40.

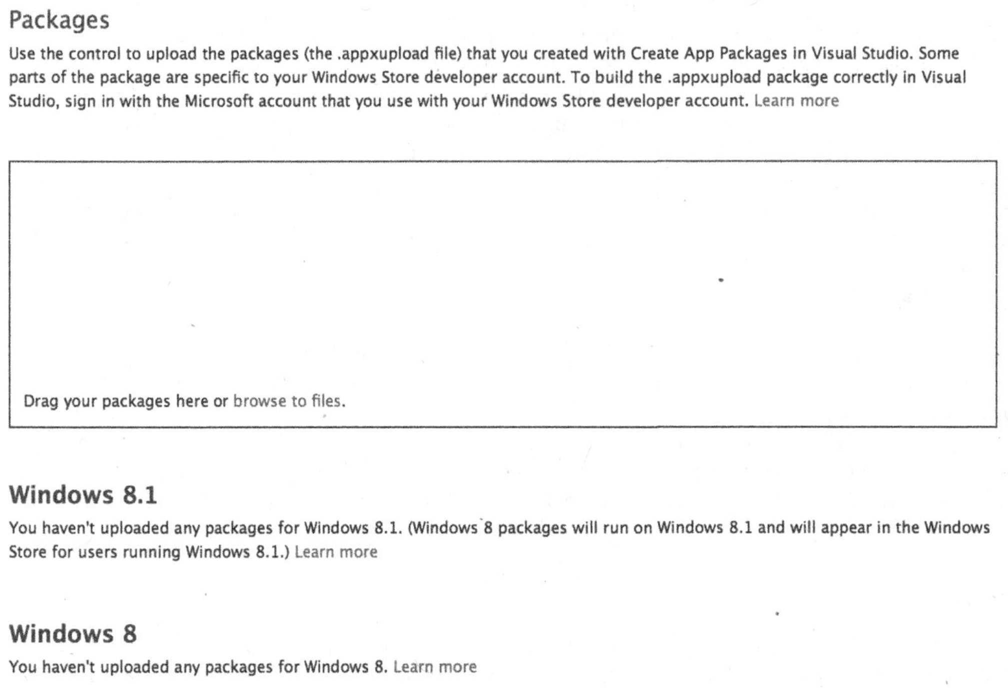

Packages

Use the control to upload the packages (the .appxupload file) that you created with Create App Packages in Visual Studio. Some parts of the package are specific to your Windows Store developer account. To build the .appxupload package correctly in Visual Studio, sign in with the Microsoft account that you use with your Windows Store developer account. Learn more

```
Drag your packages here or browse to files.
```

Windows 8.1

You haven't uploaded any packages for Windows 8.1. (Windows 8 packages will run on Windows 8.1 and will appear in the Windows Store for users running Windows 8.1.) Learn more

Windows 8

You haven't uploaded any packages for Windows 8. Learn more

Figure 11-40. *Uploading your app package to the store*

When the package has been uploaded successfully, click Save to continue to the next step to provide details on your application.

Description

Within the Description page, you must enter information about your application, which will appear in the Windows Store, as shown in Figure 11-41.

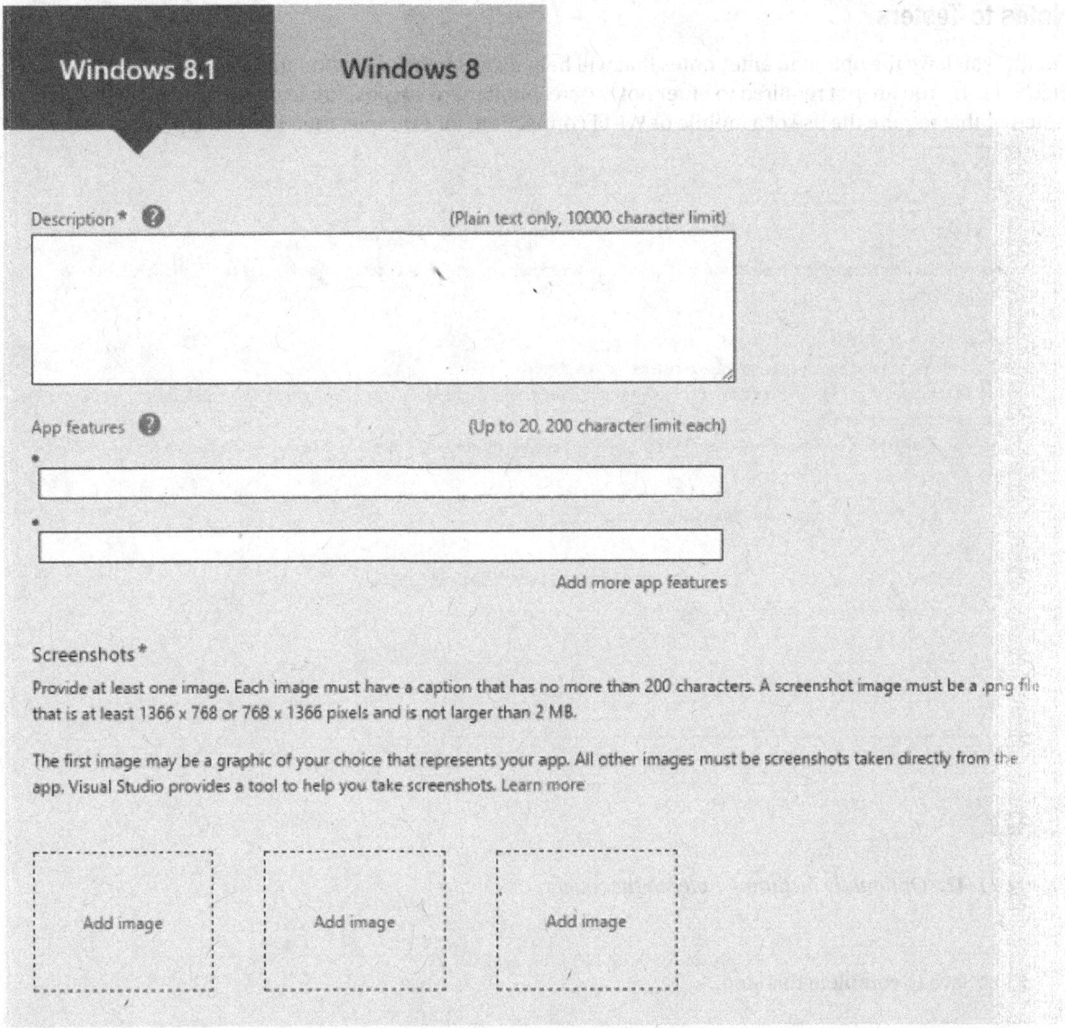

Figure 11-41. *Filling in the metadata associated with your app, which will be displayed in the store*

The metadata provided in this section will be information displayed to potential customers looking to install new apps on their PC or tablet, so be sure to sharpen up your marketing skills and provide a description that will peak their interest. You must also include at least one screenshot of your application, so be sure that it shows off the best features of your application!

You must also include copyright and trademark information, as well as a support e-mail address that will enable users to contact you in the event of any issues. Optionally, you can designate keywords to associate with your app so that users can discover it when searching the store based on those keywords. You can also choose to provide promotional images in the event that your app is featured in the store. If you do not provide these images, then your app will not be eligible to appear as a featured app.

Notes to Testers

Finally, you have the option to enter notes that will help testers better test your application, as shown in Figure 11-42. You are not required to enter notes here, but if there are obscure features that you would like tested or that require the use of a mobile or Wi-Fi connection, for example, then this is the place to make note of it.

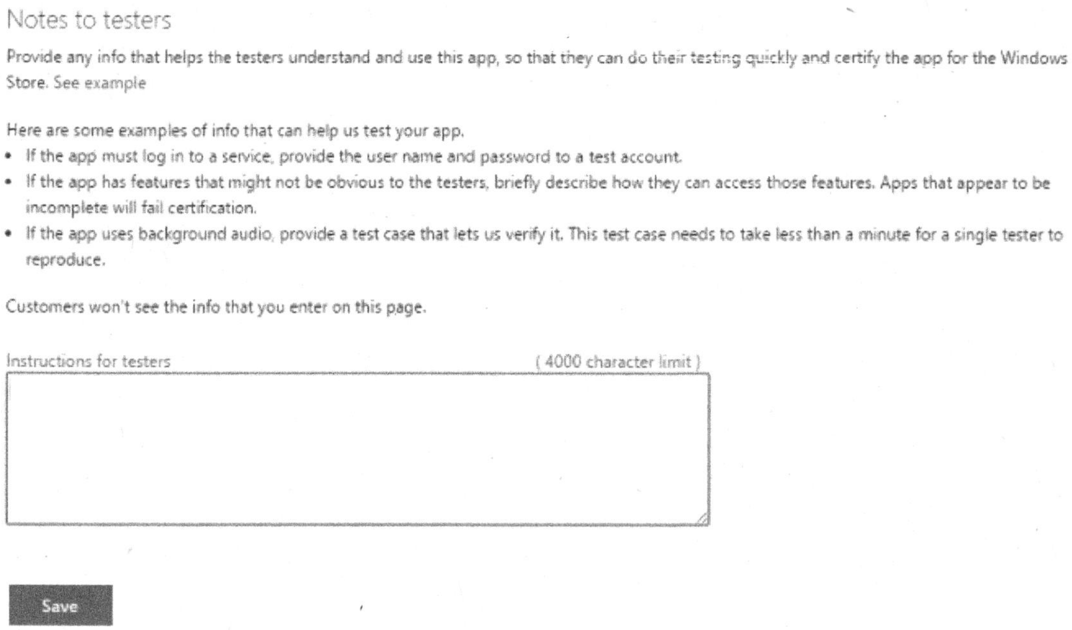

Notes to testers

Provide any info that helps the testers understand and use this app, so that they can do their testing quickly and certify the app for the Windows Store. See example

Here are some examples of info that can help us test your app.
- If the app must log in to a service, provide the user name and password to a test account.
- If the app has features that might not be obvious to the testers, briefly describe how they can access those features. Apps that appear to be incomplete will fail certification.
- If the app uses background audio, provide a test case that lets us verify it. This test case needs to take less than a minute for a single tester to reproduce.

Customers won't see the info that you enter on this page.

Instructions for testers   (4000 character limit)

```

```

Save

Figure 11-42. Optionally including notes to the testers

Click Save to complete this step.

Submit App

Once all the steps have been completed in the app submission process, you will be able to review and edit your release information or submit your app for certification to the store, as shown in Figure 11-43.

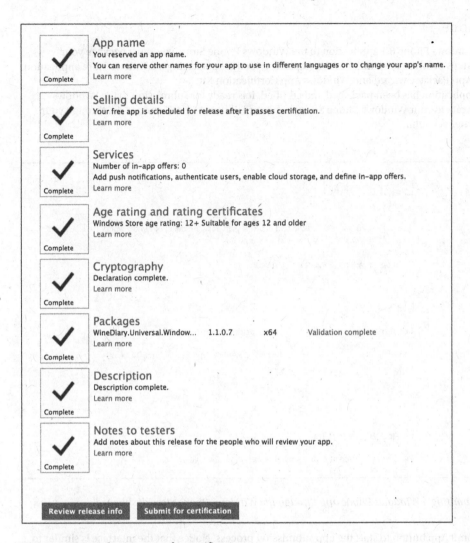

Figure 11-43. *Submiting app for certification*

Once you submit your app, it will go through the necessary stages for certification. If there are no issues with your application, you will receive an e-mail indicating that it passed certification and it is ready to publish to the store. If you configured it to publish automatically on certification, then your app will appear in the store within 24 hours.

If your app failed certification, you will receive an e-mail indicating this with details on the issues that need to be resolved. This will require you to repeat the packaging and app submission process.

Windows Phone

To submit your Windows Phone 8.1 application to the Windows Phone Store, you must package your application. The steps involved are similar to the steps described for packaging a Windows Store application, using the Create App Package wizard and Windows App Certification Kit.

Once your application has been packaged and certified, it is ready for submission to the Windows Phone Store. Navigate to your Windows Phone Store dashboard, illustrated in Figure 11-44, through your Windows Dev Center account.

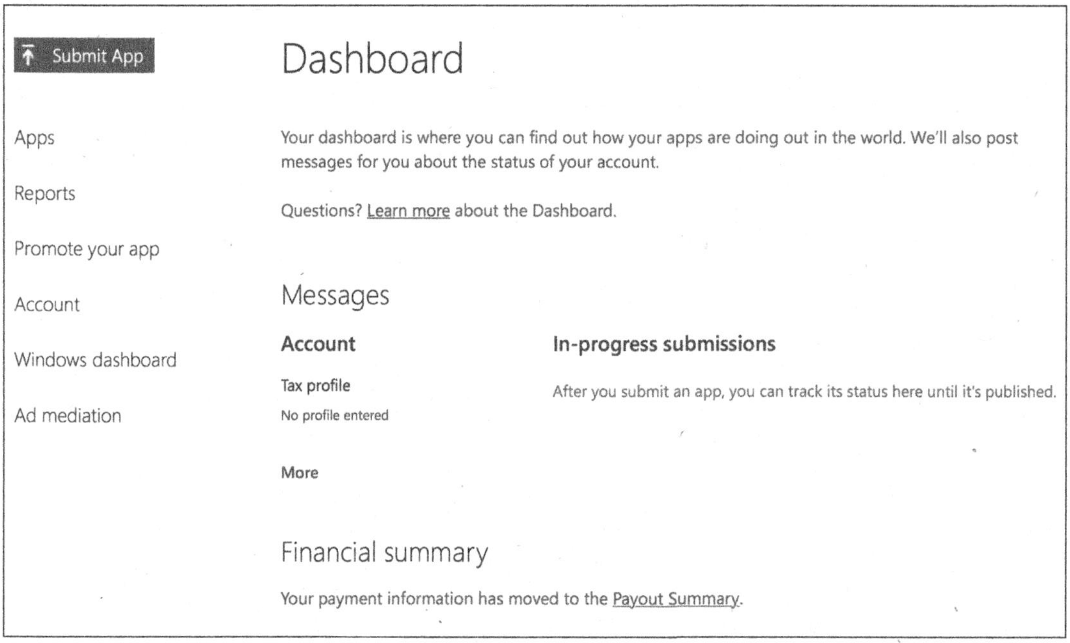

Figure 11-44. *Submiting a Windows Phone app through the Windows Phone Store dashboard*

Click the Submit App button to start the app submission process. Notice that the interface is similar to the Windows Store experience, with fewer steps involved, as shown in Figure 11-45.

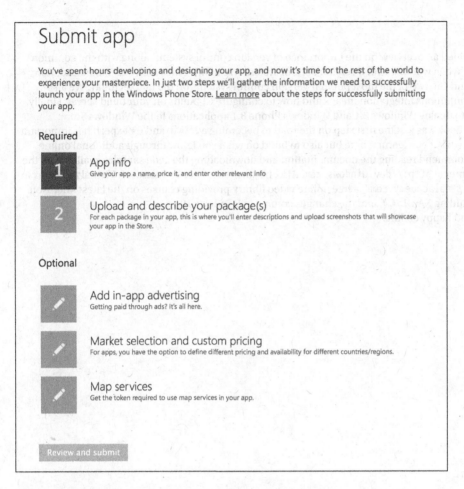

Figure 11-45. *Windows Phone App submission process*

Step through the process to reserve the app name for your Windows Phone 8.1 app. If this app submission is related to an app that already exists in the Windows Store, you can select the reserved name in the App Info page to associate the phone app with its Windows Store counterpart.

For a detailed walk-through on the remaining steps in the app submission process for Windows Phone, check out Chapter 14 in the book *Windows Phone 8 Recipes: A Problem-Solution Approach* by Lori Lalonde and David R. Totzke (Apress, 2013).

■ **Note** During the summer of 2015, Windows Dev Center publisher accounts will be migrated to use a new dashboard, which will provide a single submission process for apps targeting one or more Windows devices. Although the app submission process may look different in the new dashboard, the main concepts that we discussed in this chapter for store submissions will be the same.

Summary

This chapter provided an overview on the importance of version control systems, along with the common terminology used when working with a version control system. We took a quick look at Team Foundation Version Control and Git, two of the most popular version control systems on the market today. We also discussed what continuous integration means and how to configure CI builds on your build server. Finally, you learned how to deploy Windows 8.1 and Windows Phone 8.1 applications to the Windows Store.

Reading this book was just the first step on the road to becoming a XAML and C# expert. It is important to put into practice what you learned here but also to build on what you know through additional online resources. We recommend reading the documentation and downloading the code samples available on the Windows Dev Center at `http://dev.windows.com`. Also, be sure to register for Microsoft Virtual Academy at `www.microsoftvirtualacademy.com/`, a free online video library providing courses on the latest Microsoft technologies, including XAML, C#, and the changes coming in Windows 10.

Good luck and happy coding!

Index

A

Application programming
    interface (API), 38

B

Binary Application Markup
    Language (BAML), 4

C

Class under test (CUT), 65
Code-behind file, 128
Command Query Responsibility
    Segregation (CQRS), 36
Computer-aided design (CAD), 28
Container controls, 132
    Canvas, 134
    DockPanel, 135
    Grid, 137
    StackPanel, 140
    TabControl, 141
    UniformGrid, 142
    WrapPanel, 143
Continuous integration (CI), 61
    build definition, 228
    build process definition, 232
    build server, 226
    controller and staging
        location, 231
    custom value, 234
    items selection, 233
    Johnny Broke, 226
    queue, 234
    repository selection, 230
    retention policy configuration, 234
    team explorer pane, 226
    TFS steps, 229
    trigger, 229
Cryptography, 257

D

Data binding
    DataContext, 154
    definition, 151
    dependency properties, 156
    OnPropertyChanged Event, 153
    PropertyChanged event, 153
    ViewModel class, 153
    XAML Markup, 152
Debugging strategies, 57
    defensive programming, 58
    regression testing, 59
    system testing, 58
    unit testing, 59
    user acceptance testing, 59
Declarative language, 3
Defensive programming, 58
Design patterns
    adapter pattern, 43
    architecture types, 37
    icommand interface members, 49
        Command and the TextBox Values, 53
        implementation, 52
    layered architecture, 38
        domain layer, 39
        infrastructure layer, 40
        presentation layer, 39
        service layer, 39
        user interface layer, 39
    MVVM
        domain model, 44
        in WPF, 45–49
    repository pattern, 40–42
Domain-Driven Design (DDD)
    advantages, 28
    aggregate roots, 32
    CQRS, 36
    definition, 28
    domain entities, 30
    domain events, 36

Domain-Driven Design (DDD) (*cont.*)
    domain services, 34
    source code, 30
    value objects, 34

■ **E, F**

Enterprise Library Exception Handling
        Application Block
    App.config file, 100
        exception type, 105
        handler (*see* Handler)
        policy, 101
    Click event handlers, 111
    Enterprise Configuration Console, 99
    ExceptionManager object, 110
    ExceptionPolicyFactory object, 110
    FileNotFoundException, 109
    GetFileByte method, 110
    logging
        category, 114
        configuration settings, 112
        filters, 114
        message formatters, 115
        special categories, 114
        target listener, 114
        windows device apps, 117
    Nuget Package Manager, 98
    NullReferenceException, 109
    overview, 97
    ThrowNewException, 112
    try/catch blocks, 112
Extensible Application Markup
        Language (XAML), 3–4, 15, 39
    business analyst, 21
    code-behind files, 7
    DBA, 22
    declarative *vs.* imperative programming, 4
        nested elements, 5
        WPF window, 5
    development manager, 21
    first team design meeting, 22
    guru, 21
    junior developer, 21
    MVVM deisgn pattern, 7
    Scrum Agile Methodologies, 23
    SOLID Object-Oriented Design, 15
    TDD, 16
    unit test, 16
    user interface deisgn paradigm, 3–4
    user story, 24

■ **G**

Gestures, 201
Git, 222

■ **H**

Handler
    custom exception handler, 108
    exception type, 106
    logging exception handler, 107
    replace handler, 108
    wrap handler, 107

■ **I, J**

Imperative language, 3

■ **K**

Keep It Simple, Stupid (K.I.S.S), 64

■ **L**

Line-of-business (LOB), 37

■ **M**

Margin property, 144
Metadata, 259
Microsoft framework, 73
Microsoft Live credentials, 240
Model-View-ViewModel (MVVM)
        design pattern
    code-behind file 128
    domain model, 8, 44
    references, 4
    view model, 7
    in WPF, 8–13, 45–49
Moq framework, 87
    GetAllQuizesFromDatabase method, 88
    IQuizDataAccess interface, 88
    PrepareTestQuizCollection method, 88
    QuizRepositoryMoqFixture, 90
    QuizRepositoryStubFixture, 89

■ **N, O**

NUnit framework
    calculator class, 69
    description, 65
    NuGet package manager, 67
    project references, 67
    Setup attribute, 71
    TearDown attribute, 71
    Test attribute, 71
    test runner GUI, 68

■ **P, Q**

Padding property, 145

R

Regression testing, 59
Relational database management
    systems (RDBMSs), 38

S

System testing, 58

T

Team Foundation Version Control (TFVC), 221
Test-Driven Development (TDD), 16, 60
    failed unit test, 94
    GetAll method, 93
    Passed test, 94
    refactoring, 95
    System.NotImplementedException, 93

U

Ubiquitous language, 29
Unified Modeling Language (UML), 27
Unit testing
    characteristics
        automated exeution, 61
        continuous integration, 61
        CUT, 65
        execution, 65
        fixtures, 65
        K.I.S.S, 64
        testing, 65
    dependencies
        data access class, ADO.NET, 81
        INSERT statements, 81
        IQuizDataAccess interface, 85
        SELECT statements, 80
    description, 60
    inheritance, duplicated code, 77
    Microsoft framework, 73
    mock objects, 87
    NUnit framework
        calculator class, 69
        description, 65
        NuGet package manager, 67
        project references, 67
        Setup attribute, 71
        TearDown attribute, 71
        Test attribute, 71
        test runner GUI, 68
    repository pattern, 85
    stub classes, 86
    TDD, 59
    test fixtures, 77
User acceptance testing, 59

V

Version control system
    branch, 219
    changeset, 220
    check-in/out process, 220
    get latest code, 220
    Git, 222
    master/trunk, 219
    merge conflict, 220
    repository, 219
    resolve, 220
    revert/roll back, 220
    task/bug fix, 221
    Team Foundation Version Control, 221
    Visual Studio 2013 integration, 223
Visual Studio Application Insights
    custom event, 121
    diagnostics, 122
    events notification, 120
    on Azure portal, 120
    TelemetryClient methods, 119
    Windows Store app, 118
Visual Studio 2013 integration
    explorer pane, 223
    servers button, 223
    Team Foundation Server, 223
    workspace mapping configuration, 224

W, X, Y, Z

Windows Dev Center
    application submission, 244
    individual/company account, 240
    location currency selection, 241
    Microsoft Live credentials, 240
    payment option, 243
    publisher display name, 243
    registration, 239
    Windows Developer account, 239
Windows phone application. *See also*
        Windows Store applications
    application architecture, 170
        backward page navigation, 174–175
        caching pages, 176
        navigation, 172
        navigation helper, 172–173
        NavigationParameter, 174
        page navigation, 173
        page orientation, 171
    Application Bar, 191
    background and accent colors, 167–168
    dashboard, 262
    Font Size Resources, 169
    GridView, 183
    ListView, 178

Windows phone application (*cont.*)
   predefined resources, 170
   presentation controls
      Hub control, 186
      Pivot control, 188
   SDK, 160
      multiresolution support, 161
      scale factors, 164
   SolidColorBrush Resources, 169
   submission process, 262
   template
      DataTemplate, 176–177
      ItemTemplate, 177
   Windows Phone 8, 159
   Windows Phone 8.1, 159
Windows Presentation Foundation (WPF)
   Application class, 125
      attributes, 127
      life-cycle events, 126
   Application template, 129
   Attached properties, 133
   code-behind file, 126, 128
   container controls, 132
      Canvas, 134
      DockPanel, 135
      Grid, 137
      Padding property, 145
      StackPanel, 140
      TabControl, 141
      UniformGrid, 142
      WrapPanel, 143
   Content property, 131–132
   data binding
      DataContext, 154
      definition, 151
      dependency properties, 156
      OnPropertyChanged event, 153
      PropertyChanged event, 153
      ViewModel class, 153
      XAML Markup, 152
   dynamic layouts, 134
   file share/web site URL, 237
   fixed layouts, 134
   local directory/network share, 236
   MainWindow markup file, 130
   Margin property, 144
   markup file, 127
   control's Name attribute, 128
   NavigationWindow, 130
   Page, 131
   resource
      definition, 146
      dynamic resource, 147
      static resource, 146
   solution explorer window, 236

   Style property, 148
      application level, 149
      container-level, 150
      control-level, 150
      view-level, 149
   updates, 237
   UserControl, 131
   Window, 130
   XAML Designer, 131
Windows 8.1 SDK
   contracts
      settings contract, 217
      share contract, 215
   Flyout control
      MenuFlyout, 211
      programmatic display, 213
      Styles, 214
      usage and syntax, 211
   SearchBox control
      adding search results page, 207
      ClearHistory method, 207
      DefaultViewModel, 208
      events, 206
      resultsGridView, 208
      searchManager, 209
      suggestions displayed based, 206
Windows Store applications. *See also*
      Windows Dev Center
   age rating and rating certificates, 256
   app name, 252
   app packages configuration, 247
   app submission, 250
   associate app seletion, 245
   cryptography, 257
   dashboard, 250
   description page, 258
   design principles
      Adobe Reader, 197
      bar appears, 200
      Page.BottomAppBar, 198
      Page.TopAppBar, 198
      pop-up menu options, 200
      primary and secondary application
         bars, 199
   developer license, 196
   gestures, 201
   managing layouts
      OnSizeChanged, 205
      Package.appxmanifest, 201
      storyboards and animations, 203
      Visual States, 202
   packages, 245, 257
   selling details, 254
   services, 255
   submission process, 260

testers, 260
trial versions, 254
validation tests, 249
Windows App Certification Kit, 248
Windows SDK, 195

Windows user interface
    Windows 8.1 SDK (*see* Windows 8.1 SDK)
    Windows Store applications (*see* Windows Store
        applications)
WinForms technology, 3

Get the eBook for only $5!

Why limit yourself?

Now you can take the weightless companion with you wherever you go and access your content on your PC, phone, tablet, or reader.

Since you've purchased this print book, we're happy to offer you the eBook in all 3 formats for just $5.

Convenient and fully searchable, the PDF version enables you to easily find and copy code—or perform examples by quickly toggling between instructions and applications. The MOBI format is ideal for your Kindle, while the ePUB can be utilized on a variety of mobile devices.

To learn more, go to www.apress.com/companion or contact support@apress.com.

Apress®
THE EXPERT'S VOICE™

Printed in the United States
By Bookmasters